Believe in
Yourself!!
Rebecca Rhodes

A
CIRCLE of QUIET

REBECCA RHODES
with
Karen Farley

A Circle of Quiet
Copyright © 2003 Rebecca Rhodes with Karen Farley

Nonfiction

ISBN trade paperback: 0-9729304-7-7

This book was printed in the United States.

For inquiries or to order additional copies of this book, contact:

Gardenia Press
P. O. Box 18601
Milwaukee, WI 53218-0601USA
1-866-861-9443 www.gardeniapress.com
orders@gardeniapress.com

For anyone who has ever lost hope

Acknowledgments

I wish to thank my son Aaron for his help in transcribing hours of taped interviews, my daughter Ileah for listening to endless revisions, Beth Kattleman for her faith in me, Keith Andrew for his photography, vision and late, late nights, Richard Roszko for his drive and encouragement, Paula Maynard for her friendship and support, Rich and Linda Fiore for their generosity, Bill Gavin for everything, Lorry Salluzzi for her inspiration, and Karen Farley for her brilliance, drive and terrifying bravery, without which this book could not be. Her friendship is one of the greatest gifts I have ever received, and her tireless dedication and memory helped in the co-authoring of A Circle of Quiet. Last of all I wish to thank my mother, Bonnie Rhodes, for more than I can name on a page.

Rebecca Rhodes

***

It's difficult to put all the "thank you's" into one paragraph. After several hours of revisions it's still not perfect but it's from the heart. I would humbly like to thank Doctor Peter Weil for saving my life and being an incredibly compassionate physician, Rene Pufahl for her enthusiasm and belief in Lorry and I, Doctor Stanislaw Burzynski for his brilliance and dedication, Doctor Andrea Gould for inspiring and enlightening me, Scott DeSimone for his loving friendship, Lynn Wuest for always being there for me, my son Matthew and my daughter Dana for always knowing the right words to say to put a smile on my face, my sister Lorry for her faith in me and the encouragement she gave at a time when both were void, my dear friend Rebecca Rhodes, whose dedication, sacrifice, imagination and foresight made this book possible—I cannot thank her enough for all she's done for me on many levels. My beloved husband Richard, for his unwavering courage and support. Without it, this book could not have been written. Above all, I thank OBEDIA for communicating with me and helping me to stay on the path and for teaching me that all experiences are gifts—Good and Bad. Each life experience shared imprints memory on the soul of another.

Karen Farley

Introduction

Have you ever had one of those rare moments when a stranger walks into your life and you know that you'll never be the same? Somehow, that person is important to you immediately. Even the circumstances that brought you together feel manipulated, as if the hand of God had gently stirred the chess pieces, all strategically placed for this moment. Meeting Karen Farley was such a moment for me. I believe fate stepped in and placed me in her path.

We met in New York in 1997. Trained as an artist, I had a job at a fine gift store, with a studio in the backroom where I could create. I did all the displays for the store. My window compositions had won awards, so the owners were only too happy to let me experiment.

When the holidays rolled around, I decided to make a real gingerbread house as a Christmas display for our porcelain figurines. The structure ended up being three feet high, weighed over a hundred pounds, and was written up in all the newspapers.

My assistant Tracey suggested we donate it to a children's charity after the holidays. Better yet, a fresh-baked house, covered in icing and stuffed with treats for when they broke it open. What charity to give it to, though? We hadn't the faintest idea.

A customer in the shop whom I'd never seen, before or since, gave me the phone number of a person named Karen Farley who did a lot of charity work with children. Karen arranged to visit me at the store the next day.

She sailed into the shop on a breath of crisp winter air, grinning ear to ear and splitting seams with her boisterous laugh and ferocious charisma. She was a golden, sparkle-eyed creature who knocked my breath away the moment she appeared. I loved her instantly, the way a new mother loves the baby placed into her arms for the first time. Instinctively, without reserve. I was flabbergasted.

She shook my hand with a grip of steel, telling me about her charity organization. Its goal was to produce visual and audio material to help young cancer patients fight the disease. Utilizing guided imagery and positive thinking, along with the latest medical treatments, children were taught to recognize their own imagination as a powerful ally.

Karen and I talked for hours that first meeting. She told me how she got into this field, having a first-hand knowledge of the ravages of cancer. Most of her family had been lost to it, besides Karen being stricken herself with fourth stage lymphoma while pregnant with her daughter. That was twelve years ago.

We agreed to donate a gingerbread house to the cancer ward of Long Island's *Schneider's Children's Hospital.* Karen's charity would arrange the donation and I would make the house.

It was huge and heavy and magical when it was finished, stuffed with chocolate chip cookies and Christmas candy. Tracey Champey baked the cookies and arranged donations of toys to hide inside. My daughter made fifty-five origami cranes to fill it. They were wonderful little birds with moveable wings—a symbol of good luck.

We delivered it on Christmas Eve. The children fell on it like happy locusts, which was exactly what I'd hoped. Half the fun of an edible house full of treats is tearing it apart!

I was especially struck by a boy who'd just had brain surgery. The nurse told us that he'd had such a hard time of it, and was so sick from the chemotherapy, she hadn't seen him even smile for several days. He was too ill to go home for the holidays.

There's a photo in my scrapbook of that little boy grinning ear to ear as he broke candy icicles off the roof. Magic. Sheer magic.

The gingerbread house was a roaring success, the best part being the joy it gave the kids. For just a little while, they forgot about sickness, distracted by pure fun. Comedians say humor is the most powerful weapon in the arsenal of man, and I agree. Change your outlook from the "half empty glass" philosophy to the "half full" and you can change your life. No easy task when you're battling a so-called terminal disease.

Karen and I became close as the months went by, collaborating on several other projects. She recruited me to do a lot of illustration work for her organization. I painted in my studio at the gift shop.

My office was also there, where I spent time on another passion: history. Seven years had been dedicated to the study of World War II, Pacific theater. My dear friend had been a Marine Corps BAR man on Bougainville, Guam, and Iwo Jima. I was working on a manuscript about his experiences. A strange project, and one I was shy about.

Karen dropped by the shop one day to introduce her sister Lorry to me. A certified Reiki healer, Lorry had been diagnosed with Systemic Lupus Erythematosus nine years earlier.

Lorry seemed vastly different from her sister. Whereas Karen is in-your-face, let's do it now, now, now, Lorry looks at you with wounded eyes even when she's laughing. I could see the hurt in her.

She seemed able to view hidden pain in me as well. I'd recently had surgery, which corrected years of agony from endometriosis. It would take another year before all the discomfort disappeared.

Lorry placed her hand at the juncture of her ribs, near the liver, curving her fingers in a half melon shape that exactly defined the pain I was experiencing at that moment.

"Excuse me, but are you in pain? Right here?"

Even if Karen had told her about my operation, it wouldn't explain the placement of her fingers, which was nowhere near my scar. It was a secret hurt I'd told no one but my doctor about, one he assured me would fade with time.

"And here?" Lorry shifted to another spot. It was correct also.

Now, I am open-minded enough to believe in psychic phenomena, in the strength of faith, in ghosts and things unseen. However, I also believe that a majority of the people who claim extra-sensory perceptions are prone to either exaggeration or blatant untruths. I listen to their stories with interest but little belief. That aside, Lorry's quiet words hit me in the gut, truly frightening me. I reacted with a laugh and some dumb joke, but inside it scared me like a Neanderthal watching a flying saucer land outside his cave entrance.

As they were leaving, I remembered the manuscript sitting on my desk, and grabbed it.

"Karen!"

They both turned back expectantly, these two odd sisters. I ran up and shoved the pages in Karen's hands.

"I'm writing a book on World War II. This is a copy of what I have so far. Will you read it?" I blurted out the words with no finesse whatsoever. Karen had no idea I even wrote.

"Sure," she said, with less than her usual exuberance. "I don't know how long it'll take me, I'm so busy right now ... when do you want it back?"

Knowing the *so busy* statement was a death knell of boredom, I stammered a suitable answer and watched them leave. My actions were baffling. I was utterly basket-cased without the slightest idea why. Karen Farley, alone, is a force of nature. Together with Lorry, they were intoxicating, but that still didn't explain my behavior. The manuscript wasn't something I normally handed over. I just knew I wanted Karen to read it.

The sun began to set, my favorite time of day in the shop. The light poured into the front window, gilding the stained glass and splashing the walls with rainbows from the chandelier. I sat for a while, admiring the sight, waited on a few customers, sold a porcelain box. I wandered, cleaned a display table, and fidgeted about, restless.

The phone rang.

"Rebecca, it's Karen. We just finished your chapters."

"What? Already?"

"Yeah. Look, I have to talk to you. When can we meet?"

She arrived fifteen minutes later, her hair blowzy with wind and finger-combing.

"Lorry and I want you to write our story."

I just gaped at her.

"We've always wanted to write a book about our experiences with disease. We had an author writing it, but couldn't work things out with him. We want you to do it."

"What do you mean? A biography?"

"Look. Lorry and I had to drive to the South Shore. I started reading your book to her in the car. We just sat and read in the parking lot for half-an-hour. We couldn't even go inside."

"So you liked it?"

"More than liked ... loved it! We want you to write for us."

"What? No."

"You have to."

She talked for an hour, cajoling, telling things about her past that pulled me in despite my reticence. About Lorry, and their other sister Patty. About life in Levittown, and their family's seemingly unending struggles with cancer. Karen herself battled fourth stage lymphoma when she was only twenty-seven. Lorry fought Systemic Lupus at thirty-four.

I finally agreed, drawn in not only by my love of Karen and fascination with the story, but by some strange, compelling instinct. What had they done to save their own lives, to raise their own children, despite such a family history? I was determined to find out.

Interviewing these two women was an experience in itself. I talked to them separately, Karen at night, Lorry during the day. They always brought me something to eat or drink, thinking of my comfort and well being, even when invited to my house.

Their past is both appalling and significant to their future diseases. Both suffered emotional, physical, and sexual abuse. Both are physically beautiful, but insecure with it. When asked, Lorry would say, "Now I believe I'm pretty." But tears filled her eyes when I mentioned it. Both are obsessed with grooming, but Karen can appear in public without makeup. Lorry feels the need to protect herself behind artificial color.

Karen relates trauma with wit and an unrelenting rage against the weak cruelties of others; Lorry is wounded still by ill opinion, no matter whose. They both hate and love those who have hurt them. Karen is a warrior; Lorry a garden of flowers. Karen is someone to lean on for her dynamic strength; Lorry can be as soothing as warm milk, a tonic. Both are oddly compelling, and sometimes simply odd.

This story started out a simple tale of inspiration and hardship, at least that was the original plan. After hundreds of hours of interviews, visiting various sites of importance, I, as writer and friend, have seen it evolve into a strange and wondrous story concerning the lives of these two extraordinary sisters. Lorry told me descriptions of an enlarged heart and moon-bathing with a grin on her face. I fought to keep my expression passive when Karen described her stride during chemotherapy. Her pain had been so bad, she'd had to walk with a cane. When I asked her to show me, she stumbled across my living room with a string-cut puppet-lurch so terrible, I fought tears of astonished horror that this vibrant woman had ever looked like this, or suffered so.

Visions of death, the solace of men, dreams and words cut in stone, all things of import and strange significance, weaving themselves around me, knitting together a story of incredible complexity and fascination. Even my own past illness now serves as reference material for the lives of Karen Farley and Lorry Salluzzi. I was supposed to meet these sisters. They are two women of destiny, and I am honored to tell their story.

Part One:
The Visionaries

Chapter 1: Karen

January 1991

The first thing Karen experienced when she woke was pain. It was the pain that brought her up from the anesthetic.

God, it hurts! Jesus, Mary, and Joseph, it hurts!

For the moment, that was as deep as Karen's thoughts could reach. She tried to regulate her breathing to control the instinctive panic against such agony, but a tube was down her throat. She registered the shape and acrid taste of the plastic. It hurt too.

The next thing that came back, distracting her from the waves of pain, was sound. She tried to focus on that.

The staging surgery had taken a long time, and Karen's stomach was full of blood. The tube down her esophagus was dealing with that, pumping it out with a slushing, slurry noise that was welcome in its bizarreness. She could concentrate on such a repulsive, invasive racket.

Her hearing began to clear. Sound expanded slowly, moving beyond the bed. Karen tried to open her eyes, but her lids refused to cooperate, lying heavy and immobile. The drugs still had the upper hand. She had to settle for hearing without sight for the time being.

She wasn't in intensive care. That much, she knew. They must have moved her while she was asleep.

Two women were having a soft conversation in the room. Karen didn't recognize either voice.

"This poor woman."

She froze. *What poor woman? Are they talking about me?*

"What's the matter with her?"

"Her staging surgery showed a real mess. Such a nice person, too."

"What'd they find?"

"Tumors. Probably advanced lymphoma. Every organ had something on it. They took her spleen and two large masses, then just left the rest."

"God. Didn't she just have a baby here?"

"She's got two babies. A newborn and a two-year-old."

"Poor thing."

"Yeah. She's only twenty-seven. But, you know what the real shame is? Her children. They're too young to remember her when they grow up. They'll never know their mother."

"It's just awful. Nice woman, too."

"Yeah, I know. Terrible. Come on, or we'll never finish."

They walked out, soft-footed in their hospital shoes, and Karen was left alone.

My children will never know their mother. They won't even remember me. Numb, she could think of nothing but Matt and Dana growing up without her. All that time with Matty, sleeping next to him, holding his hand, fighting for his life. And Dana? Karen hadn't even had a chance to get to know her daughter Dana. What would her first word be? Who would Richard marry to raise Karen's babies?

It was too much. After everything she had faced in her life, this was the one thing Karen couldn't bear. All the deaths, all the sorrow and illness and stink of the sickroom. Cancer had stolen her childhood. Now it was back to steal her future. When she had given birth to Matt and then Dana, Karen thought motherhood was going to be her reward for a lifetime of suffering. Something given back after so much had been taken away. These beautiful children. Her reward.

No! It's not fair!

She forced movement into her limbs and tried to thrash out her denial. The pain hit her like a knife, cutting, threatening worse if she moved again.

Even that, Karen thought. *I can't even have the luxury of panic. Just lie here and take it.*

Her closed eyes fluttered, burning. The surgery had left her dehydrated, her tears were thin and scalding. She could only manage one. It slid weakly down the side of her face, bringing no relief at all.

It was at that moment that Karen Kikel Farley got mad. Blindingly, furiously mad. She threw blackened thoughts against the wall and shattered mental anguish onto the floor of the stinking, lousy hospital.

Why? she screamed silently at God. *Why did you do it? Why did you bring me here to this awful existence? This must be the worst trick you've ever played on me, to take away my family, then give me these two beautiful children only to take them away, too? Why? So they can hate me? The way I hated my mother for leaving me?*

Movement was coming back. She thrashed her head, and the tube sloshed. The pain kicked her again, a thick slash in her belly, warning. *Be quiet. Be still, now.*

No!

It cut again, nicked her, burned her pelvis. Infuriated, Karen tried to chew through the tube in her rage, but the pain stopped her. The pain was too big for her to be defiant for long.

Why is this happening to me? What did I do wrong?

The pain hit again, harder this time, squeezing the air from her lungs. Karen began to panic.

Am I dying? Is this it?

Drugs are strange things. They take away pain and give you illusions to ponder, hallucinations that pay no mind to visiting hours or private rooms. Creatures waltz in and whisper mysteries; fear grows a face and talks of cabbages and kings, smiling at your total bewilderment.

For a moment Karen thought there was a fluttering Kleenex stuck on the window, backlit and shining in the late afternoon sun. At first that's all it was, a tissue paper distraction that seemed to grow larger the longer she stared at it. When it came through the window, gleaming and translucent like a jellyfish, she wondered about post-surgical hallucinations.

It moved about the room, a shimmering mirage of rainbow and clear energy, taking on the background of the walls and fixtures like a rippling, liquid glass. Beautiful, the sight of it strangely calmed Karen. She began to breathe again.

Tiny and glowing, the figure slipped away from the walls and floated toward her, hovering over her face. Growing bigger, it spread like a mist across the entire bed; a great transparent butterfly figure, slightly out of focus. There were no distinct edges, only shifts of color, like a rainbow through a cloud.

Somewhere between gnawing at the tube down her throat and grappling with fate, Karen heard it speak to her. There was no voice. It spoke in silence, inside her head.

"My child, you are not being punished," it said. "I have not abandoned you. I have been with you your entire life. I will continue to always be with you. You are very loved. Those who receive pain and tragedy are not the unfortunate ones. They have been given gifts of experience. You have done very well."

Karen listened, eyes wide, as it continued. Suddenly, memories were opened up, and she saw her life laid out before her. Past. Present. Future. The entity was with her every step of the way, reviewing each strategic event, explaining the whys and wherefores of every tragedy or triumph she had ever experienced. She wondered if this was it, if she really was dying, but in truth, Karen wanted to know only one thing.

Who are you?

Then she felt the heat.

Chapter 2: Lorry

November 1963

"Norbert, what the hell are you doing? She's going to drop her!"

Nine-year-old Lorry Kikel trembled as her father placed her newborn sister, Karen, in her arms. They had just driven home from the hospital where Rita had given birth, and Norbert was feeling happy. The proud papa. He finally had a fair, blonde child. Even the fact that it was a girl, and not the son they were expecting, could not dampen Norbert's joy. As a tradition in his native Austria, he wanted Lorry to carry the baby across the threshold into her new home.

"Norbert, watch her ... "

"Shut up, Rita. I know what I'm doing."

Rita Kikel grabbed the baby away from Lorry. "Are you some kind of idiot? You know how clumsy Lorry is! I can't believe you, Norbert. Don't you care about what I want?"

"I'm trying to do something nice here, and you have to go and ruin it, you stupid fat cow!"

Patty, the eldest daughter, tried to placate the situation.

"Mom, I can carry the baby."

"You're the one who always ruins everything, Norbert. Less than a week after President Kennedy is murdered, and all you can think about is your dumb Kraut traditions."

"What has Kennedy got to do with anything? This one is *my* baby, this time. I finally got a child who doesn't look like a guinea like the rest of you. If I want to do something Austrian with my blonde little girl, I'm entitled! Ah, hell," he said, "get in the goddamn house."

The day, which had started with so much joy, ended badly. Less than two-weeks-old, Karen Kikel's first sounds in her new home were of shrieking and broken crockery.

Her sister Lorry ran unnoticed to her room. She slammed the door and threw herself on the bed, cursing the new baby.

"You were supposed to be a boy," she sobbed, giving her pillow a thump. "We all wanted you to be a boy, not another girl! What am I going to do now?"

Nervous and needy, Lorry Kikel had never been an easy child. A difficult infant, then an overweight, angry youngster, she was often wide-eyed and confused with the dysfunctional nature of the Kikel household. To make matters worse, she was the spitting image of her mother. Dark, with Rita's Calabrian beauty, Lorry suffered under Norbert's hands. He resented her obvious Italian heritage, aching for the young woman he had married each time he looked at her. Lorry was too cruel a reminder, in his eyes, of what his beloved Rita had become.

Rejected by her father, Lorry turned to Rita, who schooled her in self-loathing.

"Me, me, me," Rita complained. "That's all you think about, Lorry. I can't listen to your problems; I've got to drive Grandma Lorenzo to the hairdresser's. If Daddy hit you, you probably deserved it."

Patty, the eldest daughter, had long since given up trying in their family.

"Just keep your mouth shut, Lorry. All you have to do is obey and be quiet. Then he'll ignore you."

Five years Lorry's senior, Patty never made waves. She knew obscurity and obedience were the answers in the Kikel home.

Lorry was cut from a different cloth. Needy for drama and romance, she often made up daydreams about herself, beautiful and thin, irresistible to men. Rita always told her a woman's looks were all-important. Lorry wanted men to worship her, desire her, shower her with gifts and loving reverence. She wanted joyous thoughts of men. The only happy memory she had with her father was when he used to lift the bed covers up and let her dive in. That was five years ago.

Now, with this new baby sister, it was going to be even harder to get attention. Lorry glared at the crib and changing table in her bedroom and screamed into her pillow.

Patty, in her own gentle way, had plans of her own. Fourteen-years-old, she was quietly waiting for her chance to get away. College was her goal. When she graduated high school, she was going to study psychology so she could avoid her parents' mistakes and help other people with theirs.

I'll find a good man and we'll start a family of our own. We'll love our children, and my husband will never harm them.

That dream kept Patty going. She kept her grades up, was meticulous in her grooming, and very beautiful. In Lorry's eyes, Patty was flawless.

As the months went by, it appeared that Patty was also very good with infants. She became a second mother to little Karen.

Lorry, forbidden to hold the baby because of her own clumsiness, clung even harder to her mother's skirts.

Everybody in the Kikel family dreamt their impossible dreams of freedom, retreating from each other into their own various hobbies. Patty studied mythology. Lorry became interested in Freud's theories of the mind. Rita, a frustrated singer, listened to opera and read romance novels.

Norbert Kikel was a collector. He kept meticulous documentation of a large variety of things: coin collections, rock collections, shell displays, star maps. Often littering the house with dozens of charts, he toted little Karen about with him.

Lorry watched him lavish love on the youngest daughter and hated him for it. "Why, Mommy?" she cried to Rita. "Why does he hate me so much? Why does he love Karen more than me?"

"He's jealous; that's why he pays so much attention to the baby," Rita said. "She looks like him. You look like me. There are two types of people in this world, Lorry: Italians and those who wish they were Italian. Daddy's just jealous, that's all. Don't you worry about him. How about poking around the house and finding his empties for me? You're such a good girl at that."

For her mother, in matters concerning Norbert, Lorry always obeyed without question.

Chapter 3:

Egghead and Sibling Rivalry

"Mommy, I can't sleep in there anymore!"

Rita rolled over in bed, frowning as she looked at the clock. Three in the morning. Lorry stood in the doorway, shuffling her bare feet, liquid-eyed and weepy. Norbert snored wetly under the covers.

Rita waved her out of the room, then got up. They went into the kitchen, where Lorry burst into tears.

"It's so scary in there, Mommy. Why does Karen have to sleep in my room?"

Rita was good at this; she'd had plenty of practice. Ever since the baby was born, Lorry complained about everything. *Daddy loves Karen, not me; you never sing to me anymore; you just sing to her; I wish she'd never been born; she's ugly; I hate her; blah blah blah.* Rita stifled a yawn.

"The little egghead is back," Lorry whimpered, "He's trying to climb up the crib bars again. He scares me."

"You and your stories, Lorry." Tugging her daughter's black hair, Rita yawned. "You're a regular little Sarah Bernhardt. I'm always telling my friends, *Who knows what she'll make up next? Lorry lives in her own dream world.*"

"But I see him, Mommy. Karen likes him. He scares me."

"Enough. I'm too tired to listen to anymore of your nonsense." Rita stood up. "I want to go to sleep."

Lorry balked at returning to her room, so Rita made up a bed on the couch. It would be Lorry's sleeping arrangement for the next twelve months.

Rita's health problems began soon after Karen was born. Pains in the abdomen, depression, women's complaints, and an even shorter temper than usual. By the time Karen was a year old, polyps had appeared in Rita's uterus. Her doctors decided these problems were best dealt with under the knife, and scheduled her for a full hysterectomy.

Norbert sat at home the night before the surgery, his arms flanking a bottle of scotch and a jug of sherry, lost in his own thoughts and bitter memories. He was devastated.

A hysterectomy. Christ. No son for Norbert. My luck's running to par, as usual.

He poured another drink, nursing bitterness and rage against the fate that had placed him here. Years of resentment had colored his memories, and one flawed truth stood out amongst the sodden mess of his thoughts. He was born to be betrayed. That was it. His father disowned him, his brother cheated him, his mother died too young.

"Born to be betrayed." He laughed in his scotch. "Yeah. I was born to be shit on."

The sins of the father had been passed down in Norbert Kikel. The long-standing hatred of his dad would last the rest of his life. Beaten one time too often, he'd broken all ties with his father after Patty was born. The proud grandpa had taken a hand to the baby girl when she'd upset him in the garden.

Norbert had come running at her cries. He found Patty down in the dust, crawling to escape, with his own father yelling about her lack of discipline. She was two-years-old.

Norbert had picked her up, turned a face of ice to his dad and said, "You'll never touch her again, you bastard." Then he walked away. It was the last time father and son ever saw each other. The old man was left bitter and vengeful, his son broken-hearted and angry. Norbert thought of the son he, himself, would never have now and swallowed another shot.

It was a strange night, the eve of Rita's hysterectomy. Karen was fussy, and kept trying to climb out of her crib. Norbert's mother-in-law, Mary Lorenzo, had come over from Levittown the day before. She slept in Lorry's bed, to be near the baby. Lorry was curled up on the living room couch.

Norbert sat alone in the TV room and drank himself through half-a-gallon of sherry, chasing it with an occasional scotch. His head was full of noise, and the majority of it concerned his wife.

I love that fat slob.

That was the thought that kept spinning through his mind; the passion he felt for Rita. Her skin, that voice like velvet when she sang and razorblades when she chastised, the obscene cackle when she was amused. Their constant sex. They could fight tooth and nail during the day, but at night, in bed, she was always warm. *God, don't let her die. I can't make it without her.*

He fumbled in his pocket for a cigarette, hands shaking so much he could barely spin the flame on his Zippo. *Hell, the things you think of when you might lose somebody.*

His mind wandered, tripping over memories of youth and courtship, of Rita in blue, a little cornflower nonsense of a hat perched on her head. She was something back then, and he'd been knocked for six. Such a smile. Such a million-dollar smile.

" ... and that bitch wouldn't let you sing," he muttered. "You could of been a star. They wanted you. She should have let you go."

As a young woman, Rita had been offered the chance to study opera in Italy. Mary Lorenzo, her mother, had stopped that with a well-timed case of hysteria.

I love you, my Rita! You're my daughter. You cannot leave me!

Norbert shook these memories away and drained another glass. Then he stumbled into the living room where Lorry was asleep on the couch. It didn't matter that she was only ten-years-old. He needed a shoulder to cry on, and she was there.

"Lorry, wake up." He shook her. "Wake up. Your mommy could be dying. What's the matter with you? How can you sleep?"

Rita survived the surgery. She came home with baskets of flowers, stacks of cards, and a raging case of menopause. She was up out of bed long before the doctors advised, cleaning the already spotless house, much to the chagrin of her daughters.

"Killing me," she gasped, pushing the vacuum cleaner. This was her favorite litany. "You're all killing me. I can clean and clean, and you still get it dirty."

"Gonna rip your stitches," Norbert warned. "Your guts are going to spill out all over that clean carpet."

"Shut up and move your feet!"

Lorry started to cry. "Mommy, let me help. If you just tell me what to do ... "

Rita shook her head, doubled over with pain.

"Forget it. None of you ever do it right. Everybody expects me to do it all. This house is filthy."

Norbert loved that first year of menopause. Rita burst into tears, burned up at night, cried for human contact, voiced insecurities, and best of all, avoided Mary Lorenzo. The man couldn't have been more pleased. He despised his mother-in-law.

It was a happy time for Lorry, too. She trotted to and fro, fetching sweets and slippers for her mother. Best of all, Rita had a kiss for each errand. The baby was shoved into the background.

Patty took over diaper changing and afternoon strolls. It was Patty who unearthed the ancient potty chair, coaxing a stubborn Karen into making use of it, Patty who took over many meal preparations when Rita was too tired. For a short time the family was content.

Unfortunately, happily-ever-after only lasted one year. Norbert was too scarred by his past, and Rita too subservient to hers, for it to be any longer. His father had beaten pettiness into him. Rita's mother had squeezed independence out of her from the day she was born. An old bout with angina in her mid-fifties was all the excuse Mary Lorenzo needed to bring her daughter under control again.

"My Rita, you never visit me anymore," Mary complained. "I need you. You're always running, running running. You never have time for me. My heart is empty without you. See what happens when I don't have my darling Rita with me? I could have died. Promise you won't leave me anymore."

"I'm sorry, Ma. You know I love you."

"Your father has been doing everything. All the shopping, all the driving. It's not a man's job to do those things. It's a daughter's."

"What do you need? Do you have enough groceries?"

"How can I have enough groceries when there's nobody to shop for me? You know I can't drive."

"I know, Ma."

Mary Lorenzo sighed, and her thick lower lip quivered. "If it's not too much trouble, do you think you could pick up some lamb?"

"Of course."

"Go to Rigetti's. They have the best cuts."

"Okay."

"I'll need some fresh vegetables to make the sauce. You can get them at the green grocer's in Westbury. The owner's son is married to my neighbor's daughter."

"Would you mind if I just got them at the farm stand near Rigetti's? Their stuff is good."

"It's not as fresh as the one in Westbury. You know that, Rita. Oh, and some bread. The bakery in Hicksville has a nice Italian loaf."

"Sure."

"And, if you can, pick up some wine. Don't go to that place near your house. Their liquor is no good."

Rita obeyed. Save for that one brief year after her hysterectomy, obedience had long ago become the sum of her existence. Her husband, children, herself; they all came a distant second to her mother. Three whole days a week were spent running errands for Mary.

Karen was often left with her grandmother or Aunt Emily while Rita shopped. She spent her formative years in homes smelling of pine and old woman, the air fragrant with tomatoes and sausages, cigarettes and game shows.

And the talking. Mary Lorenzo never stopped talking, ever. "You could slit that bitch's throat, and she'd still talk for a week," Norbert always said.

He was constantly annoyed about the Lorenzos' views on raising little girls, views Rita shared. Norbert's own opinion and advice were mostly ignored. As the years went by, Rita and Mary molded the three girls' perspective on proper feminine conduct. A woman's two main goals in life were to be good to her parents and get married. Rita brought her daughters up to be attractive to men. Their age was of little consequence.

"Men like a nice figure. You should show it off. Wear makeup. Give them a treat."

Lorry was comfortable with this advice. Patty was naturally modest, but Lorry was more extroverted, a trait which Rita encouraged. Before she was even in middle school, Lorry was adept with makeup.

Naturally conservative, Norbert objected to this, considering even T-shirts too immodest on a female. "Look at her, Rita," he shouted one day, pointing at Lorry's red lipstick and blue eye shadow. "She's painted up like a street walker!"

Rita, downstairs dusting a lampshade, frowned at her husband's big mouth. "I can't hear you, Norbert."

"I said your daughter's painted up like a street walker." He turned to Lorry. "You're not going out of this house dressed like that."

"Mom, he's bothering me again!" Lorry yelled.

Rita sighed.

"Mom!"

She put down her duster, and went up the stairs. "What's the problem, Norb?"

"She's been blow-drying her hair for thirty goddamn minutes," he said. "Is she going to pay the electric bill in this house?"

"Leave her alone, Norbert. Why don't you go have another drink, and mind your own goddamn business?"

"This is my goddamn business, you whale. I have a say in my own daughter's life."

"You know, you don't give a damn about any of us, Norbert. We do everything for you, and all you do is complain. You don't give us anything. Go complain to your bottle. You love it more than us."

Norbert gobbled like a fish, deeply wounded, then stormed off, slamming the door to the TV room.

Rita turned to Lorry. "Do you have to blow your hair dry now; when he's in the house? Hurry up. I don't need to get into another argument with him because of you, Lorry. You people are killing me."

Family nights in the TV room were another lesson in stress. Noise of any kind was anathema to Norbert while he was watching television. Coughing, chewing, shifting in your seat ... all of these were taboo. Lorry crunched on potato chips, and Norbert would glare at her for the noise.

"Fat food, Lorry," he said. "Keep eating those chips. You're gonna get as blubbery as your mother and grandma, that big fat elephant."

Lorry squirmed nervously in her seat.

"Stop moving," he hissed through clenched teeth.

She tried to suck the potato chips until she could swallow them silently, fighting back tears.

Rita wasn't immune, either. She sat with a bowl of ice cream balanced on her chest, her eyes glued to the TV. Norbert turned to her.

"That's right, Rita," he began, "keep eating that ice cream."

"Leave me alone, Norbert. You're pushing me."

"Oh, sure, I should leave you alone so you can get as fat as a house."

"Leave me alone, Norbert."

Rita's leg started shaking, but she doggedly kept shoveling the ice cream into her mouth. Lorry could see there was no longer any pleasure in it.

"That's right," he jeered. "Keep eating Rita, keep eating Rita, keep eating Rita, keep eating Rita, keep eating, Rita ... "

"Shut up Norbert! Shut up! You no-good son of a bitch!"

"Keep eating! Eat that ice cream! Get as big as your mother, that fat lousy bastard. That big fat guinea," Norbert yelled, waving his arm. "Why don't you go home to Mama, Rita? That's who you really love, anyway. Why don't you go over to your mama's house and kiss her ass?"

"Shut up, Norbert! Shut up!"

"Yah, yah, yah!" He made gobbling gestures with his fingers. "Yah, yah, yah, yah! Eat up! Eat up, Rita! Eat that fat food. Fat food, Rita! Fat food!"

"You lousy bastard, Norbert!" Rita screamed. "You lousy bastard! You did it to me again!" Her voice cracked.

"Yeah, run home to Mama where everybody loves you!"

"Drop dead, Norbert!"

Rita got up to leave.

"That's right. Go take a pill, now. Go on."

It had a scent of its own, the smell of crushed feelings and cruelty. Like dust and stale air, it permeated the Kikel household, and everyone stunk of it.

The living room was Rita's haven, full of furniture from her parents and cards from loving friends and neighbors. She was a favorite everywhere but in her own home. The living room reminded her that people cared for her.

She settled herself on the couch and wiped the tears away with a shaky hand. When her breathing returned to normal, she picked up a Barbara Cartland novel, poured a glass of wine, took a Valium and escaped. Lorry snuck out to check on her, but Rita never wanted the concern. She just wanted to be left alone.

* * *

The summer before Lorry entered junior high school, she made a decision to lose weight. She looked in the mirror and cursed her reflection. "Why are you so fat, you big elephant? Why can't you just stop eating?" She was struggling with her new curves. Lorry had always been chubby, but when puberty hit, she bloomed overnight into a hothouse flower half the school mocked for its lushness. She longed for the pencil-thin figures of models in glamorous magazines.

All the fat jokes in grade school were something she didn't want carried over into the next year, so Lorry simply stopped eating. When hungry, she sucked on lemons. When starving, she ate them. Every other day, she had one meal. She subsisted on coffee and Norbert's half-smoked cigarettes, losing thirty pounds in two-and-a-half months.

Both the Kikel and Lorenzo families reacted to Lorry's new shape with enthusiasm. She was beautiful now, so was worthy of praise. Lorry basked in the attention. One particular Sunday, Uncle Marco, Rita's little brother, slid an arm around Lorry's trim waist. He grabbed a chunk of skin, and laughed, "Oh ho! What's this?"

Lorry, secretly horrified, reacted with a grin and said, "Well, the fat's got to go somewhere."

Then she went home and dieted some more, mortified that he had found a flaw.

Nineteen years her junior, Marco was Rita's only brother, and the prince of the Lorenzo household. His every whim catered to, his word was law to his parents and sister. He was a man, therefore perfect in their eyes. Even his Calabrian bride, waiting patiently back in Italy, was there only to serve him. Marco was a misogynist. He was of the opinion that women were useful for two things: food and enjoyment. A sports fanatic, he was obsessed with physical prowess and athletic beauty. A woman's mind was the least of her attributes. When Lorry was overweight, Marco ignored her. Now that she was thin, he paid attention.

The neighborhood boys soon took notice, as well.

Once ridiculed for her chubby youth, Lorry was now admired for her body.

She glowed with pleasure under the new regard from the opposite sex.

Rita glowed as well, responding favorably to every whistle or admiring glance any male gave her daughter. "Look at you, Lorry, so beautiful and thin," she said. "They all want you. I'm so proud of you."

The attention was not all positive. When she was thirteen, Lorry was grabbed and groped by a senior in high school, a furtive moment of terror and breach of privacy behind the school.

Ted was on the football team, a strong and brash kid who lived down the street from the Kikels. Rita had often encouraged Lorry to talk to him. He was very handsome.

Ted waited for Lorry after school one day as she took a shortcut across the field.

"Hey, Lorraine."

Startled, Lorry almost dropped her books.

"Hi, Ted."

He walked up and slid a finger down her arm.

"You're looking good this year. Why don't you ever come up and talk to me? I see you all the time."

"I don't know."

"Why don't you come with me now? I want to talk to you."

Lorry's heart kicked up a beat.

"What about?"

"About you."

His eyes are beautiful.

"Look how gorgeous you are now." He held out his hand and smiled. "Come on."

Lorry placed her hand in his; felt the strong fingers close around her own. He led her back behind the building.

"Hey, remember when your mom always tried to get us together? She was always pushing you on me. I got to where I was ducking behind cars to avoid her. Hell, you were a fat little kid. But, look at you now."

Lorry smiled, rosy with pleasure.

"I was always so embarrassed," she said. "I didn't want you to see me. I know I looked awful."

"Well, you don't look awful now. Come here."

He slid his arms under her jacket. She held onto his shoulders as he curved his body into hers, shifting his weight to pull her in tightly.

"Gorgeous," he whispered, spreading his hands around her waist. He kissed her neck, and Lorry jumped. When his hand closed on her breast, she tried to pull back, pushing at his wrist.

"What's the matter?" he asked. "I won't hurt you. Just let me."

"I better get home," she said, but he wouldn't let her go.

"You don't have to go right now. Come on. What's the matter with you?" He cupped her bottom.

"No," Lorry gasped, frightened, "Ted, let me go!"

The situation lost control after that. His hands were everywhere. When he reached up under her skirt, she started to fight in earnest. He barely noticed.

"Ted, no. Stop it!"

He shoved two fingers past her panties and up into her, squirming them about. His fingernail scraped her. Lorry squealed, but he held her fast. When he pulled his fingers out, he sniffed her scent on the tips, and laughed as he let her go.

"Mmm!"

Lorry scrambled to her feet, eyes frozen on his grin as he smelled her on an index finger.

"You're all grown up now, huh, Kikel?" he asked, tapping his finger against his lip. "You smell *good*."

She turned and ran. Ted's laugh chased her home.

The story soon spread like wildfire throughout the school. Ted liked to brag about his conquests. Boys came up to Lorry, smelled their fingers and went, "Mmm" in a parody of her attacker's smile.

Lorry reacted as a victim, shamed and silent-mouthed, too humiliated to complain or deny. If she talked, her family would find out. If she complained, Rita would be angry and blame her.

As the weeks passed, the weight of her fear became too much, eventually locking Lorry inside the house. She only ventured outside to go to school.

Ted rode on her bus, often sitting behind her with a gang of grinning pals, fingers to noses, humming their cruel mouthwatering hum.

The innuendoes were everywhere. Furtive grabs, elbows jabbed in her breast, the over-excited taunts of teenage boys. All this became commonplace.

Depression, which had always been a part of her life, started gaining a powerful and dangerous foothold in Lorry's mind. She started sleeping with a knife under her pillow, was ill all the time, and missed a lot of school. Rita had to force her to go back.

"What's the matter with you, Lorry? You're not really sick. Stop drawing attention to yourself all the time. I have enough to do without catering to you. Go back to school. What will people think if you stay home all the time?"

Lorry just stared at her, detached. The realization came quite dispassionately.

I don't want to be alive any longer. She was spent, worn out. *Life is too much work. I've had enough.* She decided to kill herself.

The suicide was planned for Friday night. Norbert was taking the family out to dinner. Lorry faked a cough that afternoon, knowing her parents would never tolerate a germ in public. A well-placed *hack* got Rita's attention.

"Lorry, are you getting a cold?"

"I don't know, Ma. I feel awful, and my throat's all scratchy."

Rita slapped a cool hand to Lorry's forehead.

"You do feel a little warm. Well, I'm sorry, but you can't go out to eat. You'll make the whole restaurant sick. Will you be okay here, or do you want me to stay with you?"

"No, I'll be all right. I'm sorry, Mom. I want to go, but I think you're right. I do feel pretty lousy."

It was easy.

Lorry wrote a last will and testament as her suicide note. In it, she let all her bitterness and hidden sarcasm have free reign.

To my mother Rita, I leave my dirty socks. To my sister Karen, I leave my games, only if she promises to be like me and not our mother. To my sister Patty, I leave a stock in my ass. To my LOVING father Norbert, I leave my decks of playing cards ...

The note was no joke, despite its lackadaisical wording, no sad cry for help. Lorry just wanted the bitter humor of the words to explain her actions in a romantic, obtuse way. A last fling of drama before the final curtain.

Fifteen minutes before the family left for the restaurant, Lorry went into the bathroom, poured a huge glass of water for herself, and methodically swallowed handful after handful of buffered aspirin. The bottle was a large economy-size, brand new. It took a while for her to empty it.

Head already spinning, Lorry went downstairs to lie on the couch. Rita, ever the servant of illness, offered to stay home when she saw how pale Lorry was.

"You don't look good, Lorry. Are you sure you don't want me to stay?"

"No, Mom, I'll be fine. Go. Just go."

Lorry barely heard Rita's farewell. Her ears were ringing. Norbert, already in the car, honked the horn.

"Well, if you're sure you'll be all right ... "

Lorry smiled, dreamy with aspirin, and said good-bye for the last time. The horn blared again. Rita hurried out.

The ringing in her ears grew louder. Suddenly, Lorry felt the couch snap around, like a carnival ride jerking to a start. Vertigo whirled her about.

The dizziness subsided, and she opened her eyes. Everything was blackness. Disoriented, Lorry stood up and shuffled forward, arms outstretched. *I'm not in the living room. I would have hit furniture by now. This is somewhere else.*

Satisfied and a little scared, she waited. Nothing.

Good. I must be dead. It worked.

Frightened at first, Lorry became aware of a presence beside her, urging her forward. She began walking.

As her eyes grew accustomed to the darkness, she found herself in a long, dark tunnel. A light was at the end of the corridor, a bright white pinpoint, far away in the distance. Lorry walked faster.

She reached the brightness and stepped through. It filled her, warm and irresistible. Lorry felt breathless with the sensation.

There were shapes in the light; people silhouettes who smiled at her from every direction. Some of them seemed familiar.

"Lorry, don't you want to go back?" they asked. "There's so much left for you to do."

"No. I don't want to ever go back there."

"But you're not done. Your life isn't over yet. Don't you want to finish what you started?"

"No," she said, shaking her head. "Back there is terrible."

The silhouettes kept urging her. Lorry began to understand that they wanted her to want to go back. But she didn't. She wanted to stay in the light with them.

"You need to go back, Lorry. It's important."

"I hate it there. I'm miserable back there."

"You're not done yet."

They weren't going to stop urging her until she agreed. She sighed. "I want to stay. I feel loved here. But if you want me to go back, I will."

Taking one last sorrowful look around, Lorry closed her eyes, and nodded.

She woke up vomiting. Great white streaks of undigested aspirins poured out of her as she raced to the bathroom. Her body wrenched as it violently rejected the overdose. She threw up for hours.

Spent, Lorry cleaned up the mess, then fell into bed. Her ears rang for days, and for weeks she sweated a fine white film. Rita exclaimed over her pallor and violent nausea, but Lorry was silent about the suicide attempt.

It was a full twenty-four hours before she thought to look for her suicide note. She'd put it on the coffee table by the couch.

When she crept downstairs that night, the note was gone.

Lorry never told anyone about the overdose. She watched her parents and Patty cautiously for signs of anger or concern, waiting for someone to say something. No one ever did.

Little Karen had her own crosses to bear. "Bart the Fart" was foremost among them. Three years her senior, Bart Cummings lived next door. He was the terror of their street.

Every neighborhood has one. Bart picked on anything and everything smaller than himself, enjoying each minute of the mayhem he created.

Like a painter with his canvas, he searched for a subject to enshrine, something special that would make him immortal, if only in his victim's eyes. Bart found everything he could have dreamt of, and more, in Karen Kikel. He began stalking her when she was four.

"Mr. Kikel got a nickel then he bought a Karen Kikel. Hey, Kikel, Satan's coming for you! You're going to hell. You're gonna burn! Your dad's a drunk and your mom don't care. Satan will get you!"

Bart was obsessed with the devil.

He became the bane of her existence, the thing under the stairs, the monster under the bed, all rolled up into the boy next door.

Every day, Bart was waiting when Karen got off the school bus. Telling her mom about his petty torments just labeled her a tattletale; Rita wasn't about to chastise any of the neighbor's children, especially a boy.

"Why can't you just get along with the other kids? Don't bother your father, it'll cause trouble. I'll take care of it. Just stay away from him."

Easier said than done. Bart would not allow avoidance. As the months went by with no chastising, he grew bolder. The first time he beat her, Karen screamed with pain and fear, and Bart felt a rush of adrenaline like nothing he'd ever experienced. He made her eat mud pies full of bugs and earthworms, tied her up to the apple tree in the neighbor's backyard and lobbed apples at her. This behavior continued for years. When Karen was in First Grade, Bart tried to hang her in the garage.

When Norbert complained about it, Rita was there to stop him.

"I don't like Karen playing with that Bart kid, Rita. He's too rough with her, and he's way too old. Did you see her back?" She's got a bruise the size of an orange. I oughtta go over there and kick his ass."

"Oh, sure, Norb. Go over there and start a fight so none of us talk anymore. They're our neighbors, you know."

Patty was in college by this time and knew nothing of Bart. Lorry knew in an absentminded way, but had never thought to intervene. After hearing about the hanging incident, she questioned Rita for the first time.

"I'll handle it, Lorry. Don't worry about it."

"But ... "

"I said, drop it."

Troubled, Lorry went looking for her sister. She found Karen playing with a set of plastic florist shop animals. Rita was saving all her money for her daughters' weddings; nothing could be wasted on anything as frivolous as toys.

Karen was arranging plastic elephants in a circle when Lorry walked in.

"Hey, how's it goin'?" Lorry asked.

Karen shrugged.

"You know I keep change in that dish on my dresser," Lorry said, sticking her hands in her pockets. "Whenever the ice cream truck comes by, you can grab a couple quarters and get some ice cream if you want."

Lorry turned to leave, embarrassed by her own generosity. Karen, never one to miss an opportunity, blurted out, "Just for today? Or whenever I want?"

"Whenever you want," Lorry said. "It's okay."

The music box chords of the ice cream truck were never again heard with despair.

Chapter 4:

Satan Comes to Town

Patty was happy. In her third year at Stony Brook University, where she studied psychology, she was in her element. With lots of friends, legions of admirers, and excellent grades, she dated only sporadically, disliking the fumbled gropings of most of her suitors. In her heart, she longed for a gentleman to love and trust, a man who thought of more than just sex. Her dreams of a perfect husband were fueled by both her mother's teachings, and her own passion for romantic fantasy.

She paid for her education by working at Sears in Hicksville, student loans, and careful measuring of her life savings. It was at Sears that Patty met Bill Kelly. Here, at last, was her gentleman.

Bill was a tall man with an abnormally large head, exacerbated by a big hairstyle, heavily groomed. Dark, with thick black sideburns, he had a bobbing, jerky sort of smile and an eagerness to please.

Patty caught his eye with her docile nature, quiet good humor, and tiny frame. He loved small females; the tinier the better. Bill dazzled her with his courtly behavior and sycophantic nature. A voracious reader of historical romances, Patty felt she had at last found a tall dark knight to save her from the tower.

Her family loved him. Bill was respectful and inquiring of Norbert, fawning servitude with Rita and Grandma Lorenzo, and utterly charming to Aunt Emily and Uncle Joe. Emily was Mary Lorenzo's older sister.

Best of all, Bill was wonderful with Karen. Patty watched her little sister glow under the attention. Even Lorry liked him. Bill Kelly was more than welcome in the Kikel house.

Patty finished her last year of college with an outstanding GPA. She convinced Norbert and Rita to let her have a graduation party at the house. It took a bit more wrangling to get them to vacate the premises for the evening. They agreed, on the provision that Bill be present to oversee things.

The day of the party arrived, and the Kikel daughters spent hours preparing. Lorry was a vision in green, Patty glowed with excitement, and six-year-old Karen sat squirming with her hair in rollers. Norbert and Rita went over to a friend's house for dinner and an evening of poker.

The guests started arriving around six. Record player blaring, the party was soon in full swing. Everybody was smoking, drinking, and having a good time.

Patty had a lot of friends. Lorry found herself surrounded by handsome young men who drew her out despite her insecurity. She shyly practiced the art of flirtation and found she had a hidden talent for it.

Karen skipped about the crowded living room, dancing and laughing in her party dress. Bill looked at Karen and smiled, bending down to take her hand.

"You look like a little angel."

Karen followed him around like an adoring puppy, hanging on his sleeve. She caught glimpses of her sisters now and then, but they didn't concern her. Bill was the one she wanted to be with.

As the evening progressed, the music got louder while the crowd got noisier. Liquor flowed. Bill was a generous bartender and kept Patty's glass brimming. The air was hung with cigarette smoke and the Rolling Stones.

Karen found herself a little knocked-about by adults no longer steady on their feet. Alarmed, she looked around for Patty, but all she could see was a sea of legs. She opened her mouth and gave a yell.

Suddenly, Bill was there. He took her hand, smoothing her curls.

"Hey, little angel, what's the matter?"

"I don't like all these people. That man almost stepped on me."

"Come on, let's get you a drink."

He held a sheltering arm out when a dancer stumbled into her. Karen followed him into the kitchen where an array of bottles lined the counter.

"I'm going to make you my special homemade soda for big girls," he said, dropping ice into a glass. "It's real tasty when you get used to it, and it works a special kind of magic."

"Magic?"

"When you drink this, you feel like you can fly."

Karen watched as he stirred and poured, ice tinkling. He held the glass up, waved his hand over it like a magician, then bowed and handed it to her.

She took a tentative sip, grimacing at the taste.

"Don't be a baby, now," he said. "This is a drink for big girls. Swallow it all down and you'll be able to fly! Patty loves my special soda. I always make it for her."

Karen made a face, but drank obediently.

Afterward, he danced with her. Bill held her in his arms, a protective hand behind her back. Patty came, and wrapped her arms around both of them. They spun about the room, bumping and crashing into everybody, laughing. Somebody gave Karen a cigarette and she drew on it boldly, then hacked, choking. The crowd laughed. Lorry was somewhere outside in the backyard.

Karen began to get light-headed. It was all too much for such a little girl. She stumbled over to Patty, who was drunk by this time, deep in a discussion with her friends. Patty ignored her.

"I'm so dizzy," Karen slurred.

Bill caught her as she tumbled toward the floor. Laughing, he picked her up. "I think it's time this little party girl went to bed, Patty."

Patty looked at them, annoyed, then scanned the room for Lorry. She was nowhere to be seen.

"Don't worry, sweetheart," Bill said over the noise, "I'll put her down if you want."

Patty kissed him. "What would I do without you?" Then she returned to her friends.

Karen was indeed flying. Her head spun, she felt funny, her arms and legs were rubbery. It was a strange, euphoric thing, this feeling of weightlessness.

Bill took her to the back bedroom, where Rita's upright piano was. He closed the door. Karen decided she wanted to play the instrument. Bill set her down. She loved his kindness, his patience, his indulgent attention. She loved being treated like a princess. That was what he was doing. She was a princess to him. He'd told her so earlier.

She scrambled onto the piano stool, banged out a few notes, then climbed up and up. Bill steadied her when she swayed. She got on top of the piano, standing on the lid, and threw her arms wide.

"Catch me! I can fly!"

"Go ahead," Bill said, holding his arms out. He was laughing. "Come on. Fly!"

She leapt, and the world went dark. Other than a vague memory of choking, that was the last thing Karen remembered about Patty's graduation party.

* * *

Karen stood looking in the mirror, belligerent and angry at the little girl who glared back. It was the middle of the night. Her face was shiny with sleep, her hair was matted, and she had just wet the bed *again*.

The problem had started almost a year ago. As far as she knew, the first time was after Patty's party. What was the matter with her? How could she keep wetting the bed like a toddler? She was almost seven years old.

"You just stop that, you big baby," Karen said to her reflection, poking an accusing finger. "Now don't you do it, again. I mean it."

The bedwetting continued.

The humiliation of it all ate at Karen. No matter how hard she tried, the sheets would be soaked in the morning. Rita was kind, Lorry was understanding, Norbert was oblivious. It was Karen herself who chastised.

"I miss Patty," she whispered. "I want my Patty."

Patty was rarely at home anymore. She was out with Bill a lot or busy with her new job. As a teacher for emotionally disturbed adolescents, she soon found herself struggling with a discipline problem. Patty was too steeped in subservience to excel at this type of endeavor. Students pushed her around, and faculty threatened her employment if Patty tried to help too much. The politics of the system were wearing her down.

Truth be told, Patty was too fragile for her chosen profession, but she still doggedly held on. Bill worried about her. "Bill," she often said with a smile. "Thank heaven I have Bill."

* * *

Sundays belonged to family, and family meant Mary and Florindo Lorenzo. They lived in nearby Levittown, next door to Mary's sister Emily and her husband Joe.

Rita bundled the children into the car early in the morning, always urging an unwilling Norbert to come along. He usually refused.

"Norbert, come with us. How do you think it makes me feel, having to tell my parents you don't want to come? I'm tired of making excuses for you. It's embarrassing."

"Why should I spend the whole goddamn day over there with your family bitching and moaning? They hate me anyway. I don't feel like wasting my day off listening to your mother bossing everybody around and you kissing Prince Marco's ass every five minutes."

"My parents do not hate you. You're my husband."

"They hate me."

"Why would you even think that?"

Norbert stopped watching the TV and looked at her. "Because I'm not

Italian. Go on, get out of here before Mommy Lorenzo gets upset."

Rita shook her head, herded the kids out, and drove to Levittown. They always spent the whole day at her parents.

Enthroned in her living room chair when they arrived, Mary greeted them with the traditional shriek of delight.

"Aa! Flore! Look who's here! My darling Rita!"

"Hi, Ma. Girls, go give Grandma a kiss."

Mary embraced Lorry and Karen in a mammoth grip, squeezing cheeks and cracking ribs with her three-hundred-pound bear hug, only to grab and squash again with a guffaw of joy. Mary Lorenzo was like a big child in her pleasures.

"Ah, my beautiful granddaughters," she grinned, pushing her bottom teeth with her tongue. "Are you hungry?"

Food was of the utmost importance in the Lorenzo home. One couldn't cross the threshold without being plied non-stop with food and drink while Mary cackled her glee at all the cleaned plates and full stomachs. The gravest insult was to refuse any food offered.

Mary always sent Karen over to Aunt Emily's house as soon as greetings were over. Emily and Joe loved nothing better than to sleep late every Sunday after a night of heavy drinking.

Mary Lorenzo always found this too much to bear. It wasn't the drinking that bothered her. It was the sloth. If anyone slept past nine-thirty, in Mary's opinion, they were lazy bums.

"Karen, why don't you go over and see your aunt Emily and Uncle Joe? You know how he loves to go for a walk with you. If they don't answer right away, just keep ringing the doorbell. I know they're home, and they'll want to see you."

Thus, Mary would kill two birds with one stone; Karen would do her duty, and Emily would get her lazy backside out of bed.

Aunt Emily was a *pip*. That was Karen's pet name for her. Party animal, big drinker, big mouth, obsessive compulsive, Emily washed her hands a hundred times a day and covered all her drinks for fear of germs. Paradoxically, her house was messy. Emily was also a packrat. Knickknacks adorned every inch of every window. She called them her burglar alarms. If an intruder tried to get in a window, he'd knock over a statuette, and Emily would hear it. She had the hearing of an elephant. All her cold drinks had a protective sheet of plastic wrap stretched over the top with a straw poked through to guard against lint or dust. Hot drinks, like coffee, were covered with a saucer.

Her idiosyncrasies were hidden from the outside world, and the family simply put it down to being "Emily's way." She was a money launderer in the literal sense of the word; she washed all her currency, hung it up to dry in a closet strung with clothesline, then ironed each bill between two towels. The house was stale from never being aired, and they had a stinky old black dog with one eye named "Smokey" living on the end of a chain in the backyard.

Karen adored her Aunt Emily. Sundays were her favorite day of the week because she got to see Grandma, Grandpa and Aunt Emily. Skipping next door, she rang the doorbell and waited.

Time passed. After repeated rings, Karen finally just held the button down. The front door was yanked open, and Emily came spilling out.

"What? Who is it? What do you want?" she shrieked.

Karen stood grinning on the front step. Emily's face melted from a rictus to a greeting. She and Joe were always glad to see the girls.

"Did your grandma send you over?" she asked, squinting a bloodshot eye.

Karen bobbed her head.

"She said you'd want to see me, Aunt Emily."

"Hmm. Well, of course, she was right." Emily narrowed her eyes, then clapped her hands and said, "Do you want to have some fun with your Grandma?"

Karen nodded.

"Good girl. I have something for you. Come in."

They went into the kitchen, and her aunt pointed to a chair.

"Sit right there."

Emily got a clove of garlic, peeled it, and handed it to her niece.

"Eat this, Karen. Tell me how it tastes."

Karen, who loved garlic, crunched happily.

"Good?" Emily asked.

"Mmhm."

"Good. Now, Uncle Joe has to get ready before you can go for your walk together, so do me a little favor while you're waiting, yes? Go over to your grandma's, walk right up to her face, and blow really hard. Then come back and tell me what she did."

Karen scampered back to the Lorenzos, went into the living room, and perched on the arm of her grandma's chair. She started blowing covertly out of the side of her mouth.

Mary wrinkled her nose in distaste, wondering if Flore was ruining the sauce. Then her grandma realized what she was doing and grabbed Karen's cheeks, pinching until they were red.

"*Facha Bella!* I could just eat you up! Did your Aunt Emily tell you to do that?"

Karen grinned, nodding, and Mary let out a cackle of glee. This, too, was

Sunday tradition.

It was a day of play for all. Grandpa Flore taught the girls Italian and Albanian card games. Grandma taught them how to knit and crochet while watching an endless parade of cooking, variety and game shows. The television was always on.

Then it would be time to eat. Once the greens were tossed, Italian bread sliced, roasted peppers on the table, and the sauce flavored to perfection, the family sat down to steaming plates of pasta and enormous salads, the ingredients fresh from Grandpa's garden.

Only when everything was ready would Uncle Marco, who lived upstairs, come down to eat. He was interested only in food already prepared, a break from his sports shows.

A record was put on the stereo, and Italian opera serenaded them through dinner.

Mary surveyed her family with joy, patting her ample stomach. When each person had a plateful, instructions for the coming week began.

"Rita, can you take me to get my hair done this Thursday?"

"Can you make it Tuesday, when Dad and I do the food shopping? That'd be much easier for me, Mom."

"But Rita, my hairdresser's not in on Tuesdays, only Thursdays."

"All right."

"Thank you, my darling Rita."

"What time, Ma?"

"What time is good for you, dear?"

"Try to make it earlier in the day."

"Oh, and do you think that we can pick up a little something for Donna's daughter's baby shower?"

"No problem."

"Are you going to the baby shower?"

"I'm working that Saturday."

"Rita, it's Donna's daughter's shower. You should be there. She's my neighbor and a good friend. It won't look good if you don't show up. What will people say?"

"I'll have to switch days with Ronnie at work."

"When do you want to pick me and Emily up? We'll go together."

"Where is it?"

"Massapequa."

"Well, it takes about twenty-five minutes to get there, so I'll pick you up a half hour before."

"Why don't you pick us up an hour before? Even if we're early, it's better than being late. I can give you a little something to eat."

"No, thanks, Ma. We'll eat at the shower."

Marco would always be busy with his food during these conversations, never once mentioning that he could drive his mother to one, or all of her appointments. That was women's work.

The week's schedule arranged to her satisfaction, Mary looked up at her husband, her mouth full of pasta.

"Flore, could you pass the peppers?"

* * *

The national anthem played on the TV, signaling the end of another broadcast day. Norbert curled a lip in anger as the screen turned to snow. It was after midnight. There'd been another blow-up with Rita hours before, and he'd shut himself up in here to brood.

His drinking had increased with his bitterness. Norbert hated his in-laws. They had their coils in everything that should be his. As long as the Lorenzos were around, he'd always come second with Rita, and he knew it.

I could fight the old bat if it was just her mother, but the whole goddamn family? They're all against me, even Lorry. Yeah, they're grooming her good. She's a real Lorenzo now.

When he was drunk and miserable enough, Norbert staggered up in search of Karen, turning to his youngest daughter now for his nocturnal venting. Lorry was not listening anymore.

Karen listens to me. She cares about her daddy. Not like these stinking guineas, always up my ass. Karen understands me.

As the years went by, Norbert relied more and more on his youngest daughter for love and companionship. He poured out his slobbering misery into Karen's sympathetic and troubled ear, sparing her nothing. Every worry and adult fear he unburdened on a very young and impressionable girl, talking to her as he would a therapist. He damaged his daughter with such a weight, but misery likes company, and Norbert had no friends. Death, suffering, his brother's betrayal, his paranoid fear of Rita's imagined infidelity, all the hardships of a difficult life were related to his youngest child. Norbert shared everything. He felt no guilt or responsibility for Karen's sometimes obvious distress. In actuality, he felt gratitude for her childish compassion and concern. He became addicted to it.

Always, the fighting. The household became divided into two distinct war camps. Rita and Lorry. Norbert and Karen. Norbert even gave Karen instructions on how to spy on her own mother when he suspected Rita of adultery. Rita sent Lorry to talk to Karen, and the lines of battle were drawn daily.

Karen started suffering from lack of sleep. Her father's sorrows had become her own, and she floundered about in fitful dreams, unable to rest. The bedwetting continued.

She started praying to a little Virgin Mary statue beside her bed, asking for help. Mary Lorenzo suggested it. *The Virgin Mother will help you, Karen. If you pray hard enough and are a good girl, she'll hear you.*

Karen had always been a passionate creature. Locating a problem, she then invested her entire being into the solving of it. When Mary told her the Virgin could help, Karen took her grandmother's suggestion entirely to heart, praying day and night with a fervor that cut fingernail crescents into her hands. She prayed for her parents to stop fighting, for an end to her bedwetting and chronic bad dreams. She wanted to drift through something happy in her sleep, not be plagued by nightmares all the time.

Why couldn't she could be more like Patty? Beautiful, funny, gentle, and with a strange and wondrous gift; Patty could choose a dream. All she had to do was pick something she wanted to dream about, and she'd dream it. She could even continue a dream night-to-night.

"Dreams are wonderful things, Karen. My dreams are always good. You can choose to not have nightmares, you know. Just create your own dream at night, before you go to bed. You can escape your problems by dreaming."

This approach didn't work for Karen. No matter how hard she tried, she could never control her dreams. So, she turned to prayer, instead.

Having little or no formal religious upbringing, Karen nonetheless had a particular fondness for the Virgin Mary.

"Help me, Blessed Virgin," she whispered. "Help me make my family happy. I don't know how to do that by myself. Please show me how."
One night, half-asleep during her bedtime prayers, Karen experienced her first vision, or *waking dream*, as she would come to call them. Without realizing, she had begun to tap into a gift that would change her life forever.

A few months before, Rita had given her a little Virgin Mary statue to pray to. Karen kept it on the bookcase beside her bed where she could always find it in the dark. Norbert and Karen had made the bookcase together. It was comforting, her mother's statue on her father's shelf.

With her mind sleepy and relaxed, Karen felt herself sinking into the mattress. She was aware of both the bed beneath her body, and a feeling of being somewhere else at the same time. Drifting upward like a soap bubble, she looked down and saw her body far below.

Karen soon found herself in a field of white, no distinction between horizon and sky, no sense of distance. Only white. She started walking.

A light began forming in front of her. Karen stopped and tilted her head up, watching as it took shape, growing larger. Resembling a woman's silhouette, it solidified, filling with the soft blue of her little Virgin Mary's tunic. Rita's statue, come to life.

The figure hovered above Karen for several moments before drifting lower, settling a few feet above the little girl. The Lady smiled.

"Don't be afraid, Karen. I won't harm you. I love you. You're a good girl. You will do some very special things, someday. I will be there for you."

Then her face grew solemn, compassionate. "Your parents will not be with you much longer. Don't be afraid. You must be strong. There's a purpose for everything."

With a loving smile, the Lady began to pull away, fading into the white light. Karen started crying.

My parents? Why? What do you mean they won't be with me much longer?

The Lady continued to fade.

Wait! What do you mean? Tell me! Please tell me!

Karen felt a sudden chill thrum against her back, and turned. The answer to her question was behind her. Seven blurred shapes lay at her feet. Squinting her eyes, they slid into focus.

Seven coffins were lined neatly before her, their lids shut tight. Karen knew, with a terrible intuition, that her family filled these boxes. She stared at the first coffin and the box became translucent, giving her a glimpse of its occupant. It was Uncle Joe.

He's dead! Uncle Joe is going to die!

Karen woke sobbing, huddled under the covers, too terrified to move. This wasn't just another nightmare. Her uncle Joe was going to die soon. Six more would follow.

"Why am I seeing this?" Karen cried. "I'm bad. What's the matter with me? How could I do this?"

Voices came then, whispering comfort and prophecy, curling around her in soothing tones. She didn't see anything. She could only hear them.

"You're not bad. You're a good girl. This is not a dream. Don't be afraid. We're with you."

It was not the Lady's voice. This was something else. Karen wrapped her arms over her head, trying to shut them out. She cried brittle, heart-wrenching tears, and could not be comforted.

"Daddy, help me," she whispered in the darkness. "I'm scared. Please help me."

Norbert slept drunk in the other room, oblivious.

* * *

Summer passed, and Karen began to relax. The voices hadn't gone away. Indeed, they were always with her now, but she was getting used to them. None of her loved ones were ill. She watched them closely. None of them even looked sick. Maybe it was just a dream.

Then Joe was diagnosed with throat cancer and his health plummeted overnight. The leaves were changing for fall when he first heard the news. By Halloween, he was hospitalized.

The first coffin.

Karen was terrified. Death was coming. There was no right or wrong to it. She just knew it was coming. Fast.

The cancer claimed Joe on Thanksgiving Day. He was in the hospital surrounded by family, his chest vibrating with each exhausting pull of air, the sound ringing hollow and deafening in the quiet of the room.

Lorry, standing by his side, knew before his chest grew still that it was his last breath. She felt it in her whole body. Then he was gone.

Patty, crying softly, looked down at a distrait Karen, and stroked her head. "He's with God now, Karen," she said. "God has a plan."

Karen stared at the body of her uncle and wondered at the timing. *What is God thinking, to take him on Thanksgiving Day?*

Hysterical, Emily started screaming. "Don't leave me, Joe. Don't leave. Stay with me!"

Emily had always been afraid, but now with good reason. She was going to leave this hospital without her husband. Above all else, Emily was afraid of being alone.

Out of respect for Joe's passing, there was a modest Christmas tree in the Kikel household that year. Karen didn't mind its small stature, because on Christmas morning, there was a shiny blue banana-seat bicycle standing in front of it. A glittering gold tag, tied on the handle bar, read, "To Karrie Poo. Love, Patty."

All the other gifts were plain and inexpensive. The Lorenzos considered it sacrilege to celebrate the holiday at all, but Rita had put her foot down.

"My kids have got to have some joy at Christmas, Mom. Especially Karen. Joe's death hit her hard."

Mary mopped her eyes with a handkerchief. "Do what you want, my Rita. You always do anyway."

"Nothing fancy, Mom. I promise. Just a quiet little Christmas this year."

Rita instructed everyone to buy only modest gifts, but Patty disregarded the order. She knew what the bike would mean to her beloved little sister, and paid for it with her own money. Bill supported her, but cautioned against angering the family. Patty was adamant.

"Let them get upset, Bill. I'm doing this for Karen."

The bicycle was the best Christmas present Karen ever got.

* * *

Aunt Emily moved in with the Kikels after Joe's death, and soon proved as incapable of self-sufficiency as her sister Mary. Rita's errands were now doubled. In an effort to keep his wife home at least some of the time, Norbert agreed to having Emily live with them.

Karen loved having her there. They popped Jiffy Pop, and watched the wrestler Bruno Samartino conquer the world once a week on television.

Emily was a wrestling fanatic. She taught Karen all the wrestler's names and colorful backgrounds. Karen became, if not an avid fan, an avid participator in spending quality time with her aunt.

Norbert was a closet fan himself. Storming into the room during wrestling, he began with a cursory complaint.

"What is this shit? *National Geographic* is on!"

"Shut up and sit down, Norbert," Emily yelled. "Can't you see this is great stuff?"

"If you're a moron, sure. Look at that guy. Somebody should shave his ass and make him walk backwards. He'd look better."

"Don't you insult my boy!"

"Hell, Emily, everybody knows it's fake."

"I'd like to see you do it, then." Emily whacked the seat cushion. "Sit down and watch. You might learn something."

Content with his show of disdain, Norbert sat. He made fun of it all, but enjoyed the show as much as they did. It didn't matter how drunk or mean he was. Emily stood up to him. Even Rita backed off when Norbert was in a drunken rant, but not Emily. She gave as good as she got. Karen hoped one day to be as magnificent as her aunt.

Minus the compulsions. Emily drove them all crazy with those, turning lights on and off eight times whenever she touched a switch, locking the door repeatedly, turning the hot water on and off and freezing out whoever was unfortunate enough to be in the shower. She drove Lorry insane. Cleaning, separating M&M's into color groups, arranging olives in a dish so all the pimentos faced left. Her obsessive behavior was endless. And the meals; Norbert raged about the compulsive dinners.

Emily often did the cooking because Rita was working, out shopping, or upstairs with a headache. Every day of the week had its set menu. Monday was hot dogs and sauerkraut, Tuesday was hash and eggs, Wednesday was kielbasa, Thursday was leftovers, Friday was fried chicken, Saturday was Norbert's famous meat loaf, Sunday was dinner at Grandma's. Norbert accused Emily of trying to murder him. "There's enough grease in your food to clog every artery in my body, Em. I think you're trying to murder us all. That's what I think."

Emily agreed with a grin.

* * *

Lorry met Vincenzo "Vinnie" Salluzzi in 1971. Born in Naples, Italy, Vinnie had come to America as a youth. He spoke broken English, and Lorry's Italian language instructor introduced them. They soon began dating.

Rita's mouth watered at the idea of her daughter marrying a good Napolitan man, and Lorry bloomed under the positive attention.

Rita wanted grandchildren. Italian grandchildren. "He's a good man, Lorry. A good, strong Italian to take care of you. What beautiful babies you would have with him. What a good father he'd be."

To the delight of the Lorenzos, Vinnie quickly proposed. Despite being only sixteen, Lorry accepted, more for Rita's sake than her own, regardless of her many unspoken reservations. She cared for Vinnie, but there was no spark, no sexual tension, no longing to simply be with him. The lack of passion troubled her.

"The spark happens after marriage, Lorry," Rita promised. "You have to be a wife before you get those feelings. Don't worry about it."

"Sometimes Vinnie feels more like my brother than my boyfriend, Ma. Do you really think this is a good idea? Us getting married?"

"What are you talking about? Look how much he loves you. He's Italian. He's a hard worker. He'll be a good husband and father. Vinnie will be able to give you all the things your father couldn't give me. Do you want to give all that up? Do you?"

Lorry looked down at her hands, clasped together on the table. "I guess not."

The engagement would end up lasting seven years.

* * *

Aunt Emily hated Hicksville. She missed her own home and her sister Mary in Levittown. Plus, she was paranoid. "Who knows what burglars might have broken into my empty house in the middle of the night?" she ranted. "You should all move back there with me. Back to the Levittown house."

This became Emily's newest obsession. She spoke of it morning, noon and night, badgering Norbert.

"It's so much nicer there. My house is bigger than this place. You could live upstairs. Come on, Norbert, sell this house and save the money. Levittown is less expensive than here."

Expensive was the key word. Norbert was cheap. He was infamously, notoriously, Charles-Dickens-Christmas-Carol cheap. Money was of absolute importance to him.

Emily used that as her bait. It was her best lure, her shiny red refracting tailspin feathered tackle, and Norbert fell for it. Levittown would be cheaper than Hicksville. That statement sunk the hook.

He talked it over with Rita. "Sounds pretty good. This place is a money pit, anyway, and we could sure use the extra cash."

"I think it's a great idea, Norb. How soon do you think we can move?"

"I already talked to a realtor."

The Kikel house sold quickly. Everybody rushed to pack, and money from the sale was used to convert Emily's upstairs into a separate apartment.

The day of the move arrived, coinciding with a solar eclipse. Karen stood in the driveway of her old home for the last time, staring up at the nimbus, ignoring Norbert's warning of dire consequences for doing so.

Bart glared from two doors down. He would miss the Kikel brat. He would miss hurting her.

Karen felt him staring. She was glad to be moving, if only to get away from Bart, but couldn't shake a feeling of dread. Her nightmares had not abated, and the coffin visions plagued her. Parental spats were worse than usual in the weeks before the move, and everyone's nerves were on edge. Worst of all, Patty was not going with them. She was moving in with Bill. Karen would miss her always.

She looked at her parents bickering in the rental truck, observed Lorry's troubled expression, and knew there would be another scene soon.

Is this it? she thought. *Is it always going to be like this?*

She prayed again, but this time, to whatever was up there; God, Jesus, Aliens, the Great Spirit; a hodgepodge of possibilities. Anything that would listen. She asked to be taken out of here, away from this world of bickering and unhappiness.

The nightmares were the worst. They invaded her head, flooded her bladder, tortured and humiliated her. Karen wanted to be rid of this harsh and ugly existence. She was tired of life and all its hardships. Unlike Lorry, it wasn't a heavy, dull longing to escape the present. Karen was afraid of her future. She could see it coming, but there was nowhere to hide.

"Why did you leave me here?" she asked the sky in a childish whisper. "I'm not one of them. I don't want to be here. Please don't make me stay. Please, please, please take me out of here. Don't make me do it. Don't make me stay."

"Karen!" Norbert yelled from the rental truck. "Get your butt in here. Hurry up. We're leaving!"

Glaring at the black sun, she ran to the truck.

Chapter 5:

Levittown

Levittown, New York was built after World War II, an experiment in the, as yet, unknown world of suburban housing. Hundreds of thousands of American fighting men were coming home from the war, and they needed a place to live. Housing was scarce, demand high.

The town was a clever gamble that made a fortune for the builders, if not the homeowners. All the properties were identical, cookie-cutter houses stretching for blocks in all directions like the tombstones in Arlington; regimented, rectangular, the same.

The project, started as a dream, would have been perfect if humanity were impeccable. But people, blemished by memories of war and suffering, were far from flawless. The houses filled up with veterans returning from the war, eager to find work in New York City, only a few miles away. Levittown became one of the first suburbs. The initial feeling was of hope and goodwill, flooded with relief to be anywhere but overseas in a stinking foxhole.

It wasn't to last. Long work hours, baby-boomer children, insufficient schools and medical facilities, not to mention unimaginable emotional scars from the war, trapped hundreds in misery. Everybody had the same horrendous experiences but nobody to discuss them with. Speaking ill of the war or one's trauma from it was frowned upon. America was now rich. It was considered immoral and self-indulgent to be upset over anything that happened overseas.

Several generations of stewing in poverty, alcoholism, overcrowding and welfare seasoned the mixture. Into this environment, the Kikels were dropped.

Lorry was a senior in high school when the family moved. She wanted to finish out her education in the Hicksville District, so she drove herself back and forth to class everyday. Half the school year was over before the oversight was discovered, and Hicksville High School allowed her to finish out the remaining two quarters. She was an honor student, so they let the matter slide.

It was Karen who had to discover the violence of the Levittown School District. Bullied at school, she avoided drugs in the public bathrooms, but was tormented in class. Glad to be rid of Bart, she found herself safe from neighbor kids at home, but threatened by others at school. No longer having Patty to talk to, nervous habits began to form.

She started eating a lot of junk food. Her weight ballooned, making her an easy target for the other kids. Norbert started making comments, as well.

Uncle Marco, who lived next door with his parents, noticed Karen's weight gain immediately. "You better watch Karen, Reet. Remember what happens to the Lorenzo women. Don't let her get fat, too. She's already got thunder thighs. Men don't like Zoftig women."

Karen was sitting at the table with them, having an after school snack. Marco spoke as if she weren't in the room.

"That's it, Karen," Marco said, laughing. "Take another bite of that biscotti for those beautiful juicy, big behemoth thighs."

"Leave her alone, Marco."

"Ah, I don't mean anything by it. Karen's got a big, gorgeous fat ass. It's not like yours, Rita. You've all got those flat butts. But Karen ... " He grinned, and made *wide load* hands on either side of his hips.

"Karen so stroongg. Zoftig, big healthy girl!"

Never content with her looks to begin with, Karen began suffering from a rapidly declining self-image. She combed her long hair forward to hide a soft jawline and wore loose clothes to hide a soft waist. Hidden. A large part of her thinking was dedicated to staying hidden. Camouflage consisted of the obvious hairstyle and baggy clothes, plus the more subtle use of humor and personality. Outwardly, Karen was funny and extroverted. Inside, she was huddled in a corner, licking wounds.

The move to Levittown was a mistake for the Kikel family. Grandma and Grandpa Lorenzo lived next door, and in their lap. Marco was also demanding Rita's attention. Norbert almost never saw his wife alone, anymore. There was always a Lorenzo around. The families began to root together, twisting, inevitable, overcrowded. Rita was over at Grandma's house, or Grandma was over at Emily's.

Lorry, who had a car of her own now, began running errands for her mother.

"Go to the store and pick me up a pound of lamb, will you, Lorry? Make sure you go to the butcher's in Huntington ... "

Lorry was growing up, and Rita was grooming her for a life of servitude. Lorry's entire existence began to consist of obeying her mother. Obedience had become her world. Everything, from her free time to the clothes she wore was influenced by Rita.

"Why don't you wear that short skirt you just got, Lorry? You have such pretty legs. Give the boys a treat."

Lorry was beautiful now. Having grown another two inches in height, she remained trim and lusciously curved. Her outfits became tighter, her waist smaller, hair longer. Years of makeup experimentation and a clever eye enhanced her already formidable looks, and she began to enjoy the attention her sensuality brought. An admiring stare, she had learned, was something to be proud of. Lorry flirted and played the game, but always remained the good girl her mother demanded. Good meant virgin. Vinnie respected this. He knew she was chaste, one of the reasons he wanted to marry her.

Bill Kelly took note of her as well. Patty and he were married on October 31, 1971, and Halloween was an appropriate day for such a ceremony. The devil had come to town and married the firstborn. The newlyweds lived in an apartment fifteen minutes away from the Kikel and Lorenzo houses.

Patty began to change soon after her honeymoon. Her vivacious color started to fade, green eyes grew dull, and she became querulous and demanding. Any kind of slight, real or imagined, could send her into a rage. Worried, the family was grateful she had Bill to take care of her.

He encouraged Patty to quit her job as a teacher, citing the strain on her emotions, as well as the long commute.

"Patty, that job is just too much for someone as sensitive as you," he said. "You're not strong enough. I don't want my wife working in such a dangerous place. Why don't you just quit? It's tearing you apart, and I can't stand it."

He exaggerated problems, pointed out pitfalls, and stressed the negative as often as possible, planting thoughts of fear and paranoia in his highly receptive and romantic wife. He wanted her to have no will of her own and no independence.

As the months went by, she began to rely on Bill for everything. He even discouraged her from driving the car, so Patty called Lorry for shopping favors.

Already overburdened, Lorry secretly welcomed the added chores. It was fun at Bill and Patty's, and she visited their apartment often. Any excuse to get away from the Kikel house was good enough for her.

Bill and Patty treat me like an adult. Bill even mixes drinks for me and lets me smoke. He doesn't think I'm a kid.

Lorry spent hours with the Kellys, often spending the night because she was too drunk to go home.

Patty began to rely on Lorry's company. She rarely visited Rita or the Lorenzos anymore, preferring the family to come to her. Bill was always pleasant, hovering over his wife, seeing to her every comfort. Lorry admired this. She liked the way he served them. Women, in Lorry's experience, were supposed to be subservient to men, but with Bill, the roles were reversed. Patty and she were waited on hand and foot. Nothing was too grown-up for her at their apartment. Drinking, smoking, anything. Her age didn't seem to matter to Bill or her sister. He got Lorry drunk often. Patty was already miles down the road toward alcoholism. She encouraged Lorry's drinking, as well. Bill never touched liquor himself, but he was a generous bartender.

In their bathroom, Lorry found at least half-a-dozen prescription bottles at any given time. Patty explained about depression and dealing with repressed feelings from childhood. The drugs helped her cope.

"You know what it was like growing up with Mommy and Daddy. I'm having a hard time right now. Thank God for Bill. He's helping me through it."

This became Patty's dirge.

Lorry was repulsed by her sister's weaknesses and irritated with her attitude, but she still accepted glass after glass of red wine every visit. It was social drinking, a desirable occupation at their house, and Lorry enjoyed the fuzziness of being sloshed, the seductive forgetfulness of it.

Bill encouraged the two sisters, bringing fistfuls of medications to his wife with a loving grin. Lorry kept silent about the prescription drugs. Any hint of criticism sent Patty into a rage, so it was easier to just keep her mouth shut.

Rita was the only person Lorry confided in, and Rita didn't see anything seriously wrong with her eldest daughter.

"As soon as Patty has her first baby, she'll be better," Rita said. "Being a mother will make her happy. Then she'll be more responsible. You'll see, Lorry. A baby will turn things around. It always does."

Time proved this happy future unlikely. Patty couldn't get pregnant. As the infertile months passed, she grew more and more unstable. It was fast, so fast, the deterioration of a once beautiful woman. Eyes greasy with drink, skin like sweaty cauliflower, she was a gruesome caricature of the lovely creature she'd once been.

Through Patty, Lorry saw a vision of her own possible future; a weak-spirited, whining, demanding loser with a monster for a mate.

Lorry's concern took different routes. Already saddled with Rita, Emily and Grandma, Lorry was afraid of even more responsibility. She ran almost all the errands now, including chauffeuring them to endless appointments. If Patty slid too far, became too unhinged, Bill might leave her. Lorry knew the job would fall on herself to pick up the pieces and shoulder one more demanding woman.

This very real fear brought a fresh supply of guilt, and Lorry gnawed at her own selfishness like a rat on an open wound. With the stubborn naiveté of a teenager, she decided to personally shoulder the problems of both Patty's drinking and her bottomless sorrow.

Psychiatrists are for crazy people. This was ingrained in the Lorenzo/Kikel psyche. Lorry knew that route was impossible. Norbert and Rita were both opposed to anyone in their family going to some shrink. What if someone found out? Therapy was unacceptable. Patty could train to be a psychologist, but she could never seek the help of one.

Lorry started reading books about child abuse and dysfunctional families long before there were such terms. She tried to understand Patty's relentless slide into depression and attempted to put on the brakes single-handedly. It didn't work. Lorry was halfway down the cliff herself. The interference was futile. Patty wanted the misery.

Bill watched all this from the sidelines, offering his beautiful young sister-in-law help and hindrance in a two-fisted eagerness to please.

"I'm so grateful for your concern, Lorry. I can see you really love my Patty. You mean so much to us both," he said. "Thank you for being so thoughtful. Your visits mean the world to Patty. She always cheers up when you're here."

Lorry blushed with pleasure. She appreciated any positive male interest, even that of a man she was uncertain of. Young and ingenuous, she hesitantly basked in his praise. Maybe Bill didn't understand about Patty's depression and the danger of all those prescription drugs. Lorry knew he didn't realize the harm he was causing his wife. He just wanted to keep everybody happy. Perhaps she could get through to him.

"I trust you, Lorry," Bill said. "You seem to understand everything so well. I know I can tell you my troubles and you'll have an answer. You always give good advice. You're such a comfort to Patty, and such a help to me. Thank you for that."

They would talk in the kitchen a lot when making dinner or mixing drinks, while Patty was in the other room. Over and over again, Bill thanked Lorry for her insight; she was so understanding, such a good listener, so intelligent. Lorry ate it up.

***

"Ready to go to Agway, Karen?"

"Yeah. We gonna buy the garden stuff today?"

Norbert had discovered a new hobby. Mary and Flore Lorenzo had a monumental vegetable garden next door. Hours were spent admiring their tomatoes, and Norbert was sick of it. Rivalry reared its ugly head, and he was determined to outdo them with a garden of his own. Karen was his partner.

"If we want our vegetables to be twice as big as your grandma's, we'll need to mix our own special soil."

"You really think our vegetables can be twice as big?"

"Of course."

"How?"

"We'll build gardening boxes in the backyard and fill them with our own blend of soil. Vermiculite, peat moss, topsoil, Miracle Grow, and horse manure. The boxes will prevent weeds. Then you can sell what we grow. You'll make a lot of money with your own vegetable stand."

"Oh, wow! I can keep all the money?"

"Sure. Well, after we deduct what we spent on supplies. There's the dirt, wood for the boxes, nails, the seedlings, plant food ... you can pay me back from your vegetable stand earnings."

"Oh ... okay."

Always eager to exercise his scientific background, Norbert had hatched the idea to garden in long seven-foot boxes, in an attempt to curtail the weeds. He bought the lumber, hammered the nails, filled the boxes with dirt, and planted his vegetable garden. Karen read his detailed notes, and was as eager as he to prove the brilliance of such a gardening breakthrough. They filled the containers with carefully nurtured plants.

The boxes, seven in all, looked like two neat rows of open coffins. Karen thought uncomfortably of her dream. Mary Lorenzo labeled it the *coffin garden*, which enraged Norbert.

"Those vegetables are growing in dead man's soil, Norbert. I'm not going to eat anything that was grown in a coffin."

"They're not coffins, Mary. The boxes prevent weeds from spreading."

"I'm still not eating anything grown in those things. It's a stupid idea."

"You think of that this summer when your husband's breaking his back pulling weeds. I'm telling you, this is the way of the future. I'm saving all that work."

Sadly, Norbert hadn't taken into account the fact that many seeds were carried through the air. Weeds sprouted just as well in the boxes as outside of them, a fact Mary and Rita wasted no time in pointing out.

"Great job, Norb," Rita said, laughing. "Those boxes really worked. Looks like another one of your inventions falls flat on its face."

Mary shook her head, folding her massive arms over her bosom. "It's a good thing our garden is doing so well, or we wouldn't have any fresh vegetables this summer."

It became a war zone of sorts, the coffin garden. Lorry, always eager to please, joined her mother in mocking the failed experiment. "Nice cemetery in our backyard. When we all die, Daddy can grow tomatoes on us."

"And marigolds, Lorry," Rita said. "You'd grow some nice big colorful ones."

"With my luck, he'd plant weeds in my box."

Stung, Norbert went on the attack. "You have a big fat nasty mouth, Lorry, just like your mother. Very nice, Rita. You taught her to be just like you."

He cut his daughter to the bone with those words, robbing her of breath. She ran into the house.

After that, Lorry abandoned her psychology books, and any quest for self-discovery. There just didn't seem any time for it anymore. The shopping alone took hours each day. Lorry moved and obeyed, going about her daily routine in a sort of daze, as if she were in shock. She went to school, worked at her job, and ran errands for the women in her family. In a way, she was in shock. Lorry was tired of breathing, tired of waiting for her *great destiny*, tired of watching her parents fight and her sister drink.

She thought about the light she'd stepped into all those years ago, cursing the fate that made her return to such a miserable existence. If she talked to her grandmother about it, Mary chastised her.

"Why do you want to be happy, Lorry? Nobody is happy. You have so much life to live. Look at everything you've got. You're young; you're engaged to a man who will make a lot of money someday. How can you be unhappy? It's ridiculous!"

Vinnie was equally supportive.

"Happy? There's a saying in Italy," he said. "Happiness, Happiness. Everyone is chasing him, but no one ever catches him." Then he shrugged, and turned away.

Lorry began to wish she were invisible.

Too visible to God. I don't want to be seen anymore. If He sees me, He'll do something else.

If she stayed under the covers, or didn't leave the house, everything would be all right. It would pass over. It wouldn't get her that day. She wasn't sure what *It* was, but assumed that it must be God.

Lorry's vision became disjointed. She could look at her hair, but not her face at the same time, or look at her body, but not above the neck. Put makeup on the eyes, but don't look at the lips or cheekbones at the same time. Exhausted physically, mentally, and spiritually, she sank into a sullen anger.

Drinking became the answer, the escape she discovered worked the best.

Aunt Emily hassled her about drinking and smoking at home. Norbert bitched about his gallon jugs getting watered down. Rita nagged about everything, and Karen *The Brat*, as Lorry called her, got on her nerves. Norbert liked Karen best, anyway, and that in itself was painful to witness.

Karen was oblivious to Lorry's feelings. She was too young to understand, and Norbert kept tight control of her. Karen was the last, the only one of his children who hadn't turned against him. He would fight to keep her.

Those goddamn Italians won't take Karen away from me. She's mine!

The war zone inside his home was much of Norbert's own making. He didn't concern himself with Lorry's feelings. She was part of the enemy. Karen was an ally.

Patty and Bill were the safe haven for Lorry, the lesser of two evils. There, drinking was not only permitted but encouraged, and Bill fixed them for her himself. Lorry loved the simple solution of drunkenness to forget her problems, and at the Kelly's apartment, it was easy as well as free.

She began spending the night more often, sleeping on the couch. Sometimes she'd wake long enough from a drunken sleep to feel Bill's hand on her naked thigh. Sometimes she wouldn't. Denial and insecurity had Lorry mistrusting her own senses. She convinced herself that she must have been dreaming, it couldn't have been real. Bill was always so grateful for everything she did. He seemed to be the only one who realized how hard Lorry tried. How little she was appreciated. Surely, his hands on her body weren't as bad as she imagined. Bill would always whisper away these liberties in a soft argument guaranteed to confuse.

"I love you so much, Lorry," he said. "You're my sweet little sister. I wish you lived with us all the time. Then we could take care of each other and help Patty. I love Patty so much, Lorry. She's so sensitive. We have to be careful with everything we say to her, though, don't we? She's as fragile as glass. I've always kept things from her, so she won't worry. I know you do that, too. Your sister is so delicate. Thank heaven she has you. I thank heaven for you, too."

Lorry believed him. Cynicism had only begun to wind its way into her feelings, and the flattery and free-flowing alcohol were too much to resist. That, and a misguided loyalty to Patty. Patty needed her, and Lorry needed to be needed. She kept going back to their apartment, ignoring her own instincts, punching more holes into her spirit until her self-esteem was as porous and brittle as an old sponge.

Encouraged by her silence, Bill got bolder as the months went by. Lorry caught him groping her in her sleep more often. He explained it away as a tale of her guilt, not his, and Lorry was so ashamed, she'd said nothing. She remembered Ted, whose hands inspired a whole bottle of aspirin. Of home movies with Uncle Marco behind a camera, encouraging her and her sisters to flaunt their bodies. This was life. This was how men were. Sorrow was her fate, and Lorry was bone weary from fighting it.

She made one weak attempt to escape and stopped staying the night at the apartment. But they missed her. Bill called the house often. Patty whined about the shortness of her visits.

"You just drop off the groceries and leave, Lorry," Patty said. "Can't you spare a moment for your own sister? You're upsetting me and my husband. Don't you love us anymore? Why are you doing this?"

Lorry couldn't tell her.

Bill worked the sidelines, dropping endless poison into his wife's ear.

"I'm so sorry, Patty," he said. "It's not you. She wouldn't stay away because of you. It must be me. I know she's only eighteen, and teenagers are moody, but it hurts me. I really love Lorry. Do you think I did anything wrong? Do you think I said something mean or thoughtless to her? She seemed happy over here. She was always such help to you." He sighed. "I can't stand either of you being sad. I love her like my own sister."

His eyes filled with tears.

"Sorry, sweetheart. Guess I'm just over-sensitive, thinking about everything. Work is pretty busy right now, too, and I think that's ... it just makes me feel better when she's here with you, that's all. It worries me when you're alone."

"Oh, Bill, I'm so sorry she's hurting you like this."

"No, sweetheart, it's not me I care about. It's you. Lorry's your sister and you love her, and I'm keeping her away. Please forgive me. I'd rather die than hurt either of you."

Patty wasn't the only one he worked on. Bill talked to Rita about Lorry's continued absence.

"I was so much more relaxed when she was around, Mom. Patty always seemed to feel better when she was here. Lorry's got that touch, you know. She could have been a doctor."

Rita was hog-tied and willing to help in a single afternoon, chastising Lorry for her selfishness.

"Don't you ever think of anybody but yourself? This is family. Patty is blood. How can you neglect your sister like that, Lorry? She's not well. Bill is so worried. Don't you care about her at all? Why won't you go visit? Family is the only thing in this world you can count on. Family is always there for each other. You're betraying that sacred trust. You're betraying your own sister."

Lorry couldn't tell her about Bill's roving hands. She was afraid of Rita disbelieving, or worse, blaming her. Finally, Lorry gave in. At least at Patty's she could drink.

She drove over to the Kellys' apartment the next day. They welcomed her back with open arms. The gropings in the dark started soon after.

Bill began to grow anxious for more each time he touched Lorry in her sleep. Her easily manipulated guilt made her simple to control. She was so ashamed, she just kept her mouth shut. Fantasizing about her skin, Bill wanted more than just the outside of her. He wanted to be inside as well. He knew she was a virgin. And so young; still a child, really. Her skin was like a baby's, soft and poreless, like her little sister Karen's.

He justified his own terrible violations by Lorry's continued silence. *She must not be too bothered, or she'd say something. She'd tell. Maybe she likes it. Look how she dresses. Yeah, she must like it.* An inner voice whispered the truth, but Bill refused to listen.

Hatching an idea while selling a death and dismemberment plan, Bill laid the trap carefully over a span of several weeks. He calculated which words to plant in Patty's mind, how to water them; what to tell Lorry afterward to guarantee her silence. The plan obsessed him.

Patty picked up extra hours at Kearns Florist where she worked part-time with her mother.

"Bill's trying so hard to make ends meet, Mom, but the insurance business is so slow right now. My poor man feels so guilty at my having to work extra hours. I know things will get better soon."

"Of course they will. You've got yourself a good husband, Patty. Do whatever's necessary to make him happy."

The foundation was laid. Now all he had to do was lure her in.

A week after Patty started her new hours, Bill asked Lorry to go for a drive. After a lot of convincing, he got her into the car. Lorry avoided being alone with him.

They pulled into the parking lot of his favorite deli where he switched off the engine.

"I need to talk to you, Lorry."

She waited for him to speak.

Breaking down, Bill started to weep over a lit cigarette. He dragged on it fitfully, a plume of smoke in the air. Lorry watched him, appalled. Men didn't cry. This must be something horrible.

"Patty's taken a turn for the worse. I'm so scared for her, Lorry. I think she might try to kill herself. I honestly do."

He took another drag on the cigarette, then continued.

"You've read all those psychology books. Maybe you know what to do. I need your help with her. We can't afford therapy, and you know how your family feels about that, anyway."

He looked out into the parking lot, tears glistening on his cheek.

"You've always been able to help her, Lorry. You're brilliant when it comes to her needs. Please, you've got to help me. Can we meet over dinner and discuss this more on Thursday night? Patty's working late at the florist so we'll be able to talk. Do you think you could study some of those books between now and then? You're the only one I can turn to. Please. Everything will be all right if you'll just help me. She's your sister, you'll know what to do to make everything better. I love her so much. Patty is slipping away before my eyes and I can't stop it!"

His words were compelling. Bill started crying in earnest. Embarrassed, pathetic, convincing. Lorry was touched by his distress.

Maybe he does love her. Maybe he actually believes I'm the only one who can help Patty.

"You have to be there for her," he said. "She needs you. You're the only one I can trust."

Lorry was becoming addicted to such flowery praise. Rationalization put a fine coat of paint over past violations. *Maybe Bill is just screwed up. I honestly don't think he remembers the things he's done.*

Patty had related the stories about Bill's terrible childhood; his father's alcoholism, all the beatings. That had to scar a person. And he must love Patty desperately. Lorry had never seen a man cry before.

She agreed to meet him for dinner.

Rita praised her the next day. "I'm so glad you're doing this, Lorry. Patty needs you. Family always comes first, even before yourself. That's the most important thing there is. Look at your sister. She's become lost without us. Bill buys her all those damn cigarettes and booze; I keep telling him he's feeding into her bad habits, but he won't listen to me. Neither will she. Maybe you can make a difference. I'm glad you're doing this."

With Rita's blessing, Lorry was more certain than ever that she was making the right decision. She dusted off her beloved Freud, writing copious notes, trying to design a workable plan. The drugs had to be cut down first. She thought Patty might be addicted to some of them. And the drinking should be less while she was on medication. Alcohol and prescription drugs don't mix. And some outside influence to get her out of the apartment. Church maybe ... something, anything, to get Patty to socialize.

Lorry looked at her notes and felt a strange kind of hope, as if she'd stumbled onto something unexpected. Maybe this was her destiny. Maybe her mission in life was to save her oldest sister. By the time Thursday night came, Lorry was ready.

Bill picked her up at five o'clock, smiling when he saw her. Dressed provocatively in a form-fitting black dress, makeup heavy, lips a glistening red, she was stunning.

Bill looked her over, pleased with her appearance. She had prepared herself well for self-blame, and she didn't even seem aware of it.

Perfect.

He took her to the most expensive Italian restaurant in town, and proceeded to ply her with wine and delicious food. Keeping the mood light, they ate their meal over idle conversation. Lorry began to relax. It wasn't until dessert that Bill began talking about Patty.

"I'm so thankful you're willing to help me out, Lorry. I don't know where else to turn. We both know how your family can be, but I knew I could count on you. You're like my sister. Did you get a chance to figure anything out from those books of yours?"

Lorry outlined some of her ideas for getting Patty motivated. He loved them all. They finished their dessert and sat talking. Bill asked if she'd like more wine.

"Do you want another? I'm going to have one more. I don't usually drink, but this is good, isn't it?"

She nodded.

"You look a little flushed. Your face is kind of red. Just one more, okay?" He signaled the waiter.

"Why don't you go powder your nose, or whatever you girls do, and I'll get the check. Then we can go."

In the restroom, Lorry touched up her makeup and combed her hair. She smiled at her reflection. *This is good. I think everything's going to be okay now. I think it'll work.*

When she came back out, Bill was waiting with a smile and fresh drinks. She glanced at his soda and said, "Oh, aren't you having another glass of wine?"

"No, better not. I don't want to drink and drive. But that doesn't mean you can't have one. Enjoy!" He leaned forward. "Now about this plan to get Patty out of the house. Are you sure it will help? Tell me what to do and I'll do it."

They talked for another fifteen minutes, and Lorry began to wish she hadn't ordered that second glass. *The wine here is so strong.* She found it hard to string two sentences together without slurring the words.

Bill leaned forward. "Lorry? Are you drunk?"

Her head was buzzing, and she was having a difficult time focusing. *Oh, God, don't let me throw up.*

"I don't think I should drink anymore of this wine," she said, her tongue thick and uncooperative.

"This is an expensive place. I wish you'd told me you were getting drunk, I wouldn't have ordered another glass. Now I have to pay for it. The least you can do is drink it all."

"No, I ... " Lorry slurred. "I'm fine. Just better not drink anymore."

"Well, you shouldn't waste it"

Against her better judgment, Lorry reached for the glass, but her fingers were clumsy, and she almost tipped it over. Bill's hand wrapped around her wrist, steadying her. She lifted the glass to her mouth, bumping the rim against her top lip, then tipped her head back and drained the rest in one long swallow.

Bill smiled and rose from his chair, holding out his hand. "I think it's time to go," he grinned.

Lorry stood up, and the floor was suddenly very far away. She moved as if she were underwater, anxious not to embarrass herself in public.

God, I'm so drunk. I'm going to pass out.

"Lorry?" Bill's voice was hollow. "Are you all right?"

His hands supported her as they went through the foyer. By the time they got out into the parking lot, she could barely walk.

"I can't believe this. I shouldn't have let you order that second glass," Bill sounded worried. "Lorry! Look at you. I can't take you home like this."

Her head reeling, Lorry leaned heavily on him as he unlocked the passenger door and fed her into the car.

"There you go. Watch your head."

He settled her into the seat then climbed in beside her, starting the ignition.

"Sweetheart, your mom is going to kill you if she sees you in this condition. You can't go home until you've sobered up."

Lorry sat struggling with both her humiliation and her dinner as it gurgled in her stomach. She could barely hear him.

"Lorry? Listen to me. I'm going to take you to our place and get you some coffee. Get you sobered up."

Her head lolled against the seat. Bill put his foot down on the accelerator, and that was all she remembered.

Pain and weight jarred her back to consciousness. Bill was on top of her.

They were in the Bethpage apartment, on the living room couch. Lorry's breasts were bare, her legs spread wide, and her skirt up around her waist.

Bill was fumbling with his pants, and his elbow dug into her collarbone as he balanced.

"Wha ... " Lorry's belly tensed, and she tried to sit up. Bill wasn't even looking at her; his hand was a claw on her breast, squeezing hard.

"What are you doing? No. Bill, stop it!"

The pain of entry was worse than she'd imagined. Lorry felt the push as he positioned himself, then a terrible lunge and a guttural cry. It tore at her, ripping through her unprepared flesh, dry with fear. Bill was so heavy and he was inside her so quick, she barely had time to struggle.

He started pumping immediately. Fast, like a dog, and Lorry felt another wave of pain as he drove into her.

I'm ripping. He's tearing me!

It was a jagged, sandy sort of pain, without lubrication; only virgin blood smearing her thighs for his flesh to slap noisily through. Helpless, Lorry lay there crying, and waited for it to end. Her arms and legs seemed disjointed, and she moved them in weak denial. Bill was wedged tightly between them, and she couldn't break contact.

Afterward, she staggered to her feet, blood running down her thighs, and fell on the way to the bathroom. Bill jumped up and took her arm, all concern now, the monster behind its mask once again. Lorry cowered away and shut the door in his face.

Guilt was already hard at work. The mirror showed her a new horror, one she'd never seen before. Gone was the dumpy reflection of her childhood. In its stead was a long, lush temptress, a girl who hadn't fought hard enough, bra shoved up, full breasts already speckled black and blue, spilling out from the open neckline of her dress. Her eyes were streaked raccoons, her mouth swollen, blood on her teeth.

What a mess. Her hair was all over the place in a thick black witch's mane, sexy and provocative. Lorry looked like she'd spent the whole night in bed instead of fifteen minutes being brutalized.

"Why didn't you scream?" she whispered to the mirror. Had she said something that made Bill think she wanted this? She couldn't remember. What were they talking about on the couch just before?

Lorry tried to collect all the random accusations shrieking in her head, but they jumbled and fought for supremacy, all of them loud and insistent. Why had she gone out with him? She remembered being excited about showing Bill the game plan for helping Patty. When had it degenerated into this? Why had she ever thought he wouldn't try anything?

Idiot. You got what you deserved. Why did you get all dressed up?

Lorry's first clear thought was *whore*. Her second was *bastard*.

She didn't cry. The feeling was strange, as if she were distant from it all, just watching in. Why didn't she feel worse? She should be crying her eyes out. Bill just violated her, stole her virginity. Why wasn't she crying about it?

Lorry stared dully into the mirror for a long time, unemotionally noting the passage of time. She slowly combed her hair, and looked around for her pantyhose. They must be somewhere in the living room.

She cleaned up as best she could, but didn't want to risk a shower. What if Bill came in while she was naked? He might think she wanted more.

When she left the bathroom, Lorry found him sobbing on the couch, head in his hands.

"Oh, God, I'm so sorry, Lorry. You were just so beautiful, and that dress you're wearing; no man could resist you in that thing. Patty and I, we haven't … it's been so long."

His eyes widened in horror.

"Patty! Oh, no. My poor Patty. This would kill her. This'll push her over the edge! And all I wanted was for you to help us. What are we going to do? Please, Lorry, what are we going to do?"

He begged her forgiveness, then pointed out her own irresponsible behavior and ultimate blame.

"We shouldn't have had so much wine, Lorry. I told you I can't drink. You were just too beautiful, too sexy, and Patty and I are having so many problems. I didn't mean for this to happen, but I just couldn't help myself. Look at you. You're too damn gorgeous. I don't think you should wear so much makeup. Too tempting for us poor men. Are you all right? Can I do anything for you?" He looked down. "Lorry, honey, you missed a spot. There's a little blood on your ankle. Want me to get a washcloth and clean you?"

Even her clothing was to blame. *Black stockings showed a woman was begging for it.*

"I'm only telling you this for your own good. All I wanted was to help you, and look what happened. Please, what we've done is a sin."

He droned on, attentive, concerned, oily. Lorry registered only a handful of words. All she wanted was for him to take her home. If she listened long enough and nodded in the right places, he would be satisfied and take her home.

Her legs wouldn't stop shaking. Her knees were actually knocking. Lorry watched them with detached fascination. Bill kept talking, rubbing her back now, the big brother, helpful and encouraging.

"You know I love you, Lorry. We both love Patty. What are we going to do about this? Your mother is going to be broken-hearted. Maybe even angry with you. I know you're only a kid, but you have to learn to be more careful. Thank heaven it was me, and not some brute on a blind date. I'll do whatever I can to make it right. You've got to understand how serious this is. I love you, Lorry. We'll figure it out."

She shrank from his touch.

Lorry hurt. She hurt a lot, and Bill was droning on and on. *Why can't he shut up? I just want to go home.* Blood slipped down from inside her legs, and he just kept talking. *I hope I'm not staining the couch.*

By the time he finished speaking, Lorry told him everything he wanted to hear.

"Don't touch me!" she hissed, jerking away from the hand smoothing her shoulder. "Don't you ever touch me again. Don't talk to me about it, don't so much as mention it, ever again. And if you tell Patty ... if you tell *anybody* else, I'll kill you."

Bill studied her face, then sighed.

"I think you're right, Lorry. Maybe we shouldn't tell anyone. I don't want you to get in trouble."

"Just take me home."

They drove back in a monologue of gentle chastising. Lorry said nothing. She was angling her body to prevent blood and semen from leaking out onto the car seat. Her concentration was focused on that.

They pulled up into Emily's driveway. As she was getting out of the car, Bill touched her hair.

"Are you sure you're okay?" he asked. "I meant what I said. You really were very beautiful tonight."

She slammed the door and ran inside. Rita called down from upstairs.

"Lorry? Is that you? Come up here and tell me what you talked about. What'd you have to eat?"

Lorry clenched her hands and stupidly thought of the leftovers from the restaurant. She'd forgotten them.

***

She started sleeping with a knife again, something Lorry hadn't done in years. In grade school, she would lie awake in bed and listen to her parents fighting. Norbert would be screaming that he was going to kill Rita, and Rita would be shrieking threats of her own. (*Do it, Norb. Do it! End my miserable existence. I can't take it anymore!*) Lorry was always afraid she'd wake up to silence one morning and find their bodies, or hear a shot in the night, wondering if her own bedroom door was going to fly open ... if this was the night they would all die. That's when she first hid a knife under her pillow. Lorry searched for mental exercises to soothe herself, but she always fell back on a sharp edge under her pillow. Prayer did little good. The knife brought more comfort. Intelligent and imaginative as she was, the knife still won in the end.

Sneaking into the kitchen the night after Bill attacked her, Lorry rummaged in drawers, looking for her old sharp friend. There it was, in a drawer under the sink, worn and familiar. Lorry held it to her cheek for a moment, becoming reacquainted with its cool steel and battered handle.

Padding into the bathroom, she crouched down by the night-light to get a better look. So sharp; her mother insisted on razor edges for all the knives in her kitchen. *There's beauty in such an edge,* Lorry thought. She slid the blade along her arm, cutting effortlessly. She'd barely touched it to her skin. Again, gliding a hair-thin line across her forearm, no deeper than a cat scratch. It felt good. Very good. Strange.

A dozen cuts crisscrossed her inner arm before she shook herself and stood up. Lorry washed the wounds, dabbed them with rubbing alcohol and went to bed.

In the weeks that followed, Bill kept after her. Watching her furtively on Sundays when they were all at Grandma's house, he stared in a way that made Lorry's flesh crawl. He even checked the bathroom garbage to see if she'd started her period. That was one good thing. He hadn't made her pregnant.

Lorry learned to stay out of his way, and Bill was wise enough to read the fragile state of her sanity. He limited his attentions to voyeurism.

She snuck out of the house at night, standing alone in the backyard and praying for God to send lightning to kill her. Even that wouldn't be enough to assuage her own self-hatred. *No. Lightning would be too fast.*

She dreamt of death, and imagined scenarios of disease, the more drawn out, the better. A painful death would be her penance for a wasted life. She longed for it.

***

Vinnie came to her the following summer with the proposal of opening a restaurant together. His aunt and uncle were selling their place, and Vinnie wanted it.

"It's a great investment, Lorry. Come on."

Lorry agreed. She was nineteen-years-old.

She gave up Nassau Community College where she'd begun her second year of studying psychology and liberal arts. They purchased the Roman Garden in the fall of 1974.

Situated in Plainview, it was a nice upscale family restaurant co-owned by the two of them. All the relatives were roped in as employees and managers when Lorry or Vinnie were gone. Rita tended bar, Bill Kelly waited tables, (Patty had begged Lorry to hire him; they needed the money) even Vinnie's father would come do prep work and boss the young busboys around.

That left Karen. Too young to work yet, Karen writhed with frustration until Lorry promised her a job on her next birthday.

"You're only eleven-years-old, Karen," she said. "Wait until you're twelve. You can come in and help when Mommy's here."

Karen had to be content with that.

Lorry became a different person when she was at the restaurant. She was an excellent hostess; beautiful, vivacious and funny. Customers loved her, men loved her, the employees loved her, and Vinnie loved her. People flocked to the Roman Garden, and Lorry enjoyed the quick camaraderie of serving well, with the added benefit of a certain amount of deference because she was the owner. Or the owner's girlfriend. People still showed an appalling surprise at her being anything other than ornamental. They couldn't believe she was part owner.

Everyone kept telling her how lucky she was, but Lorry still felt an emptiness inside. No matter how successful the restaurant was, or how much she was admired, she felt nothing inside. Even her relationship with Vinnie left her hollow and lonely. Her moods baffled him.

"What do you want me to say, Lorry? So you're sad. So what? Life's sad. You know, I don't get you. The restaurant's doing great, everybody loves you ... what have you got to be sad about?"

Lorry just looked at him. She liked Vinnie very much, but something was missing; a fire of some sort. Her feelings for him were more like the love she would have for a brother than a mate. The lack of passion in their relationship worried her. Passion was what she craved. She'd accepted Vinnie's proposal in the first place because it would please her mother. That, and fear of the future. Vinnie was safe. He was of a world Lorry could recognize.

"I love him," she told herself. "Of course I love him."

Love was a subject often brought up in the Kikel household. Sex was taboo, but love was often discussed. Norbert insisted that animals were the only creatures capable of true love.

"Animals are kinder than people, Karen. They always give you unconditional love. People will cheat you, break your heart, betray you the first chance they get. But animals, they're loyal. Animals are the better species. They're more humane than people. Look at your dog Geronimo. You hit her, and she still loves you. She loves you no matter what. She doesn't have a big fat mouth. She has very few needs. Eat, sleep, go to the bathroom, and be loved. That's all she needs. Unconditional love is what you get back."

Karen shared her father's love of animals. Norbert encouraged her to go out and find injured creatures and bring them home. Together, they nursed everything from baby birds and frogs to an injured seagull. Norbert never helped in the actual feeding and care of the animals; he was more the delegator. Photocopying information for Karen and giving her endless instructions was the extent of his contribution. The hands-on stuff he left to his enthusiastic little daughter.

Karen formed her own animal rescue team, with her and Geronimo as the sole members. She and Gerry would trundle about on her blue banana-seat bicycle, looking for the small, furry and helpless in the area.

One Saturday afternoon in the spring, Karen made an amazing discovery behind one of the buildings. She and Gerry were riding along the back alleys on Hempstead Turnpike, when Karen came upon dozens of breathtaking fresh flowers. They had apparently been thrown out. Gladiolus and roses, carnations and lilies; every color of the rainbow was represented in that dirty little alley, and the blacktop was brilliant with fragrant color. Karen was enchanted.

A man came around the back, carrying yet another armful, which he tossed on the heap. Never one to miss such a golden opportunity, Karen said, "Excuse me, sir. Are you throwing all these flowers away?"

"Yeah. Why? Do you like them?"

"They're all so beautiful." Karen's face lit up. "If you are throwing them out, do you mind if I take some home?"

"No, go right ahead."

"How many can I take?"

"As many as you want."

Delighted, Karen began scooping them up. She would make bouquets for everybody.

Barely able to see over the handlebars of her bike after she loaded them on, she raced home and presented one bouquet each to Rita, Grandma Lorenzo, and Aunt Emily.

There was much praise, fawning and gleeful appreciation. The women made a big deal of arranging their beautiful gifts in huge vases. Karen was a hero.

For all of one hour.

Later, sitting in the kitchen downstairs, Karen and Emily were talking about how beautiful the flowers were, and what a good girl she was.

"So," Aunt Emily said. "Who bought the flowers? Did your father take you to the flower shop?"

"No!" Karen was indignant. "I got the flowers. Nobody took me to buy them."

"Well, how'd you get them?"

"I was riding my bike on Hempstead Turnpike, near the bank, and I was going behind some of the buildings when suddenly, there were all these flowers in the alley. This nice man said they were throwing them away and I could take as many as I wanted."

"What building on Hempstead Turnpike?" Emily began to look perturbed.

"You know, the one by the bank."

Emily paled. She was trying to figure out what florist shop was near the bank. There weren't any. There was Dunkin Donuts and Nu-Way Discount Store, the real estate office and ... the funeral home.

Emily's demeanor changed dramatically. Her face slid into anger. The eyebrows dropped, the forehead grew a deep crease, and her eyes narrowed.

Karen, one leg swinging carelessly, still basking in her praise, didn't notice.

"Did you get these flowers from the funeral home?"

Karen looked up, rolling her eyes in thought as she pieced together the exact location.

"Yeah. I guess it could have been the funeral home."

Emily started screaming. Hands went up in the air, wrists flailed about, and a siren wail shrieked out of her mouth.

"What are you thinking? Don't you know these flowers belong to dead people? Oh, my God. Rita. Rita!"

Rita came down the stairs to add her own shriek of superstitious horror to the cacophony. Karen stood confused in the maelstrom as they ranted about death in the house and terrible omens, baffled as to what she'd done wrong.

"Does your grandmother know where these came from?" Emily asked her, making the sign against evil.

"No ... "

A glint appeared in Emily's eye; a sadistic twinkle, a darkling glee. Rita pointed an imperious finger toward the Lorenzo's house.

"You go right over there and tell her, now."

Rita took pity enough to call her mother and prepare Mary for the horror. Karen could hear Grandma's screams over the phone from across the yard.

Quaking in her shoes, she went next door.

"Get them out! Get them out!" her grandma screamed. "Do you know what you've done? You've brought death into my house. Oh, my God, dear God, help me. Help me, my God!"

Mary Lorenzo had an Old World horror of death and the dead. If you went to a funeral, you had to go to a store, or someone else's house, or even walk through the garage, before you could enter her door. No one could bring death into her home. This was her greatest fear, her strongest phobia, the biggest danger of all. Consequently, when a beloved granddaughter brought in a bouquet of beautiful flowers, and Mary Lorenzo pushed her face into them, breathing their scent, taking them from room to room to determine where best to display them, it was the horror of horrors. The ultimate betrayal.

So, when Karen came into the house, Grandma was vociferously upset. She wailed, clasped her heart, clawed the air in drama; she held a snowy handkerchief to her nose and mouth to protect her breathing the evil air. She prayed to all the saints in Italian. Then, she insisted upon a detailed ritual for Karen to go through which would cleanse the house of the wickedness she'd brought in. Karen was to gather up all the flowers of the dead, march in silence through the house, down the hall, out the garage, and on out into the backyard, carrying the flowers before her. Then, she was to go home, and repeat the entire process there. After every last bloom was taken away, she had to return them to exactly where she'd found them, and never touch another thing from the funeral home.

Karen did it all as ordered. Together with Geronimo, she made the trip back to the alley, placed the flowers back on the pile, then returned to face her grandmother. Mary was unforgiving. This crime was far too serious to be lenient toward the little girl.

"You have brought death into our houses," Grandma said. "There is nothing worse you could have done."

After Mary was through with her, Karen slunk home to hide in her room. Emily tapped on the door, eager to hear exact details of the event. She was grinning.

***

Mary Quinn showed up in the tall mirror in Karen's bedroom soon after they moved to Levittown. The room was small, the mirror only four feet from her pillow.

One night as she got ready for bed, Karen looked up, casually glancing in her mirror. The room was never completely dark. A street lamp outside kept her in perpetual twilight.

A woman stood behind her in the mirror. Karen gasped, flipping around.

Nobody was there. She looked back at the mirror. There, very clearly, stood a woman of about thirty, with dark hair and eyes. She wore a long skirt and button-down blouse wrapped around her skinny frame. She was worn-looking, like old leather, with scraggly hair framing her face.

Karen jumped under the covers and hid. "It's not there, it's not real, I'm just making it up … " She waited for a weathered hand to grab her shoulder. Nothing. The only sound was her own breathing.

After long minutes spent cowering under the blankets, she peeped out.

The woman was still there, standing behind the bed. Karen dove back under the covers. It was the first of many ghostly visits.

After seeing the apparition nightly for several weeks, Karen realized it wasn't going away no matter how hard she concentrated. Screwing up her courage, she sat up in bed, blanket curled under her chin, and ventured a question.

"Am I really seeing you?"

No answer, just a slight smile and tilt of the head.

"Who are you? What are you doing here?"

The woman didn't speak.

"Go away," Karen said. "Leave me alone. I can make you go away."

She wrapped herself into a tight ball, squeezing her eyes shut in concentration. When she opened them, the woman was still there.

The weeks turned into months, and the woman in the mirror continued to haunt her. No one believed it. Rita thought she was having another nightmare, Lorry accused her of attention-stealing, and Norbert voiced his fear that she was turning into another Patty. Karen finally stopped talking about it. The visitations continued.

Sleep brought no relief. The woman began talking to Karen in her dreams. She said her name was Mary Quinn, a settler who'd lived on this land over two hundred years ago. Forced to watch her husband and children murdered in a series of raids, Mary was then raped and killed, her body left to rot alongside the remains of her family.

As she described the murders, Mary seemed to relive them. Her face grew goblin-like, stretching wide and shrieking, a rictus of pain and madness.

Karen exploded out of the bed.

Racing down the hall to her parents' room, she hesitated, afraid to disturb them. Her stories, more often than not, just made them angry.

A soft sound of conversation drifted up from downstairs. The television was on. She leaned over the stairwell, trying to see any movement. Emily invariably fell asleep on the couch in front of the set. Karen hesitated, then started her descent. *Aunt Emily won't mind if I just sit with her. I'll be quiet.*

Timid, she crept halfway down the stairs, then sat on the steps to wait. She could just see her aunt around the corner, snoring on the couch.

Emily was a light sleeper. The slightest noise could wake her. A creak on the landing, the soft sound of an opening door was enough to bring her out of the deepest sleep. Karen gave a little sigh, and Emily's eyes opened. She spied her niece on the step.

"Karen, darling, what are you doing up so late? Why aren't you asleep?"

"I had another nightmare."

Emily heaved herself upright, then waved a welcoming hand. "Come on down. Come here."

Karen came to her slowly. Throwing a cautious glance upstairs, she curled up by her aunt's side. Emily rubbed her head. "Now, what are you doing awake?"

"I keep having those nightmares."

"What are you dreaming about? Are they goblins?"

"I'm afraid to talk about it."

"Don't you worry. If those things bother you again, I'll rip their eyes out. Now, why don't you sleep here on the couch tonight? You've got school tomorrow."

Grabbing an extra pillow, Emily threw a blanket around her niece, then settled into her favorite chair. Karen fell sleep, safe and secure, with her fierce aunt watching over her.

The next night, she had to sleep in her bed again. Mary Quinn was waiting in the bedroom mirror.

Karen became an expert at avoiding the glass in the darkness, of turning her back to the door, of humming music and droning silently whenever Mary's harsh whisper sounded, demanding she look. The ghost was not a kind spirit, like Karen's voices. They were always gentle, albeit firm. Desperate for an audience, Mary Quinn was ruthless.

The end came suddenly. Karen woke one night to find herself suspended several feet above the bed. She couldn't move. She tried to scream, but no sound came out.

Mary Quinn glared from the mirror.

Karen began to rise. The ceiling came closer. Some unseen force was pushing her up, her arms and legs stretched wide, unable to move. She looked up, focusing on a blackness, a thick treacle darkness above her head. In her fear, Karen felt it was waiting for her. The question of this being a dream or reality was immaterial. There was no way she was going near that gaping darkness.

Unable to speak, Karen started yelling in her own mind. *Put me down. Let go of me. Put me down right now!*

She tried to kick and slap at whatever was holding her up, but her limbs couldn't obey. Fear turned to anger at her helplessness, and she raged at her unseen captor.

You let go of me! I'm telling you to let me go. Now! Right now!

Without warning, Karen felt her body drop.

Hitting the covers with a thump, she almost bounced off the bed upon impact. Dream or no, she wasn't staying in that room another second. Karen hit the ground running and raced down the stairs, but her aunt wasn't there. Emily must have gone to bed.

Lorry's door was on Karen's right. She burst in the room and dove under the covers.

Lorry reared up.

"What? What's wrong? What happened?"

The story tumbled out, helter-skelter. Lorry rolled her eyes, disbelieving.

"Can I sleep in here with you, Lorry? Please, please, please," Karen cried. "Please let me sleep in here."

"You're gonna wet the bed."

"No, I won't. Promise. Please let me sleep with you tonight."

Lorry rolled her eyes and shifted over. "All right, fine. You can stay."

"Thank you, Lorry. Oh, thank you. I won't pee. I didn't have anything to drink before I went to bed, and ... "

"Okay, okay, just go to sleep!"

Karen snuggled under the comforter and hugged the pillow. Lorry arranged the blankets over her, and fell back to sleep.

An hour later, Karen wet the bed.

Controlling her temper with difficulty, Lorry got up, went downstairs for some paper towels and soap, then cleaned up the mess. She laid a towel over the wet spot and went back to sleep.

After that night, Karen only entered her room to get a change of clothes, but never with the light off. She slept with Lorry or on the couch beside Aunt Emily. Mary Quinn stayed in the mirror. Karen never saw her anywhere else.

***

Norbert's drinking was getting worse. Beer was added to the scotch and sherry, which he'd cut down on after a diagnosis of sclerosis. The twenty-four-hour-a-day invasion of Lorenzos preyed on Norbert's moods. He became less predictable and more volatile. Until the move to Levittown, he had never beaten Karen.

Karen joined a bowling league. They didn't cost much money. Rita or Lorry drove her there on Saturday mornings, and Norbert picked her up. Rita always stressed that he be on time; the parking lot of a bowling alley in Levittown was not a good place for an eleven-year-old girl to wait.

One Saturday, Rita's brother picked her up instead of her father. Norbert, who'd been drinking all morning, gratefully accepted.

Aunt Emily was home alone when Marco dropped Karen off.

"Did you have a good time bowling?" she asked.

"Yeah, we won. They say I'm the star player."

"You hungry?"

"Starved."

Emily shuffled toward the kitchen to make lunch. Tuna fish sandwiches and potato chips, which they ate together in front of the TV.

Norbert got home an hour later, livid with fury and mean drunk. He stalked into the room and saw Karen. "Where the fuck were you?"

He'd forgotten about Marco's errand and had driven to the bowling alley to pick her up.

Startled by her father's tone and language, Karen just blinked at him. He was clenching and unclenching his fists, glaring at her. She scrambled to her feet.

"Where the fuck were you?" Norbert shouted again.

Karen backed up, trying to explain. "Uncle Marco gave me a ride home. He said he'd told you. I thought I was supposed to go with Uncle ... "

"*I* pick you up every Saturday, you little asshole." He was advancing as Karen was retreating. "You goddamn wait for me until I get there, you son-of-a-bitch. You wait for me!"

The words were slurred and wet. Karen was terrified. This was the father of Lorry's memory, not hers. She'd always been able to handle him, always had the right words to say to diffuse the situation. Until now.

She stumbled backwards, falling into the oversized chair. Norbert was on her in an instant, fists flying. Karen felt an explosion of pain as he punched her in the stomach. Trying to shield herself from the blows raining down on her face and shoulders, she was trapped in the chair, Norbert on top of her.

Aunt Emily tried to pull him off, ripping his shirt. He was like an animal, snarling and fixated on his daughter.

Emily finally got him off, and the two of them stood screaming at each other. Karen scrambled up, ran out the room, and locked herself in the bathroom.

Five minutes went by before her fear turned to anger. Karen didn't back down or forgive easily. Not for her was the understanding patience of Patty, or the sullen, desperate servitude of Lorry.

"Beat me, will you, you old bastard?" she muttered, running water in the sink. "I can't believe you did that. I didn't do anything."

She set about repairing the damage, glaring at the swollen cheek and fat lip. Her little face, so pale and infantile, was a mask of fury. Karen was angry not only about the injustice of the beating, but the awful disappointment in her father, the utter betrayal of such an act.

In the living room, Emily stood, indecisive. Norbert had stormed upstairs to his TV room some time ago, but Karen had still not come out. Emily tidied the room, straightening the chair and cleaning up the luncheon things.

An hour went by, but there was still no sign of her niece. She went to the bathroom and knocked on the door.

"Karen?"

"Not now, Aunt Emily."

Emily wandered away, wringing her hands.

Karen stood at the bathroom sink, her forehead leaning against the mirror, eyes closed. She was sick to her stomach. Norbert had been many things; despite her youth, Karen was not blind to his faults. But she'd always thought herself safe from physical violence.

She stayed in the bathroom another half-hour, ignoring Emily's periodic tappings, until she felt strong enough, in control enough, to come out. She had to wait until all traces of her tears were gone. Few things were more horrific to Karen, even at that age, than anyone seeing her cry. The family had always regarded tears as a selfish weakness.

She splashed cold water on her face until it stung, then patted her skin dry with a towel. Her expression grew cold as she glared in the mirror, willing herself to be strong. "Stay in control," she ordered her reflection. "You're all right. Snap out of it."

At Emily's next urging, she allowed herself to be persuaded.

"Karen, come out. He's upstairs in his TV room now. I'm not going to let him touch you."

Silence.

"Wrestling's on in ten minutes."

Karen opened the door. Emily patted her shoulder and led her back into the living room. They settled themselves on the couch to watch the show.

Soon, Emily was squirming in her seat and muttering under her breath, until the tension on the screen became too much.

"Come on! Get off of him, you dirty bum!" she shouted to a wrestler who'd pinned Ivan Putski, the Polish Power.

"Come on, Ivan! Come on!" She leapt up, bending over the screen, throwing a left, a right, stomping her foot and vibrating with nervous tension.

"Aunt Emily, don't worry; it's fixed!" Karen said, laughing despite herself. "Ivan'll win!"

At that moment, the Polish Power broke free and pounded his opponent into the canvas. The crowd started chanting, "Polish Power! Polish Power!" and Aunt Emily joined in, clapping with delight at her hero's snatching victory from the jaws of defeat.

The ruse worked. Sheer delight with her aunt brought a smile to Karen's face. Emily sagged with relief, then Saran-wrapped a couple of cokes for them to drink.

Norbert knocked tentatively on Karen's bedroom door later that night. He hadn't seen her since the beating.

"Karen ... " he leaned an ear to the door. "Jacques Cousteau is almost on."

She sat on her bed, back to the mirror, and didn't answer. Norbert would find out in the coming weeks the price for his awful crime. His beloved Karen was very angry.

She didn't talk to him for six months. Not one word, not even a look. She simply refused to acknowledge his presence at all. To her, Daddy had ceased to exist the moment he struck her. Threats, bribes, treats, admonitions from everyone; nothing could sway her. To be denied the affection of his beloved Karen, cut Norbert to the quick.

He grew frantic as the months passed. He saw her smile and laugh with Rita and Emily; watched her spend time with his bitch of a mother-in-law, even gaze adoringly at Lorry. Nothing for him but mulish silence. No projects to do together. No wonderful conversations. No love. Not one drop. Six months. That was his prison term.

Then one day while he was watching a program about Roswell and Area Fifty-one, Karen marched up to him, bold as brass, and asked him about life on other planets. She decided he'd had enough. Norbert almost wept in his Cheese Nips.

***

Karen started her first menstrual period in the bathroom at home on a Sunday afternoon. Not yet twelve years old, the event was practically declared a holiday. "You're a woman now," Rita said proudly, picking up the phone. "Wait until I tell everybody!"

Karen's body began to bloom. The boys started noticing, and she preened under the added attention. Lorry gave her some makeup and showed her how to use it. Karen soon felt naked without it.

Bill Kelly also took notice. Karen had tiny breasts by the summer, and he commented on her pretty new shape. She'd relaxed toward him over the years, never regaining the feelings she'd had before, but learning to tolerate his company.

Bill couldn't do enough for her. He gave her rides in his car, took her shopping, even offered her cigarettes and alcohol. "You're so mature for your age, Karen," he said. "I want you to know I think of you as an adult."

If she wanted to go bowling, he drove her there and picked her up. If she wanted pizza, he'd go and get take-out.

"You know, I sure love little Karen," he told Patty. "She's a lot of fun. I wish she'd come over more often."

Patty soon began a campaign, talking it over with her mother. "Since Bill and I got married, Ma, Karen's never spent the night at our apartment. Why won't she visit us? I want to be near children. I can't get pregnant. It's tearing me apart. I want Karen. I miss her. I need her. I helped raise her too, remember? She's as close to a daughter as I think we'll ever get."

"I never thought about it, but Karen never has spent the night with you, has she?"

Patty dashed a few tears away. "Bill thought it would be fun if she spent the weekend with us. We could have a little party, the three of us."

"Oh, Patty, I'm sure she'll want to. I think that's a wonderful idea."

Rita was encouraged by this turn of events. Patty was looking worse and worse, almost ostracizing herself from the family. Once so meticulous in her grooming, Patty was now showing signs of self-neglect. Her hair was thinning, her face wore a perpetual film of rosacea, her teeth were yellow and unkempt. She had stopped seeing doctors for routine check-ups, as well. No annual gynecological exam, no visits to the dentist, no sojourn with the general practitioner. She had no friends, no wish for parents, no dreams to occupy her waking mind. The only consistency in her life was the rare visits with the family, and the part-time job at Kearn's Florist. Bill drove her there and picked her up. Sleep was the only thing of value to Patty. She slept for sixteen hours at a stretch. Sleep and children.

If only she and Bill could have children. A son or daughter would comfort Patty, bring her back from the brink she now hovered on. This was the opinion of the Lorenzo women. It was also Bill Kelly's. If only they could have a child.

"Then my Patty would be healed."

Bill wept in the parking lot of his favorite deli as he told Karen about Patty's terrible loneliness. He'd asked her to go for a drive with him to discuss her sister.

"I don't know, Karen. There's nobody I can talk to like you. You're so mature. Hard to believe you're only eleven."

He sighed, and pinched the bridge of his nose.

"Your sister isn't doing well. I wish there was some way I could make her happy."

"What's wrong with her?"

"She's very lonely. We wanted to have children, but the doctors don't think she can ever have any. The closest thing she has to a child is you. You're her favorite. Lorry's so wrapped up in her own life that she doesn't have time for us anymore. At least we know we have you. Patty loves you very much."

"I love her, too."

"Karen, I want to tell you some things, but it has to stay a secret. You know how mean your family has been to Patty, and they just wouldn't understand. But, you always make her happy. Maybe we can plan a Saturday night together. We could all hang out and watch our favorite programs on TV. Patty could make the lasagna you love. Maybe you could even sleep over. We'll let you stay up as late as you want. That would make her so happy."

"I'd like to do that," Karen said tentatively.

"Fantastic. You're such a good little sister, Karen. How about a week from this Saturday?" Bill grinned. "Patty likes white wine, but maybe I'll get her a bottle of scotch for the sleep-over. She likes scotch, too. What's your favorite liquor, Karen? We'll have our own little party. What do you like to drink?"

Startled by the offer of alcohol, Karen stammered a reply.

"Um ... anything is fine."

"Great." He fished in his pocket and pulled out a pack of cigarettes, offering her one. She shook her head.

He drove her home, waving a cheery good-bye as he pulled out of the drive. Karen watched him leave, troubled. Trust had never come easily to her, and she didn't trust Bill Kelly. But, she did love her sister. If Patty wanted her, Karen would come.

The weekend dawned bright and sunny. Bill picked her up on Saturday afternoon.

When they arrived at the house, Patty was already drunk. She grabbed Karen in a stranglehold embrace, keening softly as if to a baby. Embarrassed, Karen patted her back, stepping away as soon as possible.

Dinner was pleasant. Patty had been cooking all afternoon, excited about her sister's visit. Bill had offered Karen a scotch and soda before dinner, but she refused. She accepted a cigarette because he pressed her, and the air was blue with smoke.

When they sat down to eat, Bill poured Karen a glass of white wine. He smiled.

"It's all right to have wine with a meal, Karen."

She drank a few sips and left it.

After they ate, Bill acted as bartender, mixing drinks all night long, for Karen as well as Patty. When Karen protested, he insisted.

"Come on, Karen, it's okay for you to drink it. Your parents will never know. You're a big girl, now, and you should be treated that way. At least here, you will be."

Even though he only drank soda, Bill made sure she was never without a glass. When he wasn't looking, Karen poured hers down the sink. Patty encouraged her drinking, as well. Now that Karen was a woman, they would treat her like one, and grownup women had grownup drinks.

Secretly, they all went into the sink.

Sometime after midnight, Bill told them he didn't feel well.

"Would you girls mind sleeping together on the sofa instead of the bed?" he asked. "The sofa hurts my back."

They made up a bed on the living room floor for Karen and Patty to share, arranging cushions and blankets into a comfortable mattress. Bill brought Patty her medication which she washed down with scotch.

"Well, I'm going to turn in," Bill said, stifling a huge yawn. "You girls have a good night."

He kissed Patty, waved to Karen, and went into the bedroom, where he shut the door.

They stayed up another hour after he left, but the life had seeped out of Patty. The evening floundered. Karen, feeling sick from the cigarettes she'd smoked, just wanted to go to sleep.

They switched off the light. Patty tumbled onto the pillow, unconscious immediately. Karen lay awake in the dark for a while, then turned over and fell asleep.

Less than an hour later, the bedroom door opened and Bill came out in T-shirt and briefs. He bent over to see if Karen was awake, and she immediately sat up.

Patty was moaning softly in her sleep. He took his wife's arm and led her into the bedroom.

"I don't think it's good for Patty to be out here when she gets like this," he whispered to Karen. "Sometimes she wakes up and starts yelling if I'm not beside her. I don't want our landlord to get mad. She'll be better in the bedroom with me." Patty shuffled to the door, Bill's hand guiding her. Then he turned back to Karen. "Good night, sweetheart. Sleep well."

Karen sat for a long time, staring into the darkness, then climbed onto the couch and pulled a sheet around herself. She felt restless and a little afraid of the shadows in the room, huddling under the covers before falling into a troubled sleep.

It was a strange noise, wet and fast, that woke her.

Bill was crouched on the floor next to the sofa, naked, his hand rubbing Karen's head. He was masturbating.

Karen tried to jerk away, and his hand tightened in her hair. Her nightgown had tangled around her waist, exposing her panties.

"What are you doing?" she cried.

"Shh. Be quiet. Hold still."

She kicked her legs, trying to pull her nightgown down. He was hurting her.

"Leave me alone. Stop it. Stop it!" She slapped at him.

Gritting his teeth, fingers working convulsively, his hand just moved faster. Karen started yelling at the top of her lungs.

"Get off me! Stop it! I'm going to tell Patty! Get off me right now!"

Bill let go and stumbled back into his briefs. He sat down on the side of the sofa, and Karen whacked him, rearing back. "Get away from me!"

"Listen to me, Karen," he said, breathless. "You were doing a very bad thing."

She wasn't buying it. Every time Bill reached for her, she yelled again.

He got up and sat on the ottoman across the room, folding his hands and staring grimly at his little sister-in-law.

"Listen to me, Karen. I am very, very worried about this. This is a bad thing. How long have you been touching yourself like that?"

Karen was thrown off balance by the strange remark.

"Your parents would be furious if they knew. Only bad girls do that. We better not tell anyone. I can help you to stop doing that. You have to trust me. I love you, and I want to help you."

He coiled words around her like a snake, manipulating, tightening, planting seeds of doubt. By the time he gave up in the face of her stony silence, Karen was inwardly very frightened and unsure of herself. Outwardly, she just glowered at him.

Frustrated, Bill got up. "I know you don't understand, but you were very, very bad, touching yourself like that."

"What are you talking about?" Karen said. "I didn't do anything. You're making it up. You're a liar."

"You may not have known what you were doing in your sleep. It's a very serious problem. No one else would understand. You were fingering yourself in your sleep. That's not normal."

Karen struggled not to cry.

"If your mother ever found out, you would be in so much trouble. She would never forgive you. Everyone would know that you have this problem. Now, I can help you, but no one must ever know."

"I want to go home."

"I'll take you home in the morning. Try and get some sleep. This will be our secret. I promise I won't tell and get you in trouble."

"I didn't do anything wrong. I know I didn't. I want you to leave me alone. If you bother me anymore, I'm going to call my mom."

Bill's voice grew comforting. "We'll talk about it tomorrow, Karen. Go back to sleep."

He went back into the bedroom and closed the door.

Karen waited an hour, ears straining. All was silence. She jumped off the couch and ran into the bathroom, where she locked herself in.

After she used the toilet, Karen looked at her fingers, examining each digit and nail. She'd recently started her period. If she'd been touching herself like he said, her fingers would be bloody. She turned her hands over. They were clean.

"Lousy liar."

Karen filled the sink with water. She scrubbed her arms with a washcloth, then climbed onto the sink basin and stuck her legs in the water, scrubbing her feet and calves until they were red. She could still smell him. The sounds he made kept playing over and over in her head, and she jammed her face in the towel to keep from screaming.

In the morning, Bill began his verbal assault again. Patty was still in bed.

"Are you all right, Karen?" he asked. "You had a bad dream last night. You were moaning and crying in your sleep."

Karen glared at him.

"I know what you did," she said. "I remember everything."

"What are you talking about?"

"I just want to go home."

"We need to talk about this, Karen. I don't think you understand what you're saying."

"I don't want to talk about anything with you. I just want to go home. Now."

"I didn't want to have to tell you this, but you were making a lot of noise last night, and when I came out, you were touching yourself. You seemed to like it."

"What?" Karen was appalled. "What are you talking about? No, I wasn't."

"I won't tell anybody. You can trust me. We'd both get in a lot of trouble, if your parents knew you were smoking and drinking, and touching yourself like that. It was really terrible."

"Shut up. You're a liar."

Unable to manipulate, Bill drove her home, keeping up a stream of recriminations the entire time. They pulled up to the driveway, and Karen was out before the car stopped.

Sunday passed in a nightmare of self-reproach and guilt. Despite Karen's grown-up attitude, she was still an eleven-year-old little girl. Fearful scenes played out in her mind. What if it was her fault? After all, she did drink the wine. She smoked, too. If she told on Bill, would he tell Mommy and Daddy about that? And what about Patty? This would kill her.

Bill had played his cards well. Once again, his best self-defense was his own wife.

School on Monday was the usual dodging rough kids and avoiding the bathrooms, but after the bell rang, Karen had a blue K-car monster waiting for her.

Bill sat in his car, dark sunglasses on, and pushed open the passenger door. "Get in."

Karen scowled at him over her armful of books, then walked away.

"Karen! Get in this car. I have to talk to you."

She kept walking.

Every day after school for the rest of the week, Bill was waiting with a new set of fears to try out on her. Every day, Karen refused to get in the car.

By Thursday, she had had enough. Karen snuck into her father's dresser and stole his air pistol. She hid it in her pocketbook all day at school, feverish with terror that a teacher would spot it.

When the last bell rang, Bill was again waiting, but this time, Karen was ready. Her friend Gina walked out of the building beside her. Gina knew all about the incident, and all about the gun in Karen's purse. The story had been told over peanut butter and jelly in the lunchroom.

Bill shoved open the car door.

"Get in this car, Karen. Right now!"

In answer, she pulled out the air pistol and pointed it at his face.

"If you don't leave me alone," she said, "I'm going to fill that ugly car of yours full of holes."

Bill blustered and gobbled, red-faced.

Karen meant every word. She kicked the car door shut and took a stance, waiting.

Bill sat undecided, jaw working with frustration, outwitted and outclassed by a Sixth Grader. He drove off with a roar, and Gina threw a rock at his car.

Karen lasted another week before the repugnant nature of her brother-in-law's crime sank in, and she began thinking logically. It all became too much.

She told Lorry and Vinnie that night. Lorry believed her, but Vinnie was uncertain.

"Karen, are you sure?" he asked. "You said you had some wine. Maybe you were drunk, eh?"

Lorry got angry.

"She wasn't drunk. She's telling the truth. I know. I know Bill Kelly. He did it to me."

Vinnie was stunned.

Karen was livid. The bastard had done it before, and nobody knew. Nobody warned her. Who knew what he'd pull in the future if they didn't get him now?

Lorry sat, both riddled with guilt and furious at Bill. He had convinced her, actually convinced her, all those years ago, that it was her fault. All this time, she'd been too ashamed to tell anyone. She just wanted it to go away. She never imagined he'd try it with her little sister.

To Karen, this changed everything. Initially, fear had played a major role, and she had considered keeping her mouth shut. But with this new information about Lorry, there was no chance of staying silent. This was something that had to be taken care of. Right now.

Lorry spoke first. "You have to tell Mommy."

Vinnie drove them to the house. Rita's reaction was not, altogether, unexpected. She ranted and raved and wrung her hands, but when confronted with exposure of the scandal, Rita blanched. *What would the family think? What would this do to Patty?*

"You don't tell anybody else," she ordered Karen, shaking a finger. "This is family business. Do you want to shame us? What's the matter with you? Don't you dare tell Daddy. He'll kill Bill and end up in jail. Not a word to Patty, either. She couldn't take this, it'd kill her. You don't want that, do you? Do you want to live with that the rest of your life?"

"Mommy, he was ... "

"Don't say it!" Rita threw her hands in the air, knotting them into fists. "I can't take it anymore! You're all killing me!" She looked back at Karen.

"You have to think about your family. Think what this will do to Patty! *I* will talk to that bastard. I'll kill him myself if he ever tries it again." Rita sighed, running her fingers through her hair. "Lorry, what do you think about this?"

"Ma, I know Bill's a pervert."

"How? It could have been some awful mistake. How do you know?"

"Because he did it to me."

Rita stared at her for a long time, then stood up and began pacing the room. "Why didn't you tell me this before?"

"I guess ... I guess I was ashamed and afraid you wouldn't believe me."

Rita's face grew beet red. She clenched and unclenched her hands. Her breath came in little pants.

"How can this happen, Lord? Why is this happening to me? I can't take anymore!" she said between her teeth. "Dear God, I can't take anymore!"

This was becoming Rita's mantra.

She noticed Karen struggling with tears, and sighed. "Don't you worry, Karen. It'll be all right. Just don't tell. This is between us, and nobody else. Mommy will take care of it."

Mommy did not take care of it. Aside from empty threats, nothing was ever done. Patty and Norbert were never told. Lorry and Karen were never to speak of it. Bill continued to work at the restaurant. He continued to grow bolder, throwing furtive glances at their bodies, sneaking peeks at the girls from outside the bathroom window when they were in the shower at home. Everyone continued their silence. Lorry just wanted to ignore it.

Karen just wanted Bill to have an industrial accident.

* * *

Two waiters at the Roman Garden were taking the summer off to backpack around Europe. Lorry suggested, half-jokingly, that she meet them in Italy.

"I'd be really useful," she said. "I speak Italian."

They took her up on it. Lorry found herself planning a vacation almost before she knew what was going on.

Rita, however, couldn't bear the scandal of such an idea. "What are you thinking? A daughter of mine, alone with two men in Italy while her fiancee stays home? Absolutely not. What would this do to Vinnie?"

Lorry sighed. "Well, what if I took somebody with me? How about Patty? Patty could go."

"Patty? She won't even drive, anymore."

"She's always talking about Italy. You're the one who put the thought in her head years ago. She'd love it. I'll talk to her, Ma."

It took surprisingly little persuasion to convince Patty to go. After years of marriage, she'd begun to question her feelings for her husband. Everyday, Bill was becoming more controlling. He didn't want her to dress too sexy or even drive. He doled out an allowance instead of letting her work full time for her own money. Patty was rebelling.

Lorry was elated. Maybe a break from Satan, as she and Karen called Bill, would snap her sister out of the funk she'd dug herself into. Naive, with a hidden agenda of her own, Lorry packed her bags and led Patty to the gate at Kennedy airport.

The hidden agenda was a tall, sandy-haired young man named Raymond. He worked part-time at the Roman Garden while attending medical school. Upper middle class, Jewish, and well-educated, Raymond could always make Lorry laugh.

He found in her an attractive woman who was more than able to follow his favorite topics. Lorry was fun to be with, sexy as hell, and returned his interest. He asked her to meet him and his friend Bob in Venice.

Lorry took it as a good sign. Perhaps Vinnie was not her shackled future, after all.

They left in June, breathless with excitement. Lorry and Patty flew to Rome, hopped a train to Venice, and met the men at the train station. The day was bright, the scenery was beautiful, and home was far away. They all stayed in the same hotel, the girls on the fifth floor, Raymond and Bob next door.

In their confined surroundings, Lorry came face-to-face with the extent of her sister's instability. Patty whined constantly, slept fitfully, demanded wine endlessly. One late night, when they ran out of alcohol, Patty threw open a window and climbed out onto the ledge, threatening to throw herself into the canal if Lorry didn't go out and buy her another bottle.

"You don't care about me, Lorry!" she screamed. "You don't love me! Nobody loves me! I've been unhappy all my life!"

"Patty, please, get in here. Of course I love you," Patty stumbled on the ledge, and Lorry felt her stomach flip.

"Get in here, Patty. Get in here right now!"

"You don't understand," Patty cried, yanking at her hair. "Nobody understands. Nobody, nobody, nobody!"

"Calm down. I'll go get you a drink, just get in here!"

"Will you go get my wine? I just need a drink, Lorry."

"Yes, I promise. Just come inside."

"You'll go get it now?"

"As soon as you come in, I swear."

Patty crawled back to the open window. Bob and Raymond, who had heard the commotion, helped her inside. Bob stayed with her while Raymond and Lorry went in search of wine.

Strangely enough, the trip became somehow magical after that. Patty relaxed, showing signs of actual good will, and even seemed to enjoy herself. She became friends with Bob, who was a gentle, soft-spoken man. Lorry was then free to spend every moment alone with Raymond.

They fell in love, somewhere amidst the water and moonlight of those languid nights in Venice. Lorry was happier than she'd ever been in her life. She hugged the silent emotions to herself, content to simply be with him, this intelligent, kind man who seemed to truly enjoy her company. She would have gone home and never told Raymond how she felt, had he kept silent as well.

One night while Patty and Bob were enjoying a quiet conversation at a cafe, Lorry and Raymond wandered off along the water. She was wearing a thin-strapped peasant blouse. The ties in back unraveled while they were standing together on a bridge, looking up at the stars.

Raymond moved behind her, his hands gentle, and re-tied the blouse. Lorry felt her heart in her throat when he slid his hands up her arms, and whispered in her ear. "Do you feel that?"

"What?"

"That funny feeling inside."

"What do you mean?"

"You know," his words smiled at her, "that funny feeling I have every time I'm around you. It's called love, I think."

He bent his face to her hair and closed his eyes.

"I'm in love with you, Lorry. And I don't know what to do about it."

"I think," Lorry whispered. "I think I'm feeling the same way."

She turned around, and tasted passion for the first time in her life. All those years of yearning, all the sad emptiness and frustration; all of it poured from her shoulders in one embrace on a bridge in Italy, in Raymond's arms.

He loves me. The words were like a symphony, dramatic and wonderful; a musical with her, Raymond, and Venice as the backdrop. *He loves me.*

After that, they were inseparable.

Patty and Bob seemed happy together, as well. It was as if Patty had found her spirit again while they toured Rome and Florence. As if her soul had been lost all these years in Italy, just waiting for her to come find it. Lorry could relate. She too felt whole, safe and loved in this remarkable land.

They went to Italy to be carefree and happy, unconcerned with time or responsibilities, and that's what they all were. It was a draught for the soul. Italy. And Patty smiling. And Raymond.

Three blissful weeks passed, then the women had to go home. Raymond and Bob continued their journey. Their next and last stop was Israel. They wanted to make a spiritual pilgrimage to the land of their forefathers.

Lorry and Patty discussed plans on the long flight home. Lorry would break up with Vinnie, then she and Raymond would get married. He would finish school. Lorry would go back to school. They would move away from her family and live a life of joy and fulfillment. Patty would move back home with Rita, get a job as a teacher again, and file for divorce.

Bill was waiting for them at the airport.

Back at their apartment, Patty had a glass of wine to calm her nerves, before launching into the monologue she and Lorry had worked out.

At the first mention of her plans, Bill fell to pieces. He turned into a weeping, dripping, pathetic figure, burying his face in his hands, clawing at his hair.

"Oh, God, Patty, don't leave me. I can't live without you. I'll die. I can't live without you, sweetheart. I love you so much. God, don't do this to me. Give me a chance to make it all up to you. You have to give me a chance!"

He begged her forgiveness, promising undying love while he poured more wine and phoned her doctor for antidepressants.

Bill's misery melted Patty's soft heart. She felt sorry for him, and Bill fed off her pity.

Family pressure also twisted her thinking. There had never been a divorce in the Lorenzo family. Such an act was sinful, evil, selfish and unfeminine. All the considerable power of guilt was brought to the fore from every angle. Rita, Mary Lorenzo, Bill Kelly, liquor and drugs; all conspired to make her see the error of her ways.

In the end, she felt she had no choice. Caving in with little struggle, gentle Patty slid back into the coils of her husband. She drank the wine, took the pills, kept her mouth shut, and began to disappear.

Lorry, on the other hand, surprised everyone. She kept the hope of a bright future in her heart, refusing to yield.

"Raymond loves me," she said, over and over again. "Raymond loves me." The words kept her strong in the face of her family's disapproval. Raymond called the house often, and they spoke of when they'd be together again.

"I miss you, Lorry," Raymond said. "I wish you were here with me. This place; it has an atmosphere like nowhere on earth. Especially Jerusalem. I can't describe it. You have to feel it yourself. Wish you were here with me."

"Me, too. I love you, Raymond," Lorry said into the phone while Rita glared in the background. "Hurry home."

"Love you, too."

Fate began to intercede. Raymond started to change during the four weeks he spent in Israel. Thousands of years of tradition wrapped him in a soft veil of ancestry. He visited the Wailing Wall, immersed himself in the history of his Jewish heritage, and began to ponder both his future and his faith.

Rita tolerated two phone calls from that Jewish boy before she decided intervention was necessary. She called Vinnie.

"Raymond is stealing your fiancee right out from under your nose, Vinnie. He's tearing this family apart. You have to do something."

Vinnie's solution bordered on the absurd. He went out and bought a cross-bow, which he waved at Lorry, swearing he was going to use it on Raymond.

Rita took Karen aside, recruiting her in the war against Lorry's free will, much the same way as Norbert had done years before in his drunken jealousies. Karen was instructed to hang up the phone every time he called, and chastise Lorry for her betrayal of the beloved Vinnie.

"Remind her of her duties to her family, Karen," Rita said. "Don't let this Raymond destroy our family. You know what a good man Vinnie is."

"But, Mommy, if Lorry loves Raymond ... "

"She doesn't love him. How can you think that? Raymond could never take care of Lorry the way Vinnie can."

"But, I like Raymond."

"If you like Raymond, you're betraying Vinnie, a man who's like a brother to you. You can't betray your own brother. You have to do this. Hang up that phone."

Karen reluctantly obeyed, torn between loyalty to her sister and loyalty to her mother. Rita won. Rita always won. Even Patty, who tried to side with Lorry, was cut down for her troubles. Norbert didn't even know.

Despite it all, Lorry stood fast.

"Hurry home, Raymond," she whispered in her bed at night. "I need you."

Raymond was facing his own trial. In Israel, he felt an Epiphany happening deep inside himself. A revelation that colored everything with a new light. Raymond found his roots in Israel. The country of his forefathers called to him, and he knew he had to be a part of that greatness. Something holy and larger than any human being had touched him, and he was changed forever.

But he still didn't tell Lorry.

Raymond was under assault at home as well. His mother threatened to cut off all funding toward his education if he didn't give Lorry up. She wasn't Jewish, and she was already engaged. Underhanded conspiracies on both sides, linked with his new spiritual connection, were too much for him.

His mother finally gave him the ultimatum of choosing between his infatuation or his family. He chose his family, and his decision broke Lorry's heart. She would have stuck it out, defied her mother for the first time in her life, turning her back on the family, if only Raymond had wanted her enough. But he hadn't. Rita and Vinnie were there to pick up the pieces.

Lorry broke down. She saw Patty swallowed whole, and knew that her fate would be the same. She would never get away now. Raymond's desertion shattered her, and the only thing left was hopelessness.

So she cried. Three days of weeping, of runny noses and scandalizing the neighbors, of chastising, and not appreciating what you had, and what a nice boy Vinnie was.

After she ran out of tears, Lorry got up, cleaned her face, and went back to work. Her eyes were dull.

Chapter 6:

Coffins

Karen wanted a new bike. She'd outgrown the blue banana-seat long ago. That was how it started. She wanted a bright red ten-speed bicycle like she'd seen her friends riding, and she plagued Norbert for it.

"If you want a bike, buy it yourself," he said.

"I don't have any money."

"Get a job, then. If you want luxuries, earn them."

That's a good idea. I'm twelve now. I'll get a job.

She started working as a dishwasher at the Roman Garden, sticking her tongue out at Steven the busboy and befriending Scott De Simone, another busser. She progressed quickly to busgirl, then waitress. Being Lorry's sister as well as the only girl on staff made things difficult for her. Karen had to work harder than anyone to prove herself. Time passed, and her responsibilities grew.

Life went along this way for the next several years. Bill Kelly always seemed to water Aunt Emily's lawn or wash the car when the girls were in the bathroom; the window was right over the shower, Grandma Lorenzo cackled her riotous cackle and set Norbert's teeth on edge, and Rita gave Lorry endless errands to run. Patty spun more and more elaborate dreams to hide in. Lorry still wanted to be loved and admired, and Karen still wanted Bill to fall down an elevator shaft.

Christmas rolled around. Lorry and Vinnie finally set the date for their wedding. They would marry in September of the following year.

Rita was ecstatic. Two daughters married, and her beloved Lorry to a nice Italian boy, who adored her. This was to be a Christmas like no other.

Holidays in the Kikel home were always incredible events, but at Christmas, Rita excelled. Decorations festooned every corner of the house. The walls were covered with garland and holly, and all the women would cook for days. Every conceivable type of Italian bakery and luscious candy was arranged about the house in festive little bowls or shallow dishes. The air was fragrant with baking from Thanksgiving to New Year.

Two weeks before Christmas, Norbert climbed the ladder to the garage attic, and passed down box after box of decorations and lights. Then the entire family would marched inside for the trauma of decorating the Christmas tree.

Rita and the girls had the live tree waiting inside, which had been set up hours before in its own unique, excruciating manner. ("No, not that way! Turn it, turn it ... can't you see that bare spot? Norbert, turn the tree, turn the tree ... ") Norbert's insistence on letting the tree settle before decorating took an average of six hours, by which time Rita was annoyed and the kids were in a fever of anticipation.

Then, the lights. Big fat bulbs with plastic bell reflectors, each and every string of lights had to be stretched the length of the living room, side-by-side. Every wrinkle had to be smoothed out, every bulb re-screwed and checked. If one was burnt out, it had to be replaced only with the same color. Then, and only then, did Norbert start the finicky business of applying them to the tree, coughing from a combination of cigarette smoke and bronchitis. He calculated how many strings were required for the bottom two rows, how to divide the tree into sections for stringing. The exact placement needed to be determined so the wires would show as little as possible. Norbert saw it as an exact science, to be done with great precision and unwavering nervousness.

Inevitably, Rita would begin to nag.

"Come on, Norbert ... aren't you done yet?"

"A few more minutes."

"Why is it taking so long? We're waiting."

"Look, if you wanted it done fast, you should've done it yourself. I took the time out of my Saturday to help you. Why? Because you asked me. Know where I'd rather be? Upstairs, relaxing and watching TV. Instead, I'm down here, doing your tree for you, and you're bitching about it. Shut up and leave me alone. I'm done when I'm done!"

Rita turned to her daughters.

"He always has to say something to ruin it for me. Your father can never just be nice and do something because he wants to. Everything has to be a project."

Twenty minutes passed while the women waited in the kitchen, the background music of Norbert's coughing and muffled curses coloring the mood. If he went over his projected time for stringing lights, which he often did, he grew more and more nervous. The TV show he'd been waiting all week for was being missed because Rita's goddamn tree was taking too long.

Rita walked back into the living room an hour later to find him still on the stepstool, meticulously arranging a bell light. "Today, Norbert. Today!"

"Goddamn these things ... "

"You know, you're never happy, Norbert. You're never satisfied."

Norbert turned to glare over his shoulder.

"Nag, nag, nag. You're just like your mother, a big motor mouth. Keep talking, Rita."

"You bastard. Don't bring my mother into it."

Norbert, his face crimson with rage, adjusted the final bulb. "There. Done. Turn the lights on."

She clicked the button on the bell switch, and the tree lit up, gloriously flawless. "Girls, come on in. Your father's done with the lights."

Norbert retreated to the TV room for a lonely drink, leaving Rita and the girls free to decorate. This, too, was a time-consuming effort. Large balls had to be on the bottom, medium balls in the middle, and small ornaments on top. Tinsel must be applied one or two strands at a time; perhaps three. Never four, and never on top of each other.

When it was done, Rita yelled up the stairs to her husband. "Norbert! The tree's finished!"

Waiting until the commercial break, he clumped downstairs, fished the camera out of a drawer, snapped several shots, and went back up.

Karen was thrilled with the evening's work. This was much better than last year, when Norbert cut too many branches off the bottom. Rita had become hysterical, screaming that he'd done it on purpose to ruin her Christmas. This year was much better. Karen sighed with pleasure. Despite the annual argument over tree placement and bulb arrangements, she loved the whole business of Christmas decorating, together as a family.

Going up to bed later, she stuck her head in the TV room to wish Norbert good night. A cloud of cigarette smoke enveloped her. Prone to colds, Norbert never opened the window, and the hallway door stayed shut because Rita didn't want the whole house stinking of cigarettes.

"Dad, the lights look great. Thank you. I think this is the best tree we've ever had."

Norbert grunted a reply, his eyes fixed on the screen. Karen waited, rewarded with a glance and a grin during the commercial.

She skipped along to her room, smiling with holiday pleasure. Flopping onto the bed, she grinned up at the ceiling, ignoring Mary Quinn in the mirror.

Daddy sure looked funny when he was doing the lights. His face was beet red.
Focusing on the ceiling, Karen heard Norbert cough in the other room.

The vision struck like a coiled snake, hidden and unexpected, knocking the breath out of her. A coffin appeared before her eyes, making her jump.

Norbert lay, gaunt and solid, inside the box, and the word *cancer* whispered in Karen's mind. She knew, as if it had already happened, that cancer would take her father. Horrified, she stammered, "What ... what kind?"

An image of Norbert flashed before her; a blink-of-an-eye visual where a thin outline of his lungs faded in and out like some odd cartoon. Then it was gone.

"Lung cancer," Karen whispered to the empty room. "My dad is going to die of lung cancer."

Her mind touched on thoughts of Rita, and she felt a cold and terrible something close over her, a rush of sensation that brought panic in its wake.

Karen lay splayed across the bed, gripping the covers, gulping air, shutting down belief in an attempt to escape the vision.

"What's wrong with me?" she cried. "How can I have these terrible thoughts?"

* * *

Winter passed into spring, summer and fall. Another Christmas came and went. Karen was growing into a beautiful girl of fifteen.

Lorry and Vinnie's wedding was fast approaching. They had a lavish engagement party that the whole neighborhood raved about for weeks, afterward. Lorry's bridal shower was as extravagant as any wedding. Hundreds of presents filled the room, and Karen was dazzled by it all. The finest china and crystal, beautiful furniture, silver, linens, every imaginable appliance; they wanted for nothing. Lorry was kept entertained by all the attention and doting from her mother and friends, and Vinnie was glowing. At last, he'd won his princess. She was all he'd ever wanted or needed. They now had everything; happiness, love, money, success, and a wedding date. Everything was perfect.

As the day of the wedding drew near, the families were in a fever of visiting and last minute preparations. Vinnie brought his parents over to the Kikel house.

After dinner, Lorry unearthed some old photo albums, which pleased Norbert. He loved his humorous chronology of family history, and sat in the living room as Lorry showed the albums to the Salluzzis.

She sat on the couch and turned the pages, translating the witty captions, and skirting over the more lurid ones. Her future in-laws were bookended on either side of her, and Lorry smiled at their startled reactions to Norbert's scribblings. What embarrassing captions would her dad have next? She hadn't looked at these photo albums in years.

She turned the next page and froze.

A sheet of paper with the heading, "LAST WILL AND TESTIMONY" was glued to the page. Lorry was dumbfounded to find herself staring at the long-lost suicide note she'd written so many years ago. After all this time the mystery was solved. Norbert, finding it amusing, had put it in the family photo album.

Lorry looked up at her father sitting in his chair across the coffee table, and was too stunned to say a word. Vinnie's parents looked questioningly at her.

"That's a note Lorry wrote when she was a teenager," Norbert said, scooting closer for a look. "She left it out in the living room for us all to see. Thought it was really funny." Enjoying the memory, he laughed, oblivious to Lorry's white face and shaking hands. "Left her sister Patty a stock in her ass! What a brat this kid was, and look at her now." He smiled at Lorry, a genuine smile of pride. "She's turned out pretty smart after all."

* * *

Lorry and Vinnie married in September. Karen and Patty were maid and matron of honor. The flowers were daisies in baskets, the seven bridesmaids were salmon and white peasant dresses, the male attendants were coffee-with-cream tuxedoes, and Vinnie was white with brown trim. The bride and bridesmaids wore hats, and the white tulle was endless.

Lorry wore Rita's wedding gown. The mirror reflected a beauty in white satin, and a smiling, tearful mother behind her. Despite the day, despite almost seven years of engagement, Lorry felt little anticipation or joy. Her mother zipped her into the gown she herself had worn, and Lorry began to tremble.

Today, Rita wore blue. She braced her daughter's spirit with wine and praise, directing her every move. Lorry stepped and turned like an automaton. She couldn't think; she only obeyed.

This was the day Rita had prepared for since Lorry's birth. All her money from Kearns Florist, all the cash from the restaurant, every dime she'd ever saved, was for the weddings of her three daughters. It didn't occur to Rita that they picked men destined to make them miserable.

Norbert gave Lorry away. They stood in the foyer of the little church, listening to the opening bars of the wedding march. Lorry felt as if she were underwater. Noises were garbled, and she couldn't figure out if she was the bride or groom, or even male or female. She had lost herself. Panic set in. There was no floor under her feet, no air in her lungs, no sight she could recognize, and it terrified her.

Norbert, unexpectedly gentle, guided her to the correct side when she tried to take his left arm.

The music continued. She started to take the first step forward, her body rigid. Norbert stopped her with a whisper.

"If you want to call this off, you know you can."

She stared at him.

"You don't have to do this if you don't want to," he said.

What is this? What the hell are you doing? Couldn't you have brought this up a week ago, Dad? Last night? Now? You say this now, like I've got a choice, standing here in the church, ready to walk down the aisle? All these expensive preparations, my mother's dress? Vinnie?

None of the questions screaming in her mind were voiced. Lorry just shook her head, eyes wide, and urged him forward, her fingers clawed around his arm.

Vinnie stood at the end of a long narrow tunnel. He was weeping. Lorry's vision blurred, growing dark around the edges, until all she saw was his shiny face, slightly sweaty in the hot autumn afternoon. The ceiling fans turned, but she couldn't hear them. The only noise that penetrated was some relative sobbing loudly. Lorry's body felt detached, chilled, and she couldn't feel the shoes that had been pinching her feet all morning. Her only sensation was cold. Her only awareness was Vinnie and her father.

Halfway down the aisle, she tensed. Escape flared in her eyes. Rita saw it, and Lorry saw Rita. She kept moving forward. Norbert handed her over to the groom.

The honeymoon in Italy was a disaster. Vinnie was upset by his bride's lack of enthusiasm, and Lorry could only see a man she didn't want to be with.

Long before they got home, Lorry ached for a divorce. Vinnie, floundering for reasons to explain her cold anger, was lost at sea. He put it down to young bride jitters. She'd settle once they got back to the restaurant.

Lorry knew she'd never settle with this man, this nice guy who never touched or talked about anything that was of the least interest to her. *Mistake.* That's all she could think of. *God help me; I've made such a mistake.*

They moved into a pleasant little place in Bethpage, the restaurant, saving their profits for a house of their own. The apartment was only two blocks from Patty and Bill.

* * *

Grandpa Lorenzo was diagnosed with esophageal cancer in April, 1979. The disease had spread quickly through his lymphatic system. Karen knew beforehand that he was going to die. The seven coffins in her vision had given her the order of deaths. First was Uncle Joe. Now Grandpa Flore. Her own father would soon follow.

She strained to understand why she saw such terrible visions, why these glimpses of future tragedy kept visiting her. She worried that she might be creating them. But, the picture of her father, the voices, whispering the cause of his coming death; Karen hadn't asked for these. She hadn't even been thinking about them. They simply came to her, unbidden and unwanted.

Rita stayed by his side. Flore Lorenzo had always been her best friend, and she, his princess. Only when visiting hours were over could she could be persuaded to leave her father.

Lorry came each night after work, sneaking up in the service elevator.

The hospital staff never covered him up properly, an oversight which grated on Lorry. Her grandfather might be cold all night if she didn't come and drape him with blankets. Each evening, when she got there, Flore was uncovered and icy to the touch. Rita watched him during the day, Karen was diligent when her mother had a quick meal, but the twelve hours between visitations, when he had no family beside him, worried them all.

Lorry's boldness in sneaking up in the service elevator was the only thing that prevented Rita from sleeping by Flore's side.

Lorry was with him on his last night. By this time, Flore had lost the ability to speak. The only noise in the room was the soft hiss of the oxygen.

"You're going to be fine, Grandpa," Lorry whispered, stroking his hair. "You're going to be just fine."

Flore closed his eyes and shook his head.

"Oh, yes you are," she said, with an over-bright grin.

He just shook his head. Flore Lorenzo couldn't handle the messy business of dying slowly. He couldn't take soiling himself; the humiliation and helplessness of being an invalid. He wanted out.

"Don't be like that," Lorry whispered. "You're going to be up, digging in your garden in no time."

A nurse came and checked on them. Lorry saw the concern on her face and felt her stomach sink.

"I'd better call your family, Mrs. Salluzzi."

They arrived less than an hour later. Rita, Marco, Patty, and Karen shuffled into a quiet circle around the bed. Each person leaned forward and kissed him, saying their quiet farewells.

Lorry continued her gentle rambling. Rita sat beside him. Flore looked at her and smiled weakly. He reached out, took his daughter's hand, and kissed it.

Then he slipped silently away.

After his death, Mary Lorenzo was useless in the planning stages of wake and funeral. Marco deferred all the arrangements to a grieving Rita, too distraught to help in the choosing of coffins and funeral homes, raging about the shallowness of such planning.

"How can you ask me to pick out a coffin? He's my father, Rita! Don't you know what this is doing to me?"

He's my father, too. Rita kept the thought to herself. She handled all the arrangements alone.

Norbert made a casual mention of the weight he himself seemed to be rapidly losing, but no one paid attention in the aftermath of Grandpa Lorenzo's shocking death.

Desperate for some show of concern, Norbert stood in the living room in front of his family and pulled his leather belt tight. The baggy waist of his pants gathered around alarmingly gaunt hips.

"Look at me," he said. "I can't get any decent food around here. Everything your mother cooks is tasteless. I'm wasting away to nothing, and no one cares."

Emily was offended. She cooked three nights a week.

"What the heck are you talking about, Norbert? I cook wonderful meals for you. You just don't want to eat anything!"

"Maybe if somebody would make it taste better, I would eat more," he barked. "There's just no flavor to anything you two make."

"You don't know what the hell you're talking about, Norbert. Everybody loves my cooking," Emily said. "My food doesn't taste good. He's got some nerve!"

Rita joined in.

"You're never satisfied, Norbert. I'm tired of guessing what you want. You plan out the menu, and we'll cook it. Just stop complaining."

He retreated to his TV room.

As he grew worse, Norbert tried privately to solicit concern. In their bedroom, he showed skinny ribs and fish-white skin to Rita, desperate for the least sign of sympathy, but she was too caught up in the arrangements of funeral and mother-comforting to notice his health.

Karen was terrified. Coffins. That's all she could think of. Coffins in a dream, lined before her, everyone she loved lying in them.

At Flore Lorenzo's wake, Norbert took Karen up to say good-bye to her Grandpa.

"That's how I'm going to go."

For an awful moment, Karen thought another strange voice was talking to her, but it was only Norbert, tapping out a cigarette as they sat down.

"Cancer. That's how I'm gonna go too."

He knows.

Karen burst into tears. Norbert watched her dispassionately, then flipped his lighter, and had a long drag on a cigarette.

The night after the funeral, Lorry laid in bed, alone and exhausted. The room was dark, save for the light streaming in from the hallway. Vinnie was at work.   Most nights, the television was on. The noise kept out both unhappy thoughts and fear of the future. But tonight, she just wanted quiet, a soothing, silent moment, so she could empty her mind and relax.

She lay on her back and stared at the ceiling, contemplating nothing; just feeling her body unwind and sink into the covers.

Suddenly, she was no longer in her room, but standing on the back porch of the Lorenzo house. Lorry blinked, disoriented. She could smell the warm sunshine in the garden, feel the porch beneath her when she shifted her feet.

She wasn't alone. Grandpa Lorenzo was there at her side, but a grandpa years before her time. Flore was young, around forty-years-old. He was looking out into the garden, where the lilac tree was in bloom.

"Grandpa!"

"I want you to take care of your mother," Flore said, looking at the tree.

"Grandpa, what are you doing here?"

"I want you to take care of your mother."

"Are you okay?" Lorry asked.

"I want you to take care of your mother."

"I will. I'll take care of Mommy. Why are you here?"

Before an answer came, he was gone.

Back in her dark bedroom, Lorry lay blinking in amazement. She hadn't fallen asleep. That was a vision, and a good one at that. When Karen described her own experiences, they always seemed to be dark and morbid, but Lorry's visit from her grandfather had been joyous.

She felt no fear about Rita. She assumed Grandpa was just telling her to take care of her mother; help her with her grief, take care of her in her old age. *Grandpa didn't have to tell me to do that. I would have, anyway.*

***

Norbert's cough worsened. He decided to give up cigarettes, replacing them with beer. A week later, he slammed his hand down on the dinner table, shoved his plate of lasagna away and knocked over his water glass. "Goddammit, Rita, you're making this food too plain. It's got no flavor. I can't taste a damn thing!"

His taste buds were failing. Another week of bland food and tasteless wine convinced him to make an appointment with his physician. The doctor took one look at his tongue and a brief listen to his chest, then demanded he go to the hospital at once for tests.

X-rays showed two lungs full of cancer. Surgery was out of the question, chemotherapy useless. Time was narrowed, suddenly, to weeks.

Lorry visited him in the hospital before she went to the restaurant every morning, then again at night after work. She brought both Rita and Norbert food every day.

Rita never left his side. Like Lorry as a child, it took grave illness to gain Rita's full attention. She gave it willingly, lovingly, faithfully; the good wife in the end.

Karen concentrated night and day, focusing on her father in a coffin. When she did this, two things would happen. First, the coffin appeared. Willing it to become transparent, Karen looked at the inside. Whoever was revealed would die next.

Norbert lay in the coffin, solid and still.

Karen cried furious, helpless tears, but was compelled to ask more.

"When?" she whispered, lip trembling.

A stone appeared before her, letters etched out with an unseen hand.

Tuesday.

Karen shook off the deep trance she'd slid into and fumbled for a pack of Marlboros hidden in a drawer.

She visited her father each day in the hospital, playing a terrible sort of waiting game, where she snatched every possible moment, knowing her time with Norbert was winding down. They exchanged a soft dialogue in that hospital room, little moments of rambling tenderness as Karen watched the life slowly seep out of him.

"I love you, Daddy," she said, squeezing his hand. She didn't make false statements of a potential recovery. They both knew what was coming.

"I love you, too, Karen. You're my baby." He struggled with the words, his eyes shiny. "I'll miss you."

He started to choke then, gagging on a thick, ropey cough. Karen stood aside, allowing the nurse to tend him.

Lorry and she started seeing faces in Norbert's hospital room; in that soft blue light of the evening ward. No longer just shadows of the imagination in an air-conditioned bedroom, no more just figments, hallucinations, childish fantasies. The furtive shapes of their childhood were well recognized. They had always been there.

Lorry refused to acknowledge them, never taking her eyes off Norbert's face.

Karen raged in silence, ordering the visions to get out and leave them alone. She was caught in the doorway between worlds she didn't want to know about, and the forced exposure incensed her.

Norbert had time to ponder his life as he caught glimpses of death in the room. Freed from the eternal jealousy that had destroyed him, he basked in the glory of being the sole focus of Rita's every waking moment. And Lorry. Who would have thought that Lorry could ever show him such devotion? Twice each day, she sat combing his hair, wiping dribble from the corner of his mouth when he coughed, telling jokes.

Toward the end, when he was slipping in and out of consciousness, Norbert felt her hand holding his and was more grateful for that feather touch than he'd ever been for anything in his whole sorry life. He tried to convey this to her, to this surprisingly beloved daughter, but the tube was shoved down his throat, feeding him oxygen, and he couldn't speak of it.

He ended a long and pathetic existence with a shuddering, thrashing struggle for breath, surrounded by the family he adored and tried to destroy.

Then he died. The only sound in the room was the shocked silence of women, and young Karen's sobs. It was Tuesday evening.

Rita, again, saw to the funeral arrangements. Norbert had a wake that lasted three days, both morning and evening sessions. People came from miles around, gravitating around Rita in a delicious, comforting circle. They loved her. Norbert was Rita's husband. That was his eulogy.

The evening of the third day, Rita went up to the coffin for one last look at her husband, a final farewell to the man who had never made her happy, but whom she now had trouble facing life without. She bent over the body and placed a soft kiss on his cold lips.

"Good-bye, my darling."

He was lowered into the ground on the fourth day.

Marco came to visit often after Norbert's death. One afternoon, while in the next room, Karen overheard a conversation between her mother and uncle. They were talking about her.

"Marco, I want you to start paying more attention to Karen. She needs a father figure."

"Reet, you know Karen and I have never gotten along. I don't like her. I never liked her. Why do you want to push her on me now?"

"She just lost her father. I want you to be her uncle. She needs you."

"Why are you putting me in this position and forcing her on me? We never liked each other. Just because Norbert's dead, it doesn't change anything."

"Marco, I'm asking you, as a sister, please do this for me. She needs you now."

"How fair is that? If she were a boy, it might be different. But she's a girl. We have nothing in common. I've got my own problems to deal with."

"Karen is suffering. I want you to help."

He became defensive. "How can you ask me that? I don't like her. I'm not her dad. I'm not going to be her dad. Why don't you ask Vinnie or Bill?"

Rita and Marco talked for a few more minutes, then he got up and left. Karen came into the room and confronted her mother at the kitchen table.

"Why didn't you stick up for me, Mom? He was saying awful things about your own daughter! Why didn't you stick up for me?"

"Oh, don't blow everything out of proportion, Karen. He didn't mean it. Leave it alone."

"But ... "

"I said, leave it alone."

* * *

Rita was diagnosed with colon cancer three months later. The surgeons removed the tumor, did a few tests, and declared her cured. It had never occurred to her or Norbert, or Grandpa, or even Uncle Joe to get another opinion. The doctor was a friend of the family. They couldn't insult him.

A week after her mother's operation, Karen gathered the courage to look to her strange visions for questions about Rita's fate. So far, everything she'd been shown as a little girl had come true, in the order it was shown. Uncle Joe, then Grandpa, then Daddy. Rita had been there, next in line.

Karen closed her eyes, asking for a picture of her mother in a coffin.

She saw Rita, lying solid and still in the box. The voices curled around her.

"Your mother will be taken away from you." Karen raged and wept at the injustice of her clairvoyance, cursing this gift she'd never wanted. This was more than a feeling. It was a knowing, as if her energy had somehow mixed with the voices, mixed with the people she was reading so unwillingly, and she simply knew what they knew, remembered what they remembered, as if the memory were her own.

"What kind of a sick thing is this," she wondered, "to be able to see all my family's death?"

There was no answer.

* * *

Life took a turn for the entire family. Hardship slid personality changes into all of them. Once so meek in public, Karen turned mean and rough at school. She was no longer afraid of physical violence or petty tortures. She almost welcomed them. The introverted young girl had become a fearless teenager. Her regular enemies no longer bothered her.

Other kids stopped messing with Karen, as well. She began to glow with an inner fierceness, no longer the timid, overweight little shadow. She radiated energy, and both men and women were drawn to her.

She began to make friends, weaving a lifeline of caring and protection around herself. They were a tough crowd of teenagers, having learnt the art of survival in the hallways of their school. They all drank and partied with a vengeance. Despite many offers, Karen had no interest in drugs, but hard liquor was often welcome. Music, dancing, cigarettes and alcohol became her best friends, and she visited them often.

After Norbert died, Karen began cutting herself with razorblades in the bathroom, blasting "Love Reign on Me" by the Who. She didn't know that Lorry had found escape in this pastime long ago. Sometimes the cuts would be deep, and she'd bleed for hours. Karen enjoyed the self-punishment. Something inside her felt it was just.

She retreated from the world, hiding behind a tough facade and a knifelike humor. Gorgeous and lethal, Karen was an irresistible virgin, an Amazon with a quick wit and quicker temper. Anger was her governing emotion.

Lorry wanted to have a child, but like Patty, couldn't seem to get pregnant. To have a baby was her sole preoccupation outside the restaurant. She went in for fertility tests, had surgery to open her fallopian tubes, where she convalesced in the maternity ward, with babies everywhere, and took prescription drugs to make her ovulate. Rita wanted grandchildren, and Patty was a long ago discarded dream in that area. Her darling Lorry had to give her a grandchild.

"If I could just hold my grandson in my arms," Rita said, sighing. "Everything would be all right."

But, Lorry couldn't get pregnant.

Vinnie, denied fatherhood, turned to petty torture for relief. Little comments meant to wound, a hint here and there of displeasure, outright jokes about the fickleness of the female sex. Lorry responded in kind and took nips at his feelings herself, tasty little bites of his ego. Waving jars of chocolate triumphantly in the air, she searched for them in much the same way she had sniffed out Norbert's empties for Rita as a child.

Karen drank scotch to hide behind, reminiscent of Norbert's self-destructive routine. The alcohol helped the teasing at work. As the only girl on staff, she was plagued with practical jokes, which Vinnie encouraged, the fouler the better. She drank to forget the pain at home, the plague of visions. She'd just had a new one recently; a great stone blazing with the number *twenty-one* in letters of fire. This was in answer to Karen's question regarding her greatest fear.

"When? When will *I* have cancer?"

She was only sixteen. Whole bottles of wine, like her father, were downed in an endless routine of glass after glass. Forget. Not the deaths that had already happened or the ones on the way, not the fear of cancer, not the grasping vampirism of her family, or the stupid petty tortures at work or school. Karen only wanted to forget that she was alive, and had to go on breathing.

"Goddammit," she said to the empty room. "I hate this place. I hate being alive. I hate people who would be hurt if I killed myself. I hate everybody who loves me."

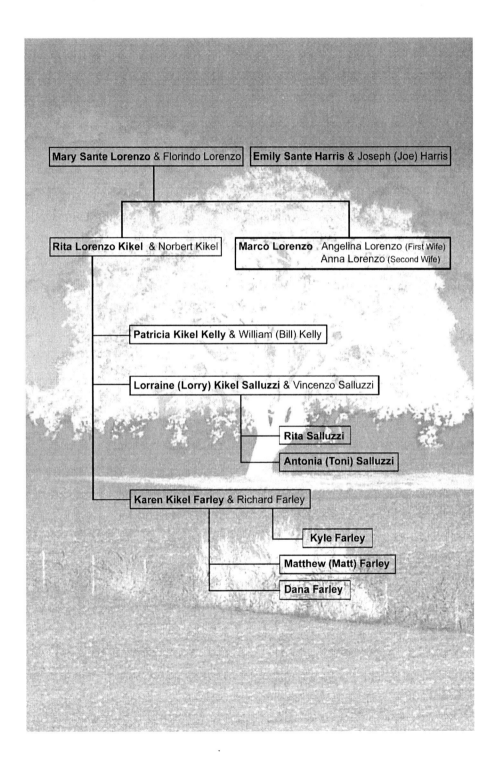

Mary Sante Lorenzo & Florindo Lorenzo   Emily Sante Harris & Joseph (Joe) Harris

Rita Lorenzo Kikel & Norbert Kikel   Marco Lorenzo   Angelina Lorenzo (First Wife)
                                                                        Anna Lorenzo (Second Wife)

Patricia Kikel Kelly & William (Bill) Kelly

Lorraine (Lorry) Kikel Salluzzi & Vincenzo Salluzzi

Rita Salluzzi

Antonia (Toni) Salluzzi

Karen Kikel Farley & Richard Farley

Kyle Farley

Matthew (Matt) Farley

Dana Farley

Mary & Flore Lorenzo's
Wedding Day

Norbert Kikel
College Graduation

Young Norbert & Rita
in Love

Norbert & Rita's
Wedding Day

Patty
age 2

Lorry
age 9

Teenage
Patty & Lorry

Karen
age 5

Karen & Lorry
Patty's Wedding Day

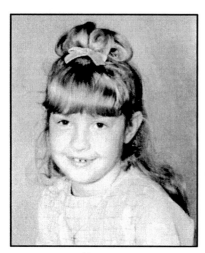

Karen
age 6

Karen
age 13

Karen with her Bookshelf
Age 11

Norbert
in his TV Room

Norbert & Rita
1977

Mary Lorenzo's
Birthday

The Seven Coffin
Garden

Aunt Emily
watching Wrestling

Karen & Patty
Lorry's Wedding Day

Norbert walking Lorry
down the aisle

Karen
in Texas

Karen & Lorry (pregnant with Rita)
at the Roman Garden

Emily with Rita Salluzzi

Lorry & Rita Salluzzi

Lorry's Daughters
Rita & Toni

Karen & Richard
1986

Richard & Karen
High School

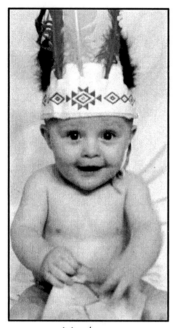

Matthew's
First Birthday

Matthew
at 7 months

Dana & Matthew
Christmas 1990

Rita & Toni

Obedia

A Vision in Stone

Karen

during Chemotherapy
June 1991

(Note Catheter in her Chest)

Karen's
30th Bithday

Richard & Matt
1993

Lorry
1993

Will to Live: Having a reason to go on.

Creating Future Goals: Looking ahead.

Turning Negatives Into Positives: The desire to help others by sharing my experiences.

Positive Thinking: Focus on the good things and raise the quality of daily life.

Edgar Cayce Remedies: His remedies have helped thousands.

Counseling: Choose a psychologist carefully; few things are more important.

Guided Imagery: Listening to Dr. Bernie Siegel cancer healing tapes, creating my own images to heal.

Detoxing Negative Thoughts & Emotions: Detoxifying negative thoughts and feelings, and replacing them with positive images and/or memories.

Diet & Juicing: Macrobiotics, organic, no sugar or processed foods. Drinking fresh juices with live enzymes to conserve the energy used in digesting fiber. Eat to heal and build strength.

Research: Study cases of how terminal cancer patients survived, research doctors, hospitals, chemotherapy and radiation regimens; everything.

Medical Support System: If you're not comfortable with your doctor, don't be afraid to change.
I had a secondary medical support system with my primary care physician as a welcome backup.

Positive Cell Conditioning: Talk to your individual cells, using positive affirmations.
Condition yourself on both conscious and subconscious levels.

Healing Crystals: Utilize the beauty and positive earth energies of crystals.

Aromatherapy: Scent is a powerful tool on many levels. Different scents affect different parts of the psyche.

Love & Support from Family and Friends: Love for my children made me want to fight harder and stay for them.
Love and Support from my family and friends was invaluable.

Hands on Healing: Human touch is a powerful healing tool.

Healing From Within: Connect with the true healing power inside yourself, rather than searching outside.

Spiritual Connection: My spiritual connections were through God, myself, other people, the entity,
my individual gifts, experiences and staying on the path.

Chapter 7:

The Red Flower

"Ma, look at you! Will you go to the doctor?"

Christmas day, 1980, and Rita couldn't get up the stairs. Her back hurt, her legs hurt, everything felt terrible. The anguish was so intense she shied away from imagining the cause, too frightened to think of it. It was a familiar pain, one that was supposed to have been cut out of her.

The first little niggle was felt around Halloween, but she'd kept silent. In charge of decorations for the neighborhood *Spookfest*, Rita couldn't disappoint the children. Besides, she loved all the little costumes.

Using the toilet became a problem in mid-November, but Thanksgiving was coming up, and it wasn't really that bad.

By Christmas Eve, she knew. But, in typical Rita-fashion, family and the annual Christmas party came first. Sugar cookies and a holly tree were far more important than saving one's own life.

Lorry and Karen bullied Rita into going to the doctor on January second, a week sooner than she'd planned.

"Girls, I just want to wait until we've settled into the New Year a bit more." This was a ridiculous excuse as well as a lie. Rita was afraid.

The cancer had returned and was growing aggressively. A large tumor had wrapped itself around a good blood source in the colon. Near the base of her spine, it was also on the move. Surgery was imperative.

Two small tumors were removed, along with a section of Rita's colon. She was fitted with a colostomy bag. The largest tumor remained inside.

"It was too close to the spine to remove," the doctor told the family afterward.

Instant pandemonium ensued, and little could be heard over the wailing.

Karen set her jaw. She'd cry later.

"Quiet, everybody. I can't hear. Doctor, what are you going to do to help my mother now?"

Question after question followed, and the doctor found a grudging admiration for this demanding and rather irritating young woman. He felt like a first year medical student, the way she grilled him.

The morning after surgery, Lorry was called into the room where Rita was lying, and the doctor stood there with a colostomy nurse. Without an explanation, without warning of any kind, they pulled the cover back from her mother's body and showed Lorry, for the first time, the colostomy.

"Look at me," Rita said, her lip trembling. "Look what they've done to me, Lorry. It's ugly." A tear rolled down her cheek. "Isn't it ugly?"

"No, Ma," Lorry said, schooling her features. "It looks like a red flower. A rosebud. Don't worry about it."

Lorry listened to the detailed instructions as the nurse hooked up the bag to the open intestine. She was cool on the surface, but a disjointed voice, an inner Lorry, stood outside and whispered. *My mother has cancer. My mother's intestine is sticking out of her side. I can see the inside of my mother's colon.*

Rita came home after a week. Bill Kelly suggested Patty and he move into Aunt Emily's house, so they could take care of his mother-in-law.

"Karen's still in school, Lorry's working all the time, and, after all, Rita," he said, "Patty's your eldest daughter. You should let her help you."

Rita eventually agreed, but on Karen's insistence, Bill had to sleep at home. He was there for dinner every night and stayed until after eleven. This was Monday through Friday. On the weekends, he slept over.

"It's only Friday and Saturday nights, Karen," Rita said. "Patty needs him. He's her husband."

Patty did nothing for her mother, of course. In a drugged state of perpetual dreaming, the real world was a place she no longer even wanted to visit. Sleep was her haven, and no one could get her out of it.

Home became a purgatory for Karen. Every time she turned around, Bill was watching. Her bedroom offered no escape. There were to be no locked bedroom doors in the house; Emily didn't believe in them. Convinced someone would start a fire, and they'd all burn to death if there was a locked door, she forbid it. No matter how late Karen stayed out, or how quietly she turned the lock, Emily would be at the door minutes later, tapping.

"Karen, open up. Karen! No locks, you know that. I'll watch for him. I won't let him bother you. Open this door."

Karen had confided in Emily about Bill's past violations, but he was clever as to where his attentions should focus and how. It was Emily'd house, so she was courted in grand style. She was the landlady, after all, the one with the money. A useful man to have around, sycophantic and fawning, Bill ran endless errands for her, flattered her, made himself indispensable. When Karen complained about him, Emily just shrugged.

"He's already here, what do you want me to do?" Emily asked. "I can't kick him out. Besides, Patty wants him with her. He is her husband, you know."

Even Aunt Emily wouldn't champion her now.

Lorry had her own hell to contend with. Rita was a difficult patient. Undergoing the rigors of chemotherapy, the thought of caring for the colostomy bag herself was too much. Rita had never been able to bear dirt or mess of any kind, so the colostomy was her greatest nightmare come true. She couldn't see it as a miracle of modern surgery that was allowing her to survive. She was incapable of handling it. The mere sight of the bag horrified her. She couldn't empty it. Lorry would have to do it.

"I don't know what I'd do without you, Lorry," Rita said. "You know how I feel about these matters. Of all the things that could happen to me ... " she shook her head. "You're the only one I can depend on. Patty can't even take care of herself, and Karen's a child. I need you, Lorry. Don't leave me."

"Don't worry, Ma," Lorry said. "I'll always help you."

Rita used guilt with the precision of a master surgeon. She cut out free will until Lorry became what was required. Now, the shopping, the hairdresser, the visits to the pharmacy, the doctor's appointments, the restaurant, the bad marriage, the infertility; to all this was now added the colostomy bag.

* * *

For the past decade, Uncle Marco had been married to a good Italian girl named Angelina. Imported from the Mother Country, she'd seemed a perfect choice for the prince of the Lorenzos.

Ten years passed with no children between them, and the couple were now in the middle of a vitriolic divorce.

Marco went back to Italy and found another bride from a neighboring town in Calabria. She was much younger than Angelina and hopefully, fertile. Her name was Anna. She was waiting for Marco's divorce to become final before she came to America and married.

Avoiding his first wife as much as possible, Marco spent little time at home anymore. Angelina remained in the Lorenzo house until the divorce was final.

She refused to move until then, speaking of nothing but betrayal morning, noon and night. She still held onto the naive belief that he would come to his senses, but he never did. Embittered and waspish, she shared it all with Rita, regardless of her sister-in-law's white face and obvious pain.

Angelina went next door to the Kikels each morning to help with Rita before Lorry arrived. She got her out of bed, wiped up any night accidents, and got Rita showered and dressed, all the time spewing venom about Marco. Long scenarios of self-righteous rage were spun as she fed Rita breakfast and chemotherapy drugs. Black fury would lie like a fog above their heads while she held a bucket for Rita to vomit in. She wept and beat her breast at the tragedies of her own life as Rita prayed for the Demerol to take effect. This was the atmosphere Rita struggled for her life in; desperate, bitter stories, the air thick with misery not her own.

Then Lorry arrived in old pants and a sweatshirt, a change of clothes over her arm. The colostomy was often messy, and she had to go to work right after Rita was settled.

"Angelina is killing me," Rita mumbled while Lorry tended her. "She's so sad, so upset. My own brother. I can't take it, Lorry. Can't you come any earlier?"

Angelina arrived at seven each morning.

The house was never empty. Relatives came over with gifts of food and self-pity. Rita had always been a good listener, and they weren't about to give that up just because she was ill. They fed on her sympathy, draining her dry, and Lorry could do nothing but watch. Rita reminded her of her obligations any time she tried to turn them away. They were family. Family is always welcome.

Lorry began to feel ill herself. Her legs hurt, she was exhausted all the time, and sunlight was uncomfortable. This was a real blow; Lorry had been a sun-worshipper since childhood. She started having acne problems, an embarrassment she hadn't experienced for a decade. She hadn't had a menstrual period for two months.

She went to the doctor, too worn out to care about the diagnosis, and was rewarded with unbelievable, impossible news.

She was pregnant.

The whole situation at her mother's, the crumbling marriage; even Bill Kelly seemed bearable now. A new life was coming, a beautiful baby for Lorry to love and cherish, to give hope to her beloved mother.

The news was a gift to Rita. Everything seemed somehow lighter, and Lorry was grateful to be able to give her mother this wonderful present. A grandchild. At long last, her first grandchild.

Lorry miscarried before she'd reached three months.

The loss was the last straw for Vinnie. Broken-hearted, he shut himself off completely and began working more hours than ever at the restaurant. He couldn't bear to look at any of the Kikels or Lorenzos, blaming them for the loss of his child.

Lorry was broken. Shattered, bloody, empty. A terrible hollowness left her short of breath.

Rita clung tighter than before. "My poor Lorry. God must have wanted our baby. Some day you'll have another. Don't worry. You can try again."

Patty, not to be outdone, sobbed and flopped all over Lorry as well. Bill offered condolences and physical embrace with a doggedness that made her flesh crawl. Grandma and Aunt Emily waved endless shopping lists at her. Angelina told her she was better off; marriages don't last anyway. Karen tried to comfort her, but the pain was too recent to bear talking about. Lorry couldn't speak of it. She did her job like an automaton, smiling and playing the hostess with a tinny quality to her cheeriness.

If I can just get through the house one day without anyone talking to me ...

When she went over to Rita's or her grandmother's, all she could think of was speed and invisibility. *If I walk quietly, do my stuff, don't look up or make eye contact, I won't have to talk to them. Just one day of not listening to their shit. Please God, just one day. Don't make me have to talk.*

* * *

Lynn Wuest entered their lives through a tip from Jack, one of the waiters at the Roman Garden. Lynn was a professional psychic, and Jack's mother was one of her clients.

Lorry had her over to the apartment for a "psychic party." The prerequisites for a visit were simple. Lorry was to provide five people, and Lynn would do a psychic reading for each one. Karen and Patty both came.

From the first moment she saw her, Karen Kikel thrummed a signal across Lynn's mind. The girl was a volcano. Lynn was almost overwhelmed by the power and tragedy radiating out of someone so young. She saw enormous psychic ability in both Karen and Lorry, but Lorry's was stagnant with the weight of depression. If she could crawl out from under that terrible burden, Lorry would be astonishing. Lynn could feel it. Karen, on the other hand, was blazing, unstoppable energy right now. Despondency had only just begun to erode her strength.

Lynn read each separate person in private. Lorry always saw psychics as a sort of acceptable therapy, an assuagement from all the desperation and fear of daily life. When it was her turn for a reading, she entered the room with a sad sort of hope.

Lynn took Lorry's hand and read her palm, closing her fingers around it.

"You've had a tough time," she began, "Boy, oh boy, you've had a hard time. You have to take care of yourself, honey. You're going to get sick, but it's a different kind of sickness. Don't worry, though. You'll be okay. You're going to live a long life."

Lynn saw a house in the country, and a house on the water, two marriages, but only one true marriage, and a future as a well-known psychic and healer.

Lorry was startled at that one. She hadn't been surprised, or even deeply bothered, by the prophecy of serious illness. But a career as a psychic? It had been a secret dream of hers, to have a future in such a field.

"But there's something you have to do before then," Lynn continued.

"What?"

"You'll have to take care of your family. Your mother needs you. Take care of your mother."

Lorry went back to the living room visibly shaken.

When it was Karen's turn, she sat down, loud and a little cocky. To her, this was just for fun, nothing serious. No matter how much she wanted to believe, this was just entertainment for a party. Lorry was the one who followed all this weird stuff. Not Karen. If she could see it and touch it, then it was real to her. She was the ultimate Doubting Thomas despite her own strong visions. Karen didn't want to believe, yet was desperate to do so. The two feelings warred with each other.

Lynn was a gentle, soft-spoken creature. Karen saw it, felt a whisper of trust in the back of her mind, a fleeting glimpse of solidarity. Staring into Lynn's eyes, who didn't look away.

"You have a hard time coming up," Lynn began.

Stomach roller-coastering, spiraling downward, a rock in the belly. Karen was terrified.

"You'll have to fight so hard and so long, Karen. Your mother will be on this earth only as long as God wants her to be, honey. There's nothing you can do to change that."

"How long do you think my mother has?"

"Maybe, two years."

"What can I do to change that?"

"Honey, only God can do that. You have so much guilt," Lynn said, puzzled. "There's no reason for it. You have to let it go, or you'll make yourself sick. I'm very in tune with people's physiology, and I know when a person is going to have a disease. I'm telling you, if you don't watch it, you can get cancer, too.

I told Lorry that she has to start taking better care of herself. She's going to get sick first. I'm never wrong about these things, honey. Listen to me."

"What's wrong with Lorry? Are you talking cancer, too?"

"No, not cancer. Some other illness that's very serious."

"How serious?"

"Very serious. Life-threatening. Listen to me. This is no joke."

"Okay ... I got it." Karen laughed nervously. "Hey, I just wanted to ask about college."

"You take care of yourself, honey. And, let go of that guilt."

Karen staggered out of the room and back to the party, where she drank until she stopped shaking.

* * *

Karen was trapped by circumstance. The anger inside her was growing stronger, and she was growing with it. In a group of angry teenagers, she was the life of the party. Dancing every night, challenges, dares. Few people could outdo Karen Kikel. She danced hard, drank hard, played hard, and her friends did the same. Reality could be chased away by something as simple as draining a glass. She earned a reputation as a bottomless drinker, and like any person with a talent for endurance or strength, Karen was challenged often.

One night after work, John the cook challenged her to a drinking contest at his house. Shots, Karen's choice.

Pulling a long drag on her cigarette, she notched it at a randy angle between scarlet fingernails, and grinned. "Line 'em up."

They cleared a table in the dining room and set up shot glasses. Karen drank Scotch. John, Tequila. The cook had a reputation for drinking. Karen wasn't one to back down, no matter how ridiculous the challenge. John put on some South American music, and the contest began.

They did the first shots to the sound of Santana. John reminisced about his youth, when he was in the Colombian circus.

After ten shots, the music blurred. John did a knife balancing trick on his chin. After fifteen, the sound became one long raucous hum, and his eyes could no longer focus.

Lorry had stayed to keep an eye on her little sister. Now, she sat in stunned silence as Karen tossed back shot after shot, slamming the glasses down in a long row that grew more slanted as the evening progressed.

A death wish. Karen's laughing at it. She's actually enjoying it.

Karen locked eyes with the contender and entered her mindset. Once she did this, nothing could sway her. She would have drank until it killed her before she'd back down.

They decided to quit after twenty-three shots. For a last and defiant absurdity, Karen had one more. Twenty-four shots down the throat of a sixteen-year-old girl, in a challenge that had no meaning. She'd accomplished nothing by this airing of her formidable will. It was just a run-away, escape tactics that cost her two days of hideous sickness. To Karen, at the time, this was a victory.

***

Karen owned a rickety old blue Plymouth Satellite with a white roof and one red door. Since she now had a car of her own, she took up some of Lorry's shopping duties. The Plymouth also freed her to see more of her friends.

Life in Levittown continued. Rita was inundated with cards and well-wishers every day. Since the chemotherapy had made her hair fall out, she brushed and fussed with her wig each morning.

"Illness is no excuse for not looking neat," she said when Lorry teased. "What would the family think if my hair wasn't tidy?"

"Or a handsome man came calling, Ma, and saw you with a bird's nest on your head."

"Exactly. Got to look my best for Prince Charming."

They often joked tenderly like this. The girls loved it when Rita joined in.

But she wasn't getting better.

She made it to Karen's high school graduation, but only under extreme pain. They couldn't stay long. Despite an inflatable donut Lorry placed on her chair, Rita couldn't sit. The tumor was too close to her spine.

Karen, sitting in her row, could think of nothing but her mom's suffering. She almost missed her name being called to go up and receive her diploma.

***

Rita began to talk about death.

"I know your father wants me with him, Karen. He can't leave me alone. For the first time in my life I can truly enjoy myself. But, no, he just can't leave me be."

Karen and Lorry knew they were running out of time. Rita was barely able to walk anymore. Even sitting up was difficult. Her cane was no longer of any use. She was deteriorating fast.

A neighbor suggested *Sloan Kettering* in New York City, famous for its long strides in the battle against cancer. The family hoped for a medical miracle.

"I'm fed up with all these screwups who can't give us any answers," Karen said. "She's not getting any better. Let's go somewhere where the doctors are more innovative. We need to take her to Sloan Kettering."

They made an appointment the next day. The oncologists at Sloan Kettering spent a month poking and prodding and administering pain medication; first in pills, then in a morphine patch. Rita wasn't admitted; instead she stayed at home and drove into New York for each test.

After much deliberation, the doctors said that they agreed with the treatment Rita was having on Long Island. They would change nothing. Let her stay where she was.

Depressing as that suggestion was, the family got an astonishing surprise a few days later.

Rita passed stool naturally, without the colostomy bag. This was, according to the doctors, fabulous news.

"The only reason this could be happening is that your mother's tumor is shrinking. We're going to schedule her for surgery right away and take it out. This is very good news."

A miracle. Lorry and Karen stared at each other, hardly daring to breathe. Shrinking. The tumor was shrinking.

Their relief was short-lived. After the operation, the surgeon called the entire family into a consulting room. Lorenzos, Kikels, Salluzzis and Kellys were all present. The doctor sat down at the desk and folded his hands. Karen watched the fingers press together. Her stomach sank.

"The news isn't as good as we'd hoped," he began. "It seemed, since she had passed stool normally, that the tumor had shrunk. In actuality, it has wrapped itself around the spine and repositioned itself. That's why Mrs. Kikel had a normal bowel movement. I'm afraid it's inoperable." The family stared at him in shock.

"However, there's a surgical procedure that I know will help Mrs. Kikel. The tumor is too intrinsically wound about the spinal cord. We can't free it." He looked up at the daughters' shocked faces. "Your mother will not recover."

The words fell like a blow.

"The pain will soon become so intense, the drugs won't be able to help her. The only thing we can do for the patient now is to sever the nerve cords in her spine. Then she can have something of a quality of life without pain. This procedure will leave her paralyzed, but comfortable."

He kept talking in a confident manner, sure of himself and offering the right choice, the only choice, in his opinion. Rita Kikel would not recover. "Your mother will not recover."

Your mother is already dead. Cut the spinal cord so she can feel dead.

Lorry cried, "Oh, my God. Oh, my God!"

"We don't give up in this family," Marco shouted. "That would mean giving up. There's got to be another medicine we can try. We don't give up in this family."

"That's very noble," the doctor said. "But your sister is in a lot of pain, and it's going to get worse. This is all we have left to offer you. I understand your pain, but we have to do what's best for Rita. Do what you have to do, but remember, this option is always open."

His words rang strange and garbled in Karen's ears, like a bizarre underwater gurgling, impossible to take in. She struggled to wrap her brain around sentences that pierced her heart, but she felt odd, dizzy, detached from her motor functions. Norbert in a coffin. Rita in a coffin.

Three years, she thought stupidly. *I've been without a father for three years. I can't lose my mother, yet.* The image of Rita's spinal cord being cut for no other reason than to prepare her for death seemed monstrous.

The surgeon was still talking, but Karen had ceased hearing him long ago. Lorry stood wide-eyed and horror-stricken, Marco was pacing the room, wailing, Patty was hysterical. Everyone was settling into death mode. Everyone, in their grief, was simply accepting what this man, this stranger, was telling them. Hope was gone from their faces in an instant, and loss had taken its place.

Why? Mommy isn't dead yet. This can't be the only answer. I won't accept it.

At that moment, the mystique of the medical profession lost all its glamour for Karen. She looked at the doctor, at this formidable and highly intelligent man, and somehow felt no awe of him. He was the expert, the emperor whose opinion was godlike law. He was to be believed without question. She had been taught this. It was the religion of her upbringing.

Suddenly, for some inexplicable reason, Karen's mind changed in that crowded office with its fluorescent lighting, and she no longer feared her own ignorance. She no longer believed implicitly. She faced the surgeon as an equal, not a superior. He was just a man. Karen saw not the experience of an expert on colon cancer, but the ignorance of a person who had run out of answers. There was more to know about her mother's illness, but he didn't know it. Stumbling along with the incomplete handful of knowledge he had, which all the doctors they'd seen in the past terrible three years had had, his only answer, after weeks of tests, was to sever the nerve cords. That was not a solution. It was a surrender, and Karen Kikel never surrendered to anything, anymore. She was not going to give in to some stupid, mindless disease. The cancer would not get Rita without a fight. Karen wouldn't allow it.

"No," she said. "Nobody's cutting Mommy's nerve cords."

"It's the only solution I can offer, now. I strongly urge you to follow my advice."

Karen turned to her family. "This can't be the only answer," she said. "There has to be something else somewhere. If paralyzing Mommy is the best the doctors here can come up with, we'll find new doctors. This is not the only answer. There's always more than one solution. We just have to find it."

They refused the nerve cord suggestion.

Karen started haunting the libraries, searching for an answer, any answer, no matter how strange or crazy it might seem. She looked up the track records of dozens of various doctors in the field of cancer. She studied celebrities who had the disease. She even researched cryogenic freezing.

And all the while, Rita deteriorated. The pain became too much for a morphine patch. Panic became the emotion of the day.

Uncle Marco supported the research Karen was doing. "Rita can't die," he said. "There must be another answer." He turned to Karen. "Find the answer, Karen. I don't care what it costs. Do it. Don't stop until you find it."

Her sisters had mixed feelings. Lorry was supportive in the search for a cure. Bill and Patty contested every idea Karen came up with.

"Mommy is dying, Karen," Patty kept telling her. "We have to accept it and get on with our lives. You're not helping her by doing this."

* * *

Patty had slid even further away from the family during Rita's illness. Bill now did everything for her, even demanding she not leave the house without him. Vacations in Virginia with Bill were the only time Patty was away from the apartment overnight. She surrendered her free will. She now spoke only with his words, and if she had thoughts of her own, anymore, they were hidden.

Karen started classes at the local college, studying business. Her grades were steady despite the stresses in her life, and she was determined to succeed. Every person she came in contact with, Karen asked to keep a lookout for alternative answers to save her mother.

The son-in-law of a cousin was a doctor at Brunswick hospital, and that was enough to convince them to move Rita there. At Brunswick, she was set up with a morphine drip.

Rita began to disappear. The morphine level became so high, she was virtually comatose. Bill and Patty were managing her money. Rita had a little over fifty thousand dollars in the bank, insurance monies from a policy for Norbert from his job at Sperry's Gyroscope. The insurance was paid in one lump sum on the condition that an employee die before the age of sixty.

In the end, Norbert finally did do something right, Rita used to say. *He died before the age of sixty.*

Karen grew frantic. She refused to see her mother in a coffin in reality. The visions were bad enough. She knew Patty was next. If Rita died, Patty would soon follow.

The Phil Donahue Show came to the rescue.

Aunt Emily watched his program every day. One afternoon, Karen was draped over her favorite chair, swinging a sullen leg when the topic on the Donahue Show was terminal cancer survivors and Doctor Stanislaw Burzynski.

Doctor Burzynski had developed a radical new treatment for cancer called Antineoplaston. Unlike conventional treatment of chemotherapy and radiation, Antineoplastons "reprogrammed" neoplastic, or cancerous, cells, convincing them to commit suicide. Burzynski followed Hippocrates' philosophy of *First do no harm.*

"Antineoplastons," he argued, "do not harm normal cells. They're "biochemical micro switches." They turn off the oncogens, or cancer-causing cells, and turn on the tumor suppressor genes."

Born in Poland, Doctor Burzynski held both an MD and a PhD in biochemistry. He was a member of many prestigious medical and scientific societies, and was confident about his treatment. In 1977, he opened the Burzynski Clinic in Houston, Texas, and had rooms at Twelve Oaks Hospital, nearby. He wasn't, yet, FDA approved, but patients who had lost all hope flocked to him, and the results were impressive. Burzynski was passionate, articulate, charismatic, and what he said made sense.

Karen called the show and asked dozens of questions, furiously scribbling notes. Here was something new, something she hadn't come across in all her colon cancer research. Doctor Burzynski was in Texas. They would go to Texas.

"No!"

Bill and Patty were vociferously opposed to the idea. Karen ignored them, going ahead with plans and schedules for departure as soon as possible.

"You know it's not fair of you to make decisions without everybody's input, Karen," Patty said. "Mommy shouldn't have to suffer anymore. If she's going to die, she should die around family. You shouldn't take her away, Karen. She is going to die. Please accept it. Let her do it at home."

"Patty, where there's life, there's hope. There have been people with terminal cancer who went to Doctor Burzynski and survived. What if Mommy is one of those?"

Bill slid his fingers around Patty's upper arm, his eyes on Karen.

"Karen," Patty said, primed like a ventriloquist's puppet. "We don't have that kind of money. This stuff is too untested. Insurance won't cover it, and there's no guarantee it's going to work. Besides, you have to transfer Mommy there, not to mention your own travel expenses. How much is this all going to cost?"

Karen knew whose words these were. She looked at Bill as she answered her sister.

"But, Patty, it's Mommy's money. Maybe God left the insurance money from Daddy so it could save Mommy's life. The money is hers, and if we have to spend every last fucking cent, if we have to sell the house, we're going to. Mommy means that much."

Bill stepped forward, his eyes full of sympathy and paternal discipline.

"What if it costs more? Have you thought of that?" he asked. "You shouldn't spend the money that way, Karen. Your mother's almost dead. I know it's hard for you to accept, but she's not going to rebound from this. We went to the best doctors in Manhattan, and they can't help her. Face it. No one can. This guy is some quack who's trying to take advantage. I'm sorry. You just need to let it go."

Karen's face grew steely. "I believe we can find the answer in Texas. Stay here if you want to. You don't have to participate. But we're going."

She sailed past them, this beautiful, invincible, intelligent creature. Bill and Patty had discussed the confrontation for hours the night before. Bill had put all of his formidable talent of word manipulation into the sentences he'd primed Patty with, but they'd toppled like a house of cards before this infuriating eighteen-year-old girl. As far as Karen was concerned, talk was over. Action was what was needed, and action was quickly becoming Karen's forte.

Bill and Patty next confronted Lorry, downstairs in the kitchen.

"Lorry," Patty began, "you're not letting Karen go to Texas with Mommy, are you?"

Lorry stared.

"Oh, no, I wouldn't do that. Karen and Mommy all alone in Houston? I couldn't allow it."

Patty sagged with relief. "Thank God."

Bill smiled.

"At least you've got some sense, Lorry," he said. "I was really worried about all this nonsense."

Lorry looked from one to the other, giving them a moment to enjoy their relief. Then she said it. "I'm going with them."

Vinnie was also unhappy about it.

"It's not your place to go," he shouted when Lorry had first told him her plans. "Your place is with your husband."

Slamming the kitchen cabinet in exasperation, Lorry turned to him.

"Look," she said. "Let's just treat this whole Texas thing as a separation, okay?"

The hurt rippled across his face. "Go ahead. Do what you want." He walked out.

Karen had arranged for the ambulance which took them to the airport. By this time, Rita was in and out of coherency. She started calling Lorry and Karen *Mama*.

"Mama. Ma Ma. Ma Ma."

This endless mantra went on for the next six weeks.

They arrived at the Houston airport in the blistering heat of a late July afternoon. The air hit them like a furnace. Rita whispered how good it felt.

The bright Texas sunlight hurt Lorry's eyes even behind tinted glasses, and her legs ached abominably. At least here she didn't have to wear high heels. She'd always worn heels at the restaurant.

The ambulance drove them to an apartment complex called *The Landing* where they would live for the duration of their stay. Offering month-to-month leases, it was situated only a few blocks from Twelve Oaks Hospital.

Doctor Burzynski came that night. He inserted a port, or catheter, into Rita's chest beneath the collarbone. At the time, this process of administering intravenous drugs was relatively new. The port had a long tube coming out of it with a small rubber cap. Rita was given her first treatment of Antineoplaston that very evening.

Burzynski was a sweet, round-faced smile of a man. His confidence reassured the two anxious sisters. He showed them how to apply antiseptic solution and antibiotic ointment to the incision, and how often to change the sterile dressing over the catheter. Karen was grateful for Lorry's possessive attitude toward these particular cares. She had a low threshold when it came to body fluids.

The doctor suggested a macrobiotic diet for Rita, which had Karen and Lorry staring in blank ignorance. Their neighbor around the corner had put her husband on macrobiotics when he first came to the clinic. According to all the medical diagnoses he had had before Doctor Burzynski, her husband should have been dead two years ago. Both Burzynski and the happy couple credited the diet as well as the Antineoplaston.

Rita was just lucid enough to refuse anything so radical.

Life in Texas developed a routine. Doctor Burzynski visited often. Rita was in and out of consciousness and lost track of time. She was up chanting all night. "Ma Ma ... Ma Ma ... MaaaaMaaaaaaaaa!"

Lorry and Karen took turns caring for her. Lorry was in charge of the colostomy bag because Karen vomited every time she tried to change it. Karen washed Rita's soiled linen. They both cooked and cleaned. Rita was never alone for longer than a bathroom trip.

After the first month, the pressures of constant care and lack of free time began to wear on Karen and Lorry. They hired a nurse who came every night who encouraged them to get out of the apartment.

The complex where they lived boasted an outdoor swimming pool. The water became a haven for both sisters, a chance to unwind and socialize.

There were always people at the pool. Karen and Lorry met two handsome young cable engineers while playing water volleyball. Ricky McCaffrey and Mark Faber were a fun-loving pair with a company car, and they liked nothing better than chauffeuring the women about.

Ricky was a nice lump of a young man, handsome and boisterous, out for a good time and excellent at showing one. He noticed Karen the first day she arrived in Texas.

They settled into a happy routine of TGI Fridays and El Torritos. By the time the nurse had been coming for a week, Lorry and Karen met several new people around the complex to go out with. One of their new friends warned them about a prowling lothario named Charlie.

Charlie was here with his mother, who was battling lung cancer. Despite a wife back in Michigan, he had hit on every woman under thirty in the complex. He first approached Lorry at the pool. Young, beautiful, and insecure, she welcomed him with gratitude.

Lorry was perfect prey for a man like Charlie. He listened with a sympathetic ear to her plight, sharing his own pain regarding his mother. Projected sensitivity was his bait, but it was his eyes, shimmering with tears, that sunk the hook.

They began dating. Karen disapproved, but nothing she could say would budge Lorry. Karen had pegged him on sight, but Lorry didn't want to hear. No amount of warning, no cajoling, no anger or talk of duty made any difference. Lorry wouldn't listen to anything bad about Charlie. He needed her, and above all else, it was imperative for Lorry to be needed.

"He's so fake!" Karen yelled. "Can't you see that? Can't you see what he's after? They even warned us about him. What are you doing?"

"Karen, he makes me happy. I've never felt this way before. This is the first time I've ever been happy."

"What do you mean, the first time? What about Raymond? What about your husband? Remember Vinnie?"

"Why don't you want me to be happy?"

"Lorry, of course, I want you to be happy, but I don't trust him. He's supposed to be here to help his mother, just like we are, and all he can think about is what young chickie can he screw? He's tried it with every girl in the building. How can you be so blind?"

"He makes me happy."

That was all Lorry would say on the matter.

Karen was furious.

Charlie started in on Karen, driving the wedge deeper between the two sisters. He swore endless devotion to Lorry, and expounded on the blissful life they would have together, gently censuring Karen for her dislike. Karen began seeing uncomfortable similarities to Bill Kelly, and a new fear was added to her anxiety about her mother. Now she feared for Lorry on top of everything else.

She began spending more time with Ricky at the pool or out-on-the-town. Six weeks after they'd arrived in Texas, the two sisters were barely speaking to each other.

Worried about their lack of transportation, Vinnie paid for a rental car while they were in Texas. He sent Lorry letters which she opened, but never answered. Totally absorbed in her newest Prince Charming, Lorry thought only of Charlie and his promises for their future. Like Raymond before him, like her father before that, Lorry picked the man most capable of hurting her. Her self-destructive patterns settled back into place.

After two months, Rita had improved dramatically. Sitting up in a chair for brief periods, she was getting strong enough to demand ice cream, yogurt and attention at any and every hour of the day. She was also well enough to begin resenting her nurses.

"They're mean to me," she insisted. "I want my girls to help, not those nurses. They expect me to do everything myself. How am I supposed to learn how to program a portable infusion pump? I don't even know what that is. I'm sick! I'm very, very ill. Those nurses just don't understand. Their jobs have made them all hard. They don't have a daughter's loyalty. It's a daughter's place to care for her mother. I don't want those nurses handling me, anymore. I need my girls."

Rita was exerting control again, casting her net wide. This was a positive sign as far as Karen was concerned. She ventured a tentative glimpse into her visions, imagining Rita free from the coffin. *Texas was the right choice. Mommy is so much better.*

Relaxing in bed, she closed her eyes, willing the vision to come to her.

The coffin appeared. Karen jerked with fear. Rita lay thick and solid inside.

"How can this be?" she whispered, appalled. "Mommy's getting better. The tumor's shrinking. She's eating real food again."

The vision was wrong. It had to be. She wanted to go to Ricky, but he had left for a four-week job at sea. Karen missed him very much.

Doctor Burzynski asked Lorry if she wanted to volunteer for a test study of Antineoplaston as a cancer preventative. She agreed. Treatments began that day.

"This is going to protect you, Lorry," Burzynski said, "You're helping to prove that Antineoplaston can save lives as a preventative as well as a cancer treatment."

"Could it help me become pregnant?"

He looked startled.

"Possibly. It depends on the medical reasons for your infertility, of course. Right now though, relax."

Two weeks of Lorry's trial study had passed when Rita started coughing.

They'd done a CAT scan two days before. Everyone was encouraged by the dramatic shrinkage of Rita's tumor. Lorry and Karen called home, basking in the well-wishes and compliments of an uncomplimentary family. Even Uncle Marco had something nice to say.

They were pressed with timetables.

"When are you coming home?" Emily asked.

"Well, we're not out of the woods yet, but it looks good," Karen said, "Do you want to talk to Mommy?" Everybody was thrilled that Rita was able to talk on the phone.

The low-grade fever hit the next night. Rita faltered and struggled for breath, startled and confused. Just the day before, she'd felt better than she had in years. She was completely off the morphine, and could eat real food again. The only painkiller she was taking currently was Tylenol. Now, all of a sudden, her chest was so painful.

"What's happening?" Rita asked in a panic. "I can't catch my breath."

The nurse came for her normal shift. She called the hospital two hours after her arrival. Rita was slipping in and out of consciousness. The antibiotics were having no effect.

"I hear fluid in your mother's lungs, and she has a fever," she said. "We need to get her to the hospital."

The ambulance drove them all through the streets of Houston, and Karen was half-crazy with fear.

Your mother will not recover.

Lorry was in a daze. Everything happened so fast. In only one day. Good news was dangled in front of their noses, then gone in the blink of an eye.

They sat in the hospital lounge, waiting as the emergency team worked on Rita. The doctor soon came and told them what was happening.

"Your mother has double pneumonia. We've put her on intravenous antibiotics, but so far, she isn't responding. All we can do at this point is wait. I'm sorry."

Rita slipped into a coma that night. She was brain dead within five days, her body lying still and bloated, fed oxygen through a respirator. She was a sad and worn-looking sight, eyes closed, skin gray, arms peppered and strapped with tubes.

For sixteen hours, Karen sat with her, holding her hand, talking until she was hoarse, refusing to give up. As time passed and Rita remained still, Karen grew quiet, just stroking her fingers and kissing her hand. The silence was interspersed with the noise of the respirator.

Lorry sat back, giving Karen this moment. She watched as her sister talked herself dry, until her lips were cracked and her voice gone. *She's only eighteen. It's not fair. She's only eighteen, and she has no parents.*

Her own feelings were frozen. She sat there, stunned, waiting for Rita to die, unable to sign the papers the doctors presented, authorizing them to take her mother off the respirators. Rita was brain dead. She wasn't coming back.

I can't do it.

Lorry left the room to call home. Karen, only eighteen, made the choice to sign. She called no one. She didn't want the over-emotional opinion of anybody far away. Rita was trapped between worlds by a machine. Karen wanted her off of it.

She signed the papers.

The nurses and doctor began peeling off tape, pulling tubes from Rita's arms and rolling the IV away. Lorry slipped silently into the room and took up the chair next to Karen. They watched the life drain out of their mother in one short, staccato set of breaths. Rita's eyes snapped open and rolled up in her head, and she was gone. Both daughters felt her leave in a chill sweep across the back of their necks.

Weeping softly, Lorry went back out in the hallway and called Uncle Marco with the news.

"What do you mean she's dead?" Marco asked incredulously. "How can this be?"

"She's dead."

"Last week she was sitting up; she was eating food; we talked to her on the phone ... we all thought you'd be bringing her home soon."

"She developed pneumonia. The doctors did all they could."

"I can't believe it. I just can't believe it," Marco said.

Lorry was crying in earnest now.

"I can't talk any more, Lorry. I have to go." He hung up.

Lorry fell to pieces. Charlie came and drove her back to the complex.

In shock, Karen marveled at the magnitude of her own grief. The sorrow washed over her with sharp teeth, and she found her strength failing. This was something she couldn't face alone. She needed company. She needed proof that she, too, was not dead.

God, please. Please don't show me anymore today. I can't take it.

She wanted Ricky. Young, healthy, so full of life. She needed life.

Fishing in her pocketbook for change, she dialed his number in Galveston.

"Ricky? It's Karen."

"Hey, sweetheart, how's it going? How are you?"

Karen gripped the phone. "She's dead, Ricky. My mom's dead."

"Oh, baby, I'm so sorry."

"I don't know what to do," she whispered. "I just ... she was getting better. She was getting better. Now, she's dead."

"Where are you, honey?" he asked.

"In the hospital."

"Where's Lorry?"

"At the apartment with Charlie. I can't go back there."

"Come to Galveston, Karen. Can you drive?"

She took a shuddering breath.

"Yes."

"Come on, then."

Karen hung up the phone, picked up her pocketbook and the keys to the rental, and left.

A few miles down the road, Karen realized she had no idea where she was going. A map bought at a gas station got her to Galveston, and a phone call to Ricky got her to his hotel.

They went to his room, Karen clinging, but numb. She lost her virginity in a desperate effort to feel something, anything. Ricky hadn't planned it; hadn't thought of giving anything other than comfort. It just happened, and the intimacy was a surprise to them both.

Karen thought the sex would make her feel better, help her forget, but she just felt dirty, and more alone than ever.

She drove back to the apartment the next evening. Ricky had wanted her to stay, said he loved her, but Karen had to get back to her sister. Arrangements needed to be made to get home to New York.

They made the arrangements for the return flight, and flew back to Long Island without speaking; too heartbroken to talk much. Conversation was limited to what they would have to face when they got home.

Lorry sat, her mind in a broken whirl. Like Rita, her entire being had revolved around servitude to her mother. With Rita gone, Lorry's world had collapsed. The nucleus of the Lorenzo family was in flux; Rita had been the center, loved by everyone. Lorry was afraid of their reception. The family would show little compassion for the daughters who had taken Rita away in her final hours.

Even worse, Charlie had betrayed her. The man she had pinned her hopes on was exactly what everyone had cautioned her about. She wasn't the first nor the last woman he'd used. Everyone warning her, everyone telling her it would happen, even Karen's insistence that she hated Charlie for hurting her sister, only made it that much more bitter.

Idiot. You stupid idiot. Lorry flailed herself with the word.

The arguments began as soon as they arrived home. Grandma Lorenzo wanted the longest possible wake for her beloved Rita. Uncle Marco was appalled.

"Oh, yeah, let's just extend the torture!" he yelled. "Three days of looking at a body with no Rita in it. Three days of forced socializing because my sister is dead!"

Mary Lorenzo had her way in the end. Rita was buried on the fourth day.

The funeral parlor was so crowded that they had to get another room. Everybody loved Rita. Everybody turned up to mourn her. Hundreds of people shuffled past in a receiving line, but the sisters couldn't understand half the words of sympathy spoken to them.

Lorry and Karen listened dully to the wailings of a hysterical Aunt Emily and a dramatic grandmother as mourners gave whispered sympathy.

"I have no more daughter," Mary Lorenzo wailed, "I have no more daughter! Poor Marco ... my poor Marco. She was like a mother to him! Aah!"

Aunt Emily joined in. "Even though she was my niece, she was like a daughter to me. Ah, Rita, my Rita."

Well-wishers placed sympathetic hands on Emily, and she blotted her nose, looking up with watery eyes.

"You know she lived with me?"

Uncle Marco sat, stoic and unmoving in the back, not wanting to be near the body. His was a brooding, angry sorrow. His atheism made the ritualistic ceremony uncomfortable and ridiculous, and he wanted no part of it.

Karen sat crushed with grief. A numbness spread throughout her body. Her chest was heavy, and breathing became more and more difficult. She was developing what would one day turn into a serious chronic asthma.

The people kept filing by, murmuring their sorrow. There were no direct attacks, no outright accusations of wrongdoing, but Karen felt their blame in every look, every shoulder turned away. Her tough shell began to crack. *I can't take it. Oh God, I'm going to lose control. I can't hold it. Oh God, help me. Help me!*

Like a raft in a storm, she clung to her Aunt Emily.

Lorry sat, an island to herself, willing people not to speak to her. There was a drone in her ears; the drone of hundreds of bodies sharing grief and crudités. Lorry glanced up dully at a relative's plaintive wail of sorrow, turned her head when Mary Lorenzo blew her nose. Their sounds meant nothing. Their sadness didn't penetrate.

The only shock was Karen. Tough little Karen was crying. Lorry wondered why. She went, a vague need to comfort driving her, and stood over her sister, crying so pitifully in the corner.

"You shouldn't cry, Karen. You're the lucky one."

Karen looked up, startled. Lorry stared at her with a blank face, her words confusing. "They didn't have the time to work on you the way they did with me. You have the door open, now. They're not here to stop you. You can do anything you want. If they'd lived, you'd be nothing. Like me."

***

Now that Rita was dead, Marco decided to solidify his position in Mary Lorenzo's will. Aunt Emily was going to leave her house to Lorry and Karen. By rights, Marco should get Mary Lorenzo's. It was his home; he was her son, her only living child, and he wanted it for his own family.

Marco began pressing Mary to change her will.

"A mother should leave her belongings to her children," he began. "Well, Rita's gone now. Emily has her own house; they'll get that. The girls don't need Rita's share of the Lorenzo home, too. I'm your son. Your only son. The three girls will be fine without any more help. Look how Lorry and Karen made all the decisions to go to Texas. The girls aren't my responsibility, and they're not yours. Patty has Bill. Lorry has Vinnie and the restaurant. Hell, they're practically rich. Karen has Emily. We need to stick together now, without worrying about Rita's girls. They'll be fine."

"But they're Rita's children," Mary said. "When she was here, she helped your father and me make up this will, together. This is what she wanted, and it's what your father wanted. Don't ask me to do this, Marco. It's not right."

"I'm your son," Marco said. "I'm the one you should concern yourself with. You need to take care of family first, remember?"

Mary stood firm for three weeks. Then, Marco threatened to move out and never see her again if she didn't do what he wanted.

Having lost a husband and daughter, Mary couldn't risk losing her son, too. She became a huge child, self-absorbed with her own anguish, and unable to cope with life's difficulties. She couldn't think. It hurt too much. She just wanted someone to make all the decisions, allowing her to grieve.

She handed her free will over to Marco. He would know what to do. He was sensitive; he taught elementary school. He'd take care of everything.

Mary signed on the dotted line, and the Lorenzos turned their backs on Rita's children.

* * *

Karen found an unexpected horror waiting for her when she returned from Houston. Patty hadn't moved back to the Bethpage apartment. She was still there. Worse yet, Bill had slipped in like a thief in the night. The two of them were now living full-time in Emily's house. They slept in Rita's bedroom.

When questioned by an astounded Karen as to why the pedophile was living in their house, Emily became sullen and defensive. "What do you want me to do? He's here. I can't ask him to leave. Your sister wants him here."

Bill knew which side his bread was buttered on. He'd become indispensable to Emily. Karen had to accept it.

College was gone, too. She'd gotten a leave of absence during Rita's stay in Texas, giving Patty detailed instructions for protecting the Social Security money and her college status.

"I'll take care of it, Karen," Patty told her on the phone. "You just concentrate on what you're doing out there."

Karen automatically got Norbert's Social Security death benefits in the event of Rita's death, and it was available to her as long as she was in school. Her college schedule was made out before they even left for Texas. She'd been due back the last week of August.

Karen asked Marco or Patty to take her place in Houston so she could begin classes, but they both declined. She refused to leave Lorry and Rita by themselves, so she told Patty to get the necessary papers and make the prerequisite phone calls to protect her Social Security benefits.

Patty dropped the ball. The checks stopped coming. Every dime that would have gone to Karen's education was lost. After everything that happened, this was too much. Karen began to lose hope.

She started calling Lynn Wuest, the psychic who had foretold Rita's death so long ago. Lynn became a confidant and friend as well as a person of intuition, as she preferred to call it. *Intuitive* was her preferred title. "Psychic" had a negative connotation to most people. She started coaching Karen and Lorry both in the strengthening of their own abilities.

"Psychic powers are like any other God-given talent. Practice strengthens and improves what you've been born with. For instance, anyone can learn to play the piano. Some people will never get past chopsticks, some people are Mozarts, but everybody can play."

With an understandable phobia about cancer, Karen often asked Lynn about her own health. She remembered the vision of the number twenty-one, carved in stone. Every ache or pain sent a shudder of fear through her. Repeatedly, she asked , "Do I have cancer yet? Do you see any cancer in me?"

Lynn handled these fears with her trademark straightforwardness. "Karen, if you don't slow down, learn to smell the roses, and let go of all that awful guilt, you're going to make yourself ill. When you set your mind to something, nothing stands in your way. Don't set your mind on cancer. You need to slow your hectic pace down. Stop feeling so guilty, day in and day out. Let it go."

Karen couldn't comprehend. *Slow down? I'm not doing enough. I didn't do enough to save my mom. I didn't even try to save my dad. I've never done enough.*

Failure was the only thing she ever saw when she looked in the mirror.

Lorry took Lynn's psychic exercises more seriously than her sister, finding she enjoyed the prospect of clairvoyance. She wanted it as much as Karen wanted nothing to do with it.

* * *

Since college was temporarily out of the question, Karen went back to being a manager/waitress at the Roman Garden. The guys, happy to see her, tenderly refrained from putting Tabasco in her diet soda.

They knew she loved movies, so one Friday after work, all the guys treated her to a night at the multiplex. They didn't consider the subject matter of the film itself. It was enough to just get her out among friends.

The movie was *Terms of Endearment*. Karen sat in the dark theater and watched as a young mother died of cancer on the screen, withering away in a performance horrifying in its perfection.

A scene came where the dying mother said good-bye to her children from her hospital bed, and Karen ... warrior, humorist, tower of strength ... lost her iron control and began sobbing in the theater.

Scott De Simone, one of the waiters at the Garden and a good friend, sat next to her. Together they shared the most tender, reverent, and sad moment of his life. Scott stayed at her side. Grateful for the chance to be with this precious girl, he tried to lend her some of his own strength. He felt inadequate; Scott knew the almost boundless reserves of toughness Karen possessed, but he was thankful to simply be there for her.

Karen left the theater, unable to finish the film, and hurried into the women's restroom. Clutching her chest, she felt like she was having a heart attack. Huddled in the back of a stall, too terrified to move, Karen was experiencing her first panic attack. She had no idea what was happening.

Bill started the old game of hide-and-seek less than a week after Karen got home from Texas. Whenever she was in the shower, he always managed to be busy in the yard, peering in the window for a glimpse of damp teenager. She locked her door at night, but Emily, still fearing fire, knocked until she opened it.

Bill didn't stop there. Commenting on the lack of space in their new bedroom, he asked Patty to do something about it. "Sweetheart, I know this is hard, but we can barely move in here. You can't even hang up your clothes because the closet's full of Rita's stuff. Please take care of it."

The divvying up of Rita's belongings came several weeks after they returned from Texas. Patty initiated the event. Karen protested, claiming it was too soon.

"Patty, I'm really not ready to do this," she said. "Can't we wait?"

Patty shook her head. "No, Karen. Bill and I are living out of a suitcase. It's not fair to my husband. He's been so patient. We need to get back to a normal lifestyle, and that's impossible with Mommy's things everywhere. It's just too painful to look at. Let's move on. It won't take that long."

Lorry and Angelina came over, solemn and pale. They all filed into Rita's bedroom, and began going through everything. Patty grabbed handfuls of dresses out of the closet. Lorry delegated what should go to the poor or Aunt Emily. Angelina emptied the dressers, complaining bitterly about Marco, whose young fiancee Anna was waiting back in Italy. As soon as the divorce was final, Anna was to be flown in.

"No, Lorry," Angelina said, when Lorry tried to press a brooch into her hand. "I don't want anything. I'm not part of this family, anymore."

"No, Patty," Angelina refused another trifle, her eyes dewy. "I can't accept that. I no longer have the right."

Looking around the room, Karen felt herself unraveling. The sorrow in the room was smothering. Lorry had been crying since they started, but continued mechanically. Karen started to shake.

Patty strove ahead. "Go on, keep going. Let's get it done." She pulled another rack of dresses out of the closet. "We have to go on."

Finding it impossible to touch her mother's things, Karen didn't participate. She just watched and began to fray around the edges.

As the dresser emptied, Angelina unearthed sentimental little bits and pieces snuggled away between satin slips and undergarments. A flowered paperweight, a gift from Karen, was tucked inside a handkerchief. At the sight of it, Karen fled downstairs to hide in the scotch bottle.

Half a pint later, she staggered back up, clutching the bottle to her chest. The women were still working, eradicating all traces of Rita Kikel. Karen sat cross-legged on the floor and drank.

"Stop it," she slurred, eyes wet and bleary. "Put that back. That's my mother's. It's not yours. You put that back now!"

She got up and stumbled around the bedroom in a drunken rage, shoving herself roughly against first Patty, then Lorry, then Angelina. Going over to the closet, she threw the doors wide. "Where are my mother's clothes? You put them back in here. You put them back."

She staggered from corner to corner, a sloppy, pathetic figure, knocking into the dresser and the bed, blundering over neatly stacked boxes, yelling incoherently.

"Why don't we stop now, and do it later?" Lorry suggested.

"No," Patty said. "Bill and I need to have a room of our own. We have to do it sometime. Let's just keep going. She'll be all right. She's just drunk."

They kept going.

Another hour passed. Sitting on the floor, empty Glenlevets bottle between her knees, Karen began rocking back and forth. It was a mindless rhythm, gaining speed. She started crying, huge gasping sobs that stole her breath.

The others ignored her and kept sorting.

By this time very drunk, muscle control slipping, Karen waved an arm with one final defiant flourish, and her bladder released in a gush of warmth.

Angelina spotted the spreading urine, pointing at the mess with a nervous laugh.

"Look! Look what Karen did. She peed herself!"

Patty let out a yell of rage.

"Karen! You're staining the carpet!"

Three expressions, each unbearable, stared at her, and in a claustrophobia of grief and humiliation, Karen tried to get away. She couldn't stand up.

Lorry was horrified. She turned on Angelina. "Don't you laugh at her. Don't you dare laugh at her!"

Angelina shut her mouth, dumbfounded. In all the years she'd known her, Lorry had never raised her voice to family like that.

"Get out of here!" Lorry yelled, "Get the fuck out of here, now!"

Angelina stormed out.

Bent over, Patty was trying to lift Karen. "Come on, Lorry. Give me a hand."

They dragged her into the shower, managed to get her into her pajamas, and brought her downstairs to the couch to sleep it off. Emily kept an eye on her for the rest of the night.

In the morning, it was all done. Patty presented Karen with her share of their mother's belongings, then left the room to start unpacking her own.

***

Patty started confronting Karen about the household bills. Lights, electricity, water, food, toilet paper—these were all things Karen was going to have to start contributing money to.

"There's no free ride in this house, Karen," Patty said. "You have to start paying Bill and me thirty dollars a week to live here. You're an adult now. Bills are a fact of life."

"What are you talking about? Thirty dollars a week? That's one whole night's work. And why would I be paying you instead of Aunt Emily? This is her house, not yours."

"I'm in charge of paying all the bills."

"You know I'm never here, Patty. I'm either at work, out with my friends, or asleep in bed. I don't even eat here."

"Well, you go to the bathroom, don't you? And you use toilet paper. When you take a shower, who pays for the water? Every time you turn on the lights, or the TV, you're using electricity, which costs money. Now that Mommy's dead, it's my duty to teach you responsibility, Karen. What happens when you go out into the real world?"

"That's a joke. How would you know? You've never been in the real world. Tell me something, Patty," Karen said, hands on her hips. "Who am I talking to, you or Bill?"

Patty flounced off.

The holidays, only a few short months after Rita's death, were a nightmare. Everybody was sad and angry, bitterly resenting the loss of the best party thrower in town. Christmas Eve had always been a big deal for the neighborhood because Rita Kikel had open house. It was free food, all the Christmas cookies you could eat, and plenty of booze.

Rita had lived for the holidays. When Lorry used to confront her about her own struggles with depression, Rita had advised her to look forward to the holidays.

That's what I do, Lorry. The holidays make it all worthwhile. Everything else is just waiting in between.

Karen went to a bar on Christmas day. She'd been invited to a friend's house, but the thought of a happy, healthy family sitting around the tree together was too much. She'd just turned nineteen with nobody remembering, and she wanted to be alone.

Going to the kind of bar haunted by the lonely and rejected, Karen slid onto a stool tucked between sorrow on her left and thick grievous envy on her right. Together, they sat and toasted the holiday with an ironic hand.

Life at Emily's continued to degenerate. With the coming of the New Year, Patty began a series of drunken nightly visits to Karen's room. Appearing at all hours, she'd shake Karen awake and insist they needed to talk.

"You have to be nicer to Bill, Karen. This is serious. You're hurting him. Bill loves you like a daughter, he understands you're suffering. All he wants is to be here for you. I do, too. I want to help you. Why won't you let me help you?" Her nose was streaming, and she wiped it on her sleeve. "Listen to me. Why don't you love him? I can't understand why you and Lorry are so mean to Bill. It hurts him so much. He's such a good man. Hasn't he been good to you all these years?"

"Look, Patty, I can't tell you why. Figure it out yourself. Or better yet, ask your husband.""

"What does that mean? I don't understand."

"You know how you don't like to be pushed into talking about something you don't want to talk about?" Karen asked. "Well, don't push me."

"Well, if you don't want to tell me, then I'll ask Bill."

"Good. Why don't you do that, and leave me alone?"

No room in the house was safe for Karen, anymore, from anyone. Bill was the worst. Even Emily had to admit that she was a witness, more than once, to his voyeurisms. In the grand scheme of things, it made no difference whether she knew or not. Bill Kelly was there, and he was useful. Obsessive compulsive, trapped female that she was, Emily couldn't make him leave.

He's not hurting Karen. He never touches her. He wouldn't dare try anything while I'm around.

The rationalization rang hollow in her conscience. Emily turned away from the truth.

Things settled into a series of appalling routines. Bill crept up to windows and keyholes, Patty periodically vomited *duty* and *honor* in a drunken slobber, and Karen escaped as often as possible with Lorry or her friends.

Marco's divorce was finalized that year. Angelina was shipped back to Italy with a new fur coat, diamond ring, and a fat settlement, to nurse her bitterness in disgrace back home.

Marco asked Karen and Lorry to drive her to the airport. He had to pick up his new bride. Angelina's plane would be taking off almost as Anna's was landing. They kissed Angelina good-bye, waving as she passed through the gates. The farewell was sad, like another death.

They would never see Angelina again. She was going home to Italy in disgrace, a divorced woman. No one would ever marry her again. She was too old, too used and infertile. Angelina would be alone for the rest of her life.

Anna and Marco were married soon after.

***

On the homefront, Karen began to buckle from the pressure. Visions plagued her dreams as much as they did her waking hours. The panic attacks were growing worse by the day. The weight of her life was becoming too much; despite an enormous capacity for strength, Karen was crumbling under its girth.

Lorry struggled with her own demons. Without Rita, she felt shattered; life seemed meaningless. Everything looked dull and empty. Colors lost their brilliance, food lost its flavor, and nothing glistened anymore. Lorry was spent. She wanted to die. Nothing short of a miracle could have saved her, so that was exactly what she got.

Her periods stopped. Listlessness set in at work, and her legs and abdomen hurt all the time now. *Like Mommy in the beginning. This is how cancer started for her.* Imagination running rampant, she wandered around in profound depression, accepting a fate of cancer without the courage to have it confirmed by a doctor.

Karen and Vinnie both pressed her to make an appointment with the doctor. The diagnosis came as a complete shock. "Congratulations, Mrs. Salluzzi. You're going to have a baby."

Lorry was pregnant.

Stunned, joyous silence greeted the doctor's words. *I'm going to have a baby. A baby!* She started laughing with delight. *Finally, a gift from heaven.*

Everyone rallied around at the news, and for a time, Lorry was the center of attention for the Lorenzo family. She was going to have a child. Pregnancy was the greatest accomplishment she could have achieved.

The Roman Garden became a sort of revolving door baby shower. No day went by without a new gift. Customers loved her, and she was coddled and praised by everyone at the restaurant.

Vinnie was elated. This would snap her out of it. When a woman has a baby, there's no time for moodiness. He was proud and attentive, stroking his purring wife with love and attention.

Her body tried to reject the fetus in the first trimester, and the obstetrician gave a label of high-risk, prescribing lots of rest. Confined to her bed during the second trimester, Lorry bled if she stood or walked too much.

Vinnie catered to her. He came home and cared for Lorry, babied her, fed her the attention she'd always needed. Lorry responded with gratitude and the soft pleasure of a kitten. It was the happiest time of their marriage and the happiest time of Lorry's life.

The prospect of being an aunt delighted Karen. Setting herself up as amateur errand girl, as well as nurse, she concentrated on nurturing the health of her sister and the growing baby. She took over the shopping, provided endless magazines and snacks, laid a hand, shaking with excitement, over the first butterfly tremblings in Lorry's belly. This was what was needed; this baby was something Karen had not seen in her plague of visions. Here, finally, was a good thing, a gift from God after so much death. New life, healing their wounds and giving all of them hope again. A baby to cherish. Everyone paid homage to the unseen grandchild of their beloved Rita.

A sonogram showed a healthy daughter growing in her womb. Lorry and Vinnie chose a name long before the baby was born. Their child would be called Rita.

Even Patty stirred out of her house to visit. Bill had nurtured agoraphobia in his wife, but he encouraged her to go see Lorry. Patty sat shaking with slobbering, drunken joy, sobbing out her gratitude for the coming child.

"We were never blessed with children, Lorry, but we'll treat yours as if she were our own." Patty laughed. "Bill is so happy. He's already buying dresses for her, the prettiest things you've ever seen. He wants to know how soon we can babysit.

He just can't wait."

Lorry always cried after Patty left.

Warm and sunny, June was fraught with excitement for the family. Filled with new hope, Karen signed up for a two month European course to study hotel and restaurant management overseas. She had scraped and saved for this trip. After assuring herself that Lorry would be fine, Karen settled down to enjoy her European adventure.

The trip was a productive way for her to get away from Bill, but it was a tribute to her mother as well.

"Mom could have studied opera in Europe. She always talked about it, the dream of Europe. Be with me, Mom," Karen whispered. "We'll see it together, through my eyes."

Two months of intense study, different cultures and Old World beauty had a deep impact on Karen. It was the greatest adventure she'd ever had. Eight weeks away from the family opened her eyes to the possibilities of change. Karen returned from her trip rested and happy, grinning as she hugged and kissed Aunt Emily.

Patty's late night drunken visits began as soon as Karen returned. She came into the room like an unsteady wraith, mouthing the same tired platitudes.

"You don't pull your own weight, Karen. You go on these expensive vacations and ignore your responsibilities. You're not even civil to my husband. Why? Why are you so selfish? You don't listen to me. You need to listen to me! I'm your big sister. I have to take Mommy's place now."

Karen exploded.

"All right, Patty. You need to get the fuck out of my room. When you're sober, then we'll talk, but I can't deal with you now. Get out!"

She turned her back and faced the wall, willing her sister to leave. Minutes passed, full of liquid pain. Then, muttering, Patty shuffled out, leaving the door open.

Quick as a flash, Karen jumped up and shut the door, turning the lock with a sigh of relief. Then she climbed back under the covers and tried to go to sleep.

A gentle tapping came moments later.

"Karen? Open the door. No locks, Karen. Are you all right? Open the door. What happened with you and Patty?"

Aunt Emily had heard the lock, but apparently, not the fight.

* * *

Rita Salluzzi came into the world on November 9, 1983. Born cesarean section, the baby was healthy and strong, a beautiful little girl with a shock of dark hair.

The last nine months had taken a harsh toll on Lorry, and she was slow to recover her strength. Pain had become such a constant companion, she was unconcerned when it stayed, even after the pregnancy. Baby Rita was a sweet but demanding infant, and the lack of sleep was wearing her down even further. Even breastfeeding made her dizzy.

No one, including Lorry, paid much attention to how weary she was. Motherhood was too demanding. She had no energy to return to the Roman Garden.

Her mother showed up one afternoon, in a ghostly visit that shook Lorry to the core.

The baby started crying in her crib while Lorry was in the other room, scrubbing the kitchen sink. Wiping her hands as she walked down the hall to the nursery, Lorry heard the baby's cries turn to giggles.

She entered the room and stopped in mid-stride.

Rita stood there, leaning over the crib, smiling and making happy faces at her granddaughter. She held another baby in her arms, and Lorry watched, stunned, as she bent to lay the child beside her namesake. Rita was as real and solid as if she weren't a spirit, bending over the crib in a flowered muumuu and house-slippers.

Lorry blinked once, twice; Rita was still there. The baby saw her, too, because she was squealing with delight, looking straight at the apparition.

"Mommy ... "

Rita straightened and grinned at her. The hairs on her arm stood up.

"She's beautiful, Lorry. Just beautiful."

Then she was gone.

***

"I've come to a decision."

Patty made her announcement with all the flourish of a carnival barker. She and Karen were in the kitchen, cleaning up after lunch. Karen looked up.

"What decision?"

"I think this is a good time to try and have a family celebration. Now that we have baby Rita, I'd like to plan a Thanksgiving dinner for the whole family, here at our house." Patty smiled. "What do you think, Karen?"

"I think it's a great idea."

"Good. Now, it's going to cost a lot of money for all this."

"Oh." Karen waited.

" ... and I think, since you're part of this household, you should contribute as well. Bill and I talked about it, and the whole dinner will probably cost about $250. We need $60 from you."

"If you're hosting this dinner, why do I have to help pay for it?"

"Because you're a member of this household, and everybody contributes in their own way."

"Well, why don't I just do the baking?"

"No, I already have the menu planned out. I'm doing all that."

"Well, I don't feel that I should have to contribute $60," Karen said.

"No more free rides, Karen. You have to contribute."

"What are you talking about, Patty? A free ride? I pay my health insurance, my car insurance, gas; I'm trying to save to go back to college because you screwed up my Social Security benefits; I give Aunt Emily money for the phone; I pay for my own clothes; I chip in for the cable. Where am I supposed to come up with $60 for your party?"

"Well, you should have thought about that before you went off to Europe. Things are going to change around here, Karen, because you can't live here for free any more. Why don't you go out and see what it's like out there? Why don't you move out and see what it's like to support yourself for a change? Try renting an apartment, then maybe you'd appreciate what you've got here with us."

"Good idea." Karen's face grew hard. "I'll do just that."

"Good!"

Karen bought a newspaper that night, drawing rings all over the section *Apartments For Rent*.

She found a two-bedroom apartment in Farmingdale, signed a lease, got a roommate, and gave the news to Emily.

"Don't do it!" Emily cried, beating her breast. "Don't leave me. What am I going to do without you? Your mother wouldn't want this."

"You know why I'm doing it, Aunt Emily. I just can't live in the same house with Bill Kelly."

She moved out in January of 1984, smiling bitterly at Aunt Emily's tears, ignoring the triumph in Bill's eyes. Jessica, her new roommate, helped her move.

Patty wept as Karen drove away.

The arrangement lasted less than a year.

Jessica moved to Florida the following autumn, and Karen found herself unable to make rent or find another roommate. She asked Grandma Lorenzo if she could live with her, so she could go back to college, but Mary didn't want the responsibility or the hassle. Karen pleaded, but it was no use.

"You belong in Emily's house, Karen," Mary told her. "Anna and Marco's baby is due any day now, and there simply won't be enough room. We need the spare bedroom in case Anna's family visits from Italy."

In the end, Karen returned to Aunt Emily's, hating herself for the failure which drove her back into that house.

Her asthma, which had plagued her since Rita's death, began to grow worse. In and out of the emergency room, Karen had to carry an inhaler and an Epipen at all times. Pure adrenaline, the Epipen could be self-injected in case she stopped breathing.

Uncle Marco's wife Anna had a baby boy. They named him Marco Junior. Lorry's fifteen minutes of fame were over.

***

In 1984, Karen met Richard Farley at a nightclub in the Marriott Hotel. She was twenty-years-old. He was a young attorney; tough, charismatic, ambitious, and a big, sexy guy. That was Karen's first impression of him.

His first thought when he saw her was *blonde*. Richard gravitated toward her like a magnet in a room full of several hundred people and soon found that *blonde* was the least of her attributes.

She was radiant. That was the only description that fit; a gorgeous, blonde, radiant creature in a sexy green dress. Richard was sowing his wild oats in the aftermath of a broken marriage, and the last thing he was looking for at the Marriott Hotel was a relationship. He approached Karen because of how she looked. Within a half-hour of talking to her, he knew he needed more.

Richard Farley was far different from Ricky, who had been a balm during a crisis in her life, but faded away soon after. He was relentless in his pursuit of her. Karen Kikel was a rare prize to be won, and he soon set about securing her.

Karen fell hard. Richard was everything in a man that she had never known, but always dreamt about. Fearless. She marveled at his utter fearlessness, and regarded his devotion to her with wonder. The sexual chemistry between them startled her. It was something she had never experienced before, not to that degree, even in the boy-crazy fantasies of her teenage years. This was no boy. This was a man, and he wanted her.

Embroiled in a difficult divorce that would end up lasting a few years, and involving his young son Kyle, Richard wasn't free to commit to her, yet, but he let his intentions be known. He wanted to marry her.

Karen was more cautious. She never made a decision lightly, especially about such a serious subject as matrimony. She was drawn to him, but afraid to commit. The temptation to lean on such a strong man was very great. Richard could free her from the cage of her life. He had no fear of anyone in her family, and nothing had ever intimidated him in any way that she could see. Still, she was careful. *Is Richard the future I need?* Her voices were quiet on the subject.

* * *

Baby Rita had her first birthday in what seemed a tick of the clock, and Lorry, infertile for six years, found herself pregnant again as soon as she stopped breast-feeding. She was ecstatic as well as surprised, and not a day went by that she didn't praise Doctor Burzynski in her own mind. Lorry was convinced his treatments had made this possible. These babies, these sparkling new lives, would heal them all.

Lorry and Vinnie bought a house in Levittown. Since baby Rita's birth, they had been getting along well. Satisfied with the joy their daughter brought, they stopped looking for it in each other. This second pregnancy meant twice the happiness.

Antonia "Toni" Salluzzi was born in April of 1985, cesarean section like her sister. Vinnie was giddy with pride and happiness, Karen was ecstatic, and the Lorenzos praised the production of another baby.

But Lorry's health was failing. The pregnancy took another huge toll on her, and she'd not fully recovered from the first. Incapable of even the simplest exertion, she was perpetually exhausted. Lorry fell asleep simply talking to people.

The itching acne that had plagued her as a teenager reappeared. The sun gave her terrible headaches if she was out too long. Postpartum depression hit hard. Even the sight of her babies couldn't shake her out of a melancholy so heavy she felt like lead.

Karen babysat every chance she got, taking the girls three or four nights a week. Richard grew to love Rita and Toni as much as his own son, Kyle. They were generous in their adoration, lavishing attention on the children. Toys, stuffed animals, ice cream, trips to the amusement park, new clothes, and anything colorful that Karen could get her hands on.

Lorry's daughters were festooned in ribbons and bows. Whatever Karen didn't buy, Lorry would find. They were bright and adorable treasures, and nothing was too good for the Salluzzi babies.

* * *

Karen was gradually moving in with Richard. A pile of sweaters here, a drawerful of blouses there; the house began to have a flavor of Karen about it. Richard urged her to make it official.

Predictably, when she broached the subject with Aunt Emily, Karen had a rain of fire descend on her head.

"You're always over at his house these days! What are his intentions with you?" Emily was as ruffled as an angry mother hen.

"He says he loves me, Aunt Emily. I think he and I are going to end up together."

"Hmph. Does he know how lucky he is? Does he realize that he'll never do better than you?"

"I don't know, Aunt Emily," Karen said, grinning. "Maybe you should tell him."

"But, Karen, think of your family. What do I tell everybody?"

"What are you talking about?"

"What do I tell the family about you living in sin?"

"Tell them I don't want to live under the same roof as my pedophile/rapist brother-in-law."

"You know I watch over you and protect you, Karen! I'd never let him touch you. You don't have to leave! Why don't you wait? You shouldn't live with a man until you're married. Only tramps do that. They won't buy the cow if the milk's free!"

"Aunt Emily, let's face it, all right?" Karen said, exasperated. "My life has never been perfect, and it probably never will be, so why should I do anything the so-called *right* way?"

"If your mother was here, you wouldn't be doing this!"

"If my mother was here, that asshole wouldn't be living upstairs, either," Karen said. "Now, I love you, Aunt Emily, but I can't live in the same house with Bill Kelly anymore. You've made your decision, and I've made mine."

Karen packed her bags, kissed a teary-eyed Emily good-bye, and drove to Bellmore, where she and Richard set up house together.

Karen's asthma improved, and her panic attacks decreased. They had become a nightmare in the years since Rita's death. At their height, the panic attacks had come as often as twice a day. After she met Richard, they grew less, and Karen only had them once a day, gradually dwindling to once every other day, then once a week.

***

Patty began having seizures. She'd been ill for years now, but everyone assumed it was the dribbling complaints of a moody drunk, and nothing serious. Everyone was used to Patty's prescription drugs, the beer, the wine, the mood swings, the manic depression, the sheer repulsiveness of her addictions. These had become commonplace, and the commonplace is often overlooked, even if it's appalling. The seizures were the family's wake-up call.

A feeling of dread crept across Karen's mind, and she had to know. How ill was her sister?

The small handful of local doctors that Bill took Patty to, couldn't seem to find an answer other than another prescription. They could tell Karen nothing. She would have to look to other means to find out Patty's fate. Karen would have to look inside herself, acknowledge the awful reliability of the coffin visions.

She went into her room, laid down on the bed, and fixed her gaze on the ceiling. She didn't have long to wait.

Visions slipped in and out of Karen's head, and she didn't have the strength to turn away. They danced and poured the future into her lap, and she couldn't close her eyes; it just kept coming, more and more and more hardship. A coffin appeared, and her oldest sister was in it.

Patty. Patty was next.

Karen rolled over into a fetal position, wrapped her arms around her head and hid her face in the blanket.

"Impossible," she said through clenched teeth. "There's no way Patty's going to die. She's only thirty-five years old. She can't be next. I won't believe it!"

Karen shut her mind to the vision, slammed the door on the voices, and refused to listen. Once again, she couldn't face the truth of her own unwanted gift. *I have to talk to Lorry.* Lorry no longer scoffed at Karen's visions. Grabbing her car keys, Karen ran out.

They discussed their sister for a long time, stringing together a plan, a last ditch attempt to get Patty cleaned up and into a hospital. Bill blocked any interference with his wife, but he couldn't want her to die. Patty needed help, and soon.

Lorry sat on the couch after Karen left, thinking over the pathetic aspects of Patty's life, and finding too many similarities to her own. She was terrified of everything Patty represented. Responsibility was becoming anathema to her.

The reality Lorry spun about herself was a sticky web of duty and sacrifice, a loveless marriage the price she was willing to pay to keep her children happy. That, and she was too afraid of failure and rejection to brave a change.

When they'd first opened the restaurant, Lorry had been the center of attention, the female in the Lorenzo family who was most admired.

Now it was Karen, because she had snared an attorney. Just the mention of Richard Farley brought a smile to Aunt Emily's face. Free legal advice. No mention of Karen's bravery and strength as something to look up to or be proud of. The greatest accomplishment for the Lorenzo women seemed to be how impressive a husband they could get.

Now that Karen had become the admired one, Lorry was just another woman with children and no job. Uninteresting and unimportant.

Even Lorry degraded herself, thus. She was trapped. *You've made your bed. Now lie in it.* Guilt again, duty, and fear. Once a decision is made, everything can fall before it, but the decision must be upheld, no matter what. A bad marriage was still a marriage. It was a holy thing—more important than the husband, and certainly more important than the wife. Lorry knew it.

I'll never be free. I'm tired, and sad, and I can't get away from it. I'm turning into Patty.

Then Lorry looked at her daughters, and a spark flared. There was no way she could let anyone else raise her children. Lorry knew that if she succumbed to the depression and wasted away; if she died, Vinnie would turn Rita and Toni over to his parents and their backward ways. Mama Salluzzi still believed in curses and dowries. All the women of that family were slaves. Lorry knew Karen would die before she allowed such a fate for her nieces. Karen would be there to protect them if anything ever happened to their mother.

Lorry held that knowledge close. The thought of Karen was a comfort. The thought of Patty, a nightmare.

* * *

After the seizures began, things happened quickly. Patty was fading, repulsive; her mind was gone. Years of heavy drinking and prescription drugs had severely damaged her liver and kidneys. The listless disregard of the true addict affected every aspect of her personality, and she no longer cared how she looked or even dressed. The concern of her sisters had no effect. No talking, no tender embrace; nothing could reach Patty, anymore. She was already gone. It was just a matter of time before her body followed. Patty was impatient for its company. The doctors scribbled new prescriptions which Bill pressed into her unfeeling hand, sometimes even placing them directly on her tongue. Her kidneys began to shut down, unable to carry such a load after so many years.

Thus, the seizures. The episodes became so violent, Patty's front teeth started gaping outward at a forty-five degree angle. She'd lost most of her molars years ago, so the front teeth fanned apart, pushing against her top lip like a dislodged bone. Lorry visited, and Patty showed her a lopsided grin full of jagged gaps. She never bothered to have the teeth fixed.

Her face became swollen and distended. Mottlings of red and burgundy were discoloring skin which had looked like porcelain in her youth. Her eyes were swollen and red, their beauty lost.

She never ventured outside. Patty stayed indoors always, unless Bill drove her to a doctor's appointment. This was her life, and save for a brief stint as a Jehovah's Witness, it had been for over a decade. The wit, the intelligence, the beauty of Patty; all had been lost years ago. The only thing left was a voracious, slack-toothed black hole, devouring all joy around her with its terrible gravity.

Bill was always there, feeding his creation, increasing its nightmarish aspect, greasing his palm with money from Aunt Emily for new medications, spending his own precious savings on cigarettes and bottles of wine to pour down Patty's throat.

Lorry was a solemn witness to Patty's slide toward death. Something inside her ached for it to happen. Patty tried to use little Rita and Toni as a lifeline, but Lorry refused. Not even the love for a sister could make her compromise her children's safety.

Karen supported her emphatically in this. Patty meant Bill, and Bill meant Patty. Rita and Toni would never be in their grip.

Late night drunken phone calls, Patty wailing hysterically in her ear, sent Lorry's heart racing in panic. "I've got to get out," she whispered to herself. "I've got to get away from all this."

Thoughts of divorce, once impossible, began to rise. Rita and Toni would not suffer the same life she'd been forced into. Lorry had to take them away.

Karen watched Patty's decline with a mixture of helplessness and frustration. At every turn, Bill blocked any attempt to help her, and until the day she died, Patty thanked God for her precious and loving husband.

Karen's feelings were quite different. "So, Patty, what are the doctors doing about these seizures?"

"I'm scheduled for a bunch of tests over the next couple weeks."

"The next couple weeks? Why aren't you doing it all in one week?"

"Oh, Bill can't take off all that time, so we're spreading it out."

"You don't have to wait for Bill. I'll take you," Karen said eagerly.

"No, Bill wants to take me. He likes to talk to the doctor while I'm in there."

"Patty, I think your doctor's a jackass. What's he done for you? He writes prescriptions like they're candy. You're having seizures, for God's sake. Why don't you go for a second opinion instead of trusting your life to this asshole? See a specialist."

"A second opinion? Karen, I've had the same doctor for years and never had any complaints. Why would I need a second opinion? My doctor already knows everything about my case. It'd make no sense to go to somebody new. Besides, Bill would never let me go to a quack."

Karen felt like screaming. "If Bill loves you so much, why isn't he getting you the help you need? Why's he encouraging you to take all those drugs? Why's he buy you all that alcohol? Patty, have you looked at yourself? You can't wait a couple weeks; you're having unexplained seizures! Check into the hospital and get the tests done there."

"I hate hospitals, Karen. You know that. I'd rather die than go into a hospital."

"Patty, don't even kid about that, okay?"

"Don't worry," Patty smiled her keyboard grin, and patted Karen's hand. "I'll be fine. Bill's taking care of me. We'll have more answers in a few weeks. Everything's going to be okay, Karen."

* * *

Patty died in her sleep one late morning in July, 1985. She was thirty-five years old.

Bill had gone to work early that day. He was out of the house when it happened.

The phone rang in the afternoon. Emily picked it up, and it was Bill. He wanted to ask a favor.

"Hey, Em, I'm running late," he said. "Can you go upstairs and wake Patty for me? She's got a doctor's appointment. Just get her up and ready, and I'll be there in a bit. Thanks. I really appreciate it."

Emily went upstairs and banged on the bedroom door. "Patty! Patty, honey, time to wake up." She opened the door and went in. "Patty. Wake up, Patty. Doctor's appointment. Bill's on his way. Got to get up." Emily clapped her hands, and bounced the mattress. "Come on, now. Get up!"

Patty didn't move. This, in itself, was nothing new; she slept like the dead. It was always hard to get her up.

This time, however, there was no response at all. Pulling back the blankets, Emily gave her a poke, but Patty didn't move. Her skin was icy. Emily couldn't tell if she was breathing.

The old woman went back downstairs and told Bill. "Bill? It's Emily. I can't wake her up. I shook her and yelled right in her ear, but she didn't even move."

There was a long pause at the other end. "Is she dead?"

"I don't know. I can't tell."

"Don't do anything, Em. I'm leaving now. I'll be there in a few minutes."

Emily called Richard at Lorry's house. He listened to her jumbled panic on the phone, glancing toward the other room. Lorry and Karen were both in the house.

"Emily," he said. "Hang up and dial 911. I'm on my way."

He arrived a few minutes before the paramedics. After calming a frantic Emily, he went upstairs and found Patty cold and stiff in bed.

"Jesus ... "

The paramedics came. Richard stood back as they worked on her, his heart sick. He knew before they turned to look at him. "I'm sorry, sir. There's nothing we could do. She's been dead for some time."

How am I going to tell Karen and Lorry?

Emily was waiting at the bottom of the stairs. The paramedics stayed with Patty, preparing her for the ride in the ambulance.

"They're taking her to the hospital, Emily."

"Could they wake her up?"

He shook his head. "I have to call the girls. They're waiting."

He went to the phone, his mind working furiously. Aware of their family history, the years they'd spent with death and disease ... how was he going to break this latest news?

Richard deliberated for long minutes, words and apt phrases racing through his head. Nothing seemed to fit in any way that would alleviate this situation. In the end, there was nothing to do but make the call.

Lorry answered the phone.

"What's going on, Richard?"

His voice was quiet. "It doesn't look good."

"What do you mean? Oh, God, Richard, don't tell me it's Patty."

"They're taking her to the hospital. It doesn't look good."

"What? What do you mean? Is she dead?"

"It just doesn't look good."

Karen grabbed the phone. Lorry was already scrambling for her car keys.

They arrived as the paramedics were carrying Patty out on a stretcher, and followed the ambulance to the hospital. Driving his own car, Bill was close behind.

Emily stayed at home. She was on the phone to Mary before the car pulled out of the drive.

They pronounced Patty dead on arrival at the hospital. Karen refused to accept it. Bill started crying.

"Bill! Tell them to work on her!" Karen screamed at him. "Push them! Do something!" It was horrific. Unbelievable.

The doctors worked on Patty for a few more minutes, but it was for sympathy's sake alone. There was nothing they could do. Patty was gone.

Her sisters stood in the emergency room, numb with shock. Karen couldn't breathe, and Lorry wept bitter, guilty tears. Shaking his head in silent wonder and compassion, Richard gave what comfort he could. How much more were these two women going to have to face?

Lorry couldn't talk. *What more is there to say? Nothing. Nothing at all.*

Distraught and hand-wringing, Bill wept inconsolable tears. "She's gone. My Patty. I can't believe my angel is gone. Oh, God, I loved her. I loved her so much."

The last surviving Kikels watched the doctor put a sympathetic hand on Bill's shoulder. His grief was palpable, his tears genuine. If they'd been able to feel anything at that moment, Lorry and Karen would have hated him.

They shuffled through the emergency room as if in a dream, signing all the necessary papers, answering any questions. After it was over, Bill drove home. Richard and the sisters followed.

They filed into the kitchen together, where Emily had coffee waiting. She sat numbly at the table, nursing her cup. Bill slid into the seat next to her. Karen and Lorry stood like mannequins against the counter. Richard pushed a mug in each of their hands, and they drank mechanically.

Funeral arrangements were discussed in listless monotones; words sliding off into silence, sentences left unfinished. No one noticed. Soon after, Richard took the girls home.

After they'd gone, Bill slid up behind Emily and began rubbing her shoulders. He shook his head slowly.

"I can't believe it," he said. "Our Patty's gone. She's left us forever." His hands worked on Emily's shoulders, and he bent low over her ear.

"It's just you and me, now, Em. Just you and me. I guess you'd better change your will, now."

Richard and Karen went to Lorry's house. They all stood together in the kitchen, stunned by this new death. Their minds couldn't wrap around it. Why would such a young woman, regardless of her drinking habits, die so young?

Richard knew of drunks twice her age and habits who were still going strong. He couldn't swallow the prevailing theory of kidney or liver failure. Bill had refused an autopsy.

The phone rang. It was Aunt Emily.

"Bill wants me to change my will, Karen. He said it just now, less than fifteen minutes ago. His own wife, my niece, just died, and all he can think about is what he's going to inherit! Please, help me. What do I do?"

This, at long last, had convinced Emily of the true nature of Bill Kelly.

To Lorry, this was just one more piece of garbage from a pig of a man they would never be able to escape.

To Karen, it wasn't the straw but the two-by-four that broke the camel's back. She had gained a new perspective about men, spending so much time dating a man of courage and action. Karen turned to Richard.

He simply took charge of the situation.

"Listen to me, Karen. You need to get that son of a bitch out of that house. Tell him he has to pack up his stuff and get out within two weeks, or we'll hit him with a rape charge and subpoena his ass. We'll tell the whole world what a pedophile piece of shit he is."

They decided to wait until after Patty was buried. Karen made all the necessary phone calls to the funeral home. Lorry tried to help with the arrangements, but she found she was unable to contribute much. She just felt numb.

At the wake, her numbness fell apart. The tears flowed, out of control. Words were too difficult, too much effort. Lorry simply *was* misery; she had become its definition.

Vinnie leaned over. "Get ahold of yourself. This is the fifth death in your family. I'd think you'd be used to it by now." Vinnie meant his words to be a clumsy dose of reality, a shock to snap her out of it.

But the callous words just reinforced why she was so unhappy in her marriage. Lorry cried harder, shamed by her lack of dignity, destroyed by tragedy, loss and her own endless loneliness. All her life, she'd been surrounded by people. Family members, aunts, uncles, grandparents, the kids at school, men; despite never being alone, she'd always felt lonely. *Lonely in a crowd.* She understood those words. Even the whispered talk of the mourners showed no concern for Lorry or Karen.

"What about Aunt Emily?" She heard a pair of cousins ask each other. "What's going to happen to her?"

Bill overheard, and laid a comforting hand on each of their arms. "You don't have to worry about Emily. I'll never leave her."

Watching him, Lorry felt sick to her stomach. *I could go to sleep any night and not wake up in the morning, just be dead. It's possible for me to die before I've ever truly lived.* The thought struck her hard.

How long? She wondered. *How long am I going to go on in this tomb of an existence? This loveless, lonely, hopeless place I've created for myself.*

Lorry was there, in this room of chatty mourners, but not there. Present, but voiceless. She couldn't answer questions; she had nothing to ask. She simply waited for it to end. Lorry seemed to disappear that day, and no one noticed.

Karen wept in secret. She felt internally bruised, as if her heart had burst, and she was hemorrhaging somewhere deep inside. Breath came in short, painful bursts, and she feared another asthma attack. Memories flew, one after the other, through her mind, and she couldn't shut them out. All she could think about were the extremes that her beloved Patty had become. The nurturer who read to her when she was little. The goblin who slobbered over her bed a decade later. A blue banana-seat bicycle and a pedophile. Paradox and tragedy weighed heavy on Karen's shoulders, and she felt that she might buckle under their girth.

Most frightening of all was her inability to stop crying. At any moment of the day, Karen had to bolt for the safety of a bedroom or bathroom to sob into a towel. Privacy and humiliation at her own weakness weren't to be shared with anyone. Karen had to mourn alone, always. She couldn't bear anyone to witness her collapse. She couldn't bear to be alone. It was a tug-of-war dance she played all by herself.

A few days after the funeral, bolstered by Richard's adamant opinion regarding their brother-in-law, the sisters went over to Emily's to confront Bill.

He looked expectant and welcoming, unprepared for what was coming.

For a brief moment, as Karen looked at him, she saw him through the eyes of a child. Tall, old, and intimidating. She felt as if she were confronting the devil. In a way, she was. Bill Kelly was their own personal demon.

Then something changed. Richard's words washed over her, and Karen's vision cleared. Bill stood before her and he was just a man, nothing more. Maybe something less.

"Bill, we have something to say to you."

He held up a hand. "You don't have to worry about Aunt Emily. I have no intentions of leaving. She won't be alone. I'll take care of her."

He doesn't know. He can't see it coming. The realization stunned Karen with its audacity. Angrily, she continued.

"We've had to live with what you've done to us all these years, Bill. Every time I looked into Patty's eyes, I wanted to tell her what you did, but couldn't. The news would've destroyed her. We put up with you because we had to, but Patty's dead, now. And so are you."

He started crying.

"I thought I'd made it all up to you. I tried. I tried! I thought all that was behind us. How can you do this to me? I just lost my wife. You know Patty would never approve of—"

"Patty's dead, and we want you out of our lives," Karen said. "I could forgive you for what you did to me, but I can never forgive you for what you did to Lorry."

The tears rolled down his cheeks.

"I'm so sorry. I'm so sorry. I tried to make it up to you when—"

"You're sorry?" Karen's voice rose. "Do you realize what you did to us? How could you? I was just a child! Have you any idea how disgusting you are? Do you know what it was like when you kept bothering me over and over again? Staring at me in a holiday dress, trying to peek at me in the shower? You repulsed me. I hated you! And you knew; you knew I couldn't say anything because of Patty. You used the whole situation to benefit yourself. How can we forgive you for everything you did? You're not even a man."

Karen pulled back, and her voice grew cold. "Our sister was the only reason we tolerated you. Now she's dead. You have two weeks to get the fuck out."

"Where am I gonna go? What am I gonna do?"

"Do you think we care?"

"I can't believe this is happening. Karen, Lorry, let me make it up to you. I can make it all better. Please, let me stay here. I'll take good care of Emily and the house. Anything you want. Just don't do this to me."

"We just want you out of our lives."

Long, dripping minutes went by as Bill wept. Then he swallowed, and asked, "What about Aunt Emily's house? What about Patty's share? That should go to me as her husband. Patty would have wanted me to have her third."

"If you can get out of this without anyone knowing what you did, consider yourself very lucky. That's your inheritance." Karen eyes flashed, and he shifted uncomfortably. "My sister's dead, now. You have no place in this family anymore. And Bill ... " She leaned forward and locked eyes with the devil.

" ... if I see you near my grandmother, or Aunt Emily; if you bother Lorry, or come near my nieces, I'll fucking kill you. And I mean it."

He believed her.

Later, Richard had his own private discussion with him. Bill feared him from that day on.

He spent the next two weeks growing more frantic as his attempts to persuade Emily proved fruitless. In the end, he threw his belongings into a box and grabbed whatever valuables he could lay his hands on.

Then Bill Kelly climbed into his overstuffed car, slammed the door, and drove out of their lives.

* * *

I'm so tired. I'm so tired, all the time.

Lorry's fatigue was getting worse. Karen took over the shopping for Aunt Emily and Mary Lorenzo. She drove them to their appointments, went to the butcher, the baker, and the candlestick maker, just as Lorry, and Rita before her had always done.

Other than accepting the errands and chauffeuring, Mary Lorenzo turned away from her two granddaughters. While Emily became more modern and open-minded in her grief, Mary Lorenzo withdrew into the Italy of her past.

Patty's death, and her own guilt, were too much for the old woman. She couldn't bear to look at her beloved Rita's remaining children, for fear of losing them, too. A childish way of dealing with grief, but she had always been a childish woman. She looked at Karen and Lorry, and the sight was an open wound. They were too painful a reminder of what she'd lost; her most beloved daughter and Rita's firstborn.

She never voiced her fears or emotions, leaving Lorry and Karen in utter confusion as to *why.*

Karen turned to Richard for support. He'd become the rock for her to cling to.

Lorry asked Vinnie for a divorce. Patty's death had been the catalyst. If she was to survive, Lorry knew she had to change her life.

Vinnie refused to move out of the house.

"We're not divorced yet, and it's my house," he said. "If you don't want to be with me, then you leave."

Lorry reacted to his sarcasm with barbs of her own, and a devouring rage consumed them both. Starving in the aftermath of their decayed relationship, they both fed off other people.

* * *

Karen entered the Miss New York beauty contest at Richard's urging. She was self-conscious about doing so, but he spurred her on. He was very proud of her beauty.

Karen's eyes were soon opened to the whole pageantry scene. Rivals slashed each other's gowns, got the phone numbers of the judges, sabotaged their fellow contestants in a hundred different ways. She found the proceedings exhausting in their incessant competitions, and cruelty to others had always affected her personally. Karen was more than grateful to be cut out of the running early. Still, insecurity made her embarrassed at what she feared others would see as a failure; what she, herself, saw as a failure. She wasn't pretty enough. Her thighs needed work. Maybe that was the reason she wasn't picked. Karen set about pricking tiny holes in her self-worth, and little whistles of air spun out as her fragile ego collapsed.

Time went by, and relationships changed. Richard often alluded to the idea of marriage; Karen was receptive but cautious. Vinnie and Lorry grew more and more belligerent with each other. Rita and Toni were angels in the eyes of both parents, but it was the only real love they showered on anyone.

In ways reminiscent of their mother, Lorry began to rely on Karen for everything.

Karen was eager to help. She took Rita and Toni two or three nights a week, so Lorry could rest. Welcoming the girls, Richard was happy his son Kyle had someone to play with when he visited on weekends.

Lorry didn't look good. Severely depressed, she had a face like a pimply teenager on junk food, and walked with a limp.

Karen watched the decline of her remaining sister, feeling the same type of frustration and terror that she'd had while watching Patty's downward spiral. At least Lorry didn't have a Bill Kelly pouring alcohol and drugs down her throat.

Still, Lorry was very ill; that was obvious. Karen decided to look to her visions, and perhaps, catch a glimpse of her sister's fate.

A coffin appeared before her and revealed Lorry, semi-translucent in the halls of Karen's mind. She was confused by the sight, registering the fact that Lorry's figure was transparent with angry uncertainty. In all her other visions, everyone had been opaque.

"Well, what does that mean?" Something snapped inside, and Karen was suddenly, blazingly angry.

"Not Lorry. Not Lorry, too. I'm not going to lose anybody else. This is it. Forget it. Lorry is going to be okay. I'm going to be okay. I'm not going to lose her! I'm not going to lose anybody else, not for a long time."

She believed it.

Part 2:
Two sisters

Chapter 8:

Reborn

Selling nursery schools was not exactly what I had in mind. Karen sighed as she studied a contract for closing. *Somehow, I thought my life would be different.*

It was 1987. Patty had been gone for over two years, now. Karen's twenty-first birthday had come and gone, and despite her old vision, she still didn't have cancer. That was one heavenly sigh of relief.

Lorry and Vinnie were separated. After a year of refusing to leave the house, he finally moved back in with his parents. The breakup devastated him. They sold the Roman Garden and split the money. Vinnie was still hopeful for a reconciliation.

Richard recommended a good divorce lawyer to Lorry. The following years of emotional and legal battle sucked the life out of her. She couldn't deal with it; she didn't want to deal with it. Lorry began to dream of an illness so severe, so debilitating, that she wouldn't have to face any more court appearances. The guilt of Vinnie's misery was overwhelming. He still told her, at every opportunity, how much he loved her ... how much she was hurting him and their children.

It affected her deeply. Lorry dreamt of pain and suffering for herself the way a normal person dreams of riches. She longed for it, fantasized about it, and at long last, her wish was granted.

She clung to Karen and Richard, who welcomed her company. Richard often joked that he had two wives. Karen was like a wife, despite the lack of written word. The three of them were always together.

Lorry listened to Richard as she would a husband or father, more than happy to have her decisions made for her.

He suggested both Karen and she take classes in real estate. There was big money in that. They signed up and worked hard at getting certified.

Lorry began to gain weight. She didn't eat much more than she ever had, but her face and body began to grow spongy and soft. Horrified, she doubled her exercise routine and felt like death after each workout. Disgusted with herself, she decided that she was just in terrible shape. That's why she didn't have any energy. She started wearing ankle weights to strengthen her legs. Her thighs hurt constantly, and simple everyday tasks still exhausted her.

The dermatologist had been treating her severe acne for months now, but the Accutane prescription wasn't doing much. She was repulsed by what she saw in the mirror, slathering on makeup which burned her oversensitive skin.

Even sunbathing brought little pleasure, anymore. Lorry was an avid sun worshipper. Since Toni was born, she as often got a heat rash as a tan.

Worried by her own visions of Lorry in a coffin, Karen called her psychic. Lynn Wuest spoke of terrible illness. Cancer was the big fear.

They both knew that particular enemy. Lynn, herself, was a breast cancer survivor. She'd been the first person Karen knew who had a positive attitude when faced with cancer. Lynn had simply refused to lie down and take it. She had fought.

Lynn was also the first person who'd ever appeared transparent in one of Karen's coffin visions, unlike all her other dreams of ailing loved ones.

Except for Lorry. Perhaps transparent meant only the possibility of death, and not the certainty of it that the solid forms prophesied.

A week before, Lorry had gone to the latest in an endless stream of doctors without diagnoses. The physician had mused, openly, about Lyme disease.

Test results came back negative. It remained a mystery.

Her chiropractor recommended a rheumotologist named Alguta, an expert on diseases of the immune system.

Lorry didn't want to schedule an appointment until after her divorce hearing, less than a week away. She was too tired to think about anything else.

Things came to a head on the eve of the hearing. She woke that morning in a pool of rank sweat, stinking of urine. She'd not urinated for over a day and a half. Her belly was distended, and it was difficult to breathe.

She was walking across the room without her leg weights when it happened. Without warning, Lorry felt her equilibrium shifting as if she were walking down stairs. Startled, she grabbed the wall to keep from falling.

I'm in pain. The thought surprised her. A lot of pain—even thinking was difficult. She felt almost drunk, without the pleasantries of dulled senses. Her brain refused to consider that this might be serious. *I don't have time for this. I've got to get ready for my realtor meeting.* It was too scary. Ignoring the discomfort, she shuffled through the morning like a ghoul, bent and jerky, unable to stand up straight, or even walk normally.

The only way to propel herself forward was to *throw* her legs, one after the other, and grip the floor with her toes. The slate floor was agony on her over-sensitive feet, and she had to tread on throw rugs scattered about the room.

"Not today," she said. "Don't let anything else happen to me today."

The realtor meeting was set for the afternoon. Karen was coming over to baby-sit. This newest sensation of *walking down stairs* sent Lorry into a panic. Today was her wedding anniversary. The next morning was the day of her divorce. After so many years, Lorry found the end of her marriage both exhilarating and alarming at the same time. She couldn't face anything else right now, least of all an illness. Like a sleepwalker, Lorry fixated on one thing. She was determined to go to her realtor meeting.

By the time Karen arrived, Lorry was covered with red pimple-like lesions, her fingers were almost black, and she could hardly walk, but she was still doggedly preparing for the meeting.

Karen took one look at her and exploded.

"Are you crazy? Lorry, look at you! You can't go to any damned meeting! You need to go to the doctor right now!"

Lorry was as stubborn as her sister. "It's a contract signing, Karen. I'm a single mother now. This meeting means a lot of money for me and my children. Argue all you want, but I'm going."

Karen opened her mouth, but Lorry forestalled her.

"It's only a few blocks away, Karen. I'll be fine."

"Do you absolutely have to be there?"

"Yes, I do."

"Then let me drive you."

"No, you stay here with the girls. It won't take long."

With great reluctance, Karen agreed. She would have physically stopped Lorry if she'd had any idea of the seriousness of her sister's illness.

Lorry arrived at the meeting, and the little group waiting for her was more than kind, they were attentive. Lorry realized she must look awful. Realtors are not usually so congenial to their competitors.

She got to the meeting, witnessed the signing, and left soon after. Every minute brought more pain, and Lorry began to grow frightened at its intensity.

She started the long trek back to her car. *Walking down stairs.* She felt as if she were sinking into the ground, but her body remained upright, her vision level. It was oddness and agony, that trip to her Mazda. By the time she crawled into the driver's seat, Lorry was terrified.

She got home, saw the expression on Karen's face, and started crying.

I really am sick. Karen can see it, too.

"Thank God you're here, Karen. You'll take care of me. You always take care of everything. I'm in so much pain."

"I don't believe those doctors can't figure out what's wrong with you!" Karen was furious, balancing little Rita on a hip.

"Don't worry, Lorry," she hushed. "We'll take care of it today. We'll find out what's wrong with you, one way or another, *today.*"

Karen had phoned Lorry's chiropractor, who referred them to a general practitioner in Bellmore. They could see him that afternoon.

Karen had arranged for a babysitter while Lorry was at her meeting, and the woman was already at the house.

The walk from the car to the front step of the doctor's office was an endless corridor of pain for Lorry. Her sweat stunk, her mouth tasted like sewage, and her vision was blurry. Everything was heavy and painful, like a broken tooth with an exposed nerve.

Karen exclaimed over her appearance, was shocked at her odor, and worried about her listlessness. *Not Lorry, too.*

In the doctor's office, the GP examined her, then immediately recommended Doctor Nuri Alguta.

"I think you might have Lupus, but it's not my expertise. I want you to see Alguta today. He's an expert on immune system disorders."

"Can't we do this tomorrow?" Lorry asked weakly. "I have two babies at home. I have to make arrangements for things ... "

"No," the doctor said. "You must go today."

Alguta was at Stony Brook college, wrapping up some paperwork when he got the call. Unable to get to the hospital until after eleven, he arranged to meet Lorry in the emergency room at the hospital around midnight. Richard would watch Rita and Toni.

Doctor Alguta was a beautiful, black-haired, golden-skinned man from India with gentle eyes and a soft voice. He examined Lorry tenderly, then ushered Karen out into the hall for a talk.

"I can't be sure until we run some tests, but I think it's Lupus."

Karen sagged with relief. It wasn't cancer. Lupus, she'd never heard of.

"So, what now?" she asked. "You give her some medicine; she gets better; we go home. Right?"

Alguta shook his head. "Lupus is a very serious, chronic illness. There is no cure."

"But it's not life-threatening?"

"I'm afraid it can be."

Time stood still. *Lorry. No—*

"How is that possible?" she asked. "What do you mean, it can be?"

"I'm going to order some tests. Your sister is gravely ill right now. She has some heart palpitations, and her lungs have been affected. If you hadn't brought her in when you did, she would have died."

"But she'll be okay now, right? I mean, she's here. She'll be okay now; won't she?"

"I can't guarantee that she'll survive the night."

Karen was surprised to find herself still standing upright.

"You've got to be kidding me."

Karen called Richard and told him everything. "They said they're going to do more tests. Can you pick up Rita and Toni? I've to get back to Lorry. I'll be home soon. Thanks. I love you."

Richard brought the little girls back to his place and put them to bed. In the office, he opened a set of medical textbooks he had in the house and began to search for answers.

Karen and Doctor Alguta went in together to see Lorry. She was lying curled in fetal position.

"So," Lorry said, trying to smile. "What is it?"

"I'm going to run some tests, but it looks like you may have Lupus."

Lorry was relieved. It wasn't cancer. No colostomy bag, no tumor-filled lungs. *Now I don't have to go to the courthouse tomorrow.* Lorry sighed with relief, and the deep breath caused a spasm. *At least I don't have to face that.* She'd been praying to God all day to spare her the debacle tomorrow. Her prayers had been answered. This Lupus was a gift from God.

"Is it fatal?" She asked it as a joke, a whimsy.

"It could be."

The words hung in the air, grew fat and bright red, ballooned over her face. *It could be.* It felt like there was a crash, with no noise. Lorry looked over at Karen, registered the shock, the drain of color, but she couldn't hear what they were saying. *It could be* hung over her, oppressing her, stealing her oxygen. I. Could. Die. It. Could. Be. *Be careful what you wish for. You just might get it.*

Alguta stroked her head, soothing her distress. "Don't worry. You'll begin to feel better in a little while. The medicine will take effect soon. We'll take care of you. You're in good hands here."

Lorry couldn't take her eyes off him, pathetically grateful for the show of kindness. He left the room.

A battery of tests showed a wealth of ailments; enlarged heart, barely func-tioning kidneys, a sluggish liver, massive inflammation in her connective tissue, and problems with her lungs. Drowsy with pain meds, Lorry drifted in and out of consciousness.

Karen and Alguta went out in the corridor again.

"Please tell me honestly, Doctor Alguta. Do you think my sister's going to make it?"

"Lupus is unpredictable, but she's responding to the medication well. I think she's going to be okay."

"Should I stay?"

Doctor Alguta shook his head.

"We have her on intravenous medications right now. It's not necessary for you to stay. If there's any change, we'll call you. She'll probably sleep through the night. Come back in the morning."

"Any change at all. Make sure everybody knows to call me."

"I promise, Miss Kikel."

"Any change at all."

"Of course. Any change at all."

Karen went back in and prepared to leave. "I'm going now, Lorry. See you in the morning. Everything's going to be fine now. We've found somebody who'll help you. Thank God. Good night." She leaned over and kissed her.

Driving home, alone in the car, Karen's mask slipped and she allowed herself to cry. She cried for her sister, her nieces. She cried for herself.

Richard was busy. A natural born problem-solver, he was already researching the disease. *Systemic Lupus Erythematosus.* Everything he read was grim.

"Jesus Christ."

He showed Karen a grave face when she walked in the door, hours later. She sat beside him and read the articles, shaking her head, dry-eyed. Rita and Toni were asleep in the other room.

"Lorry kept thanking me, Richard. She kept saying, 'Thank you for making me go to the hospital. Thank you for saving my life. You're a healer, Karen. I knew you were a healer.'"

Systemic Lupus is a chronic ailment which compromises the immune system, confusing the body to such an extent that it attacks itself. Organs, connective tissue, joints—everything is a potential target. When first given a name, it was thought to be a skin disorder by most doctors. Doctor Alguta wasn't most doctors. He knew Lupus was connected with the immune system. He also knew Lorry Salluzzi was in real danger.

Lorry was in the hospital for over a week. It was her first serious Lupus flair. They placed her in quarantine because of the lack of knowledge about the disease. Fed Cortisone through her IV, she was still in agony. The suffering was so intense, she remembered a prayer to God during Rita's illness. She'd asked, "How can Mommy still want to live? She's in such pain." Lorry now had her answer.

She had struggled so long with the wish for death, that she never realized how far from her soul it truly was. She understood now, with Death hovering over her, that she wanted to live. For her girls, for Karen. Even for herself. And she was worried that it might be too little, too late, like Patty. Days before she died, Patty talking about all the plans to get her life together. Then she was dead. Lorry wondered if she, too, would follow in Patty's footsteps ... if she would also repeat the same pathetic pattern.

Karen discovered a terrible new instinct within herself. She went into warrior mode. "Nothing is going to take my sister away from her children or me. I won't allow it." She'd wrap her hands around its throat and throttle fate itself to prevent it.

All during Lorry's stay in the hospital, Karen would come in and grab her hands, holding tight, like a guardian angel, fierce and insistent.

"Give it to me," Karen growled, her eyes like fire. "Give it to me. Give me your pain!" Lorry could feel the hurt pulling, like some incredible gravity, and she would scramble to hold onto it, not wanting Karen to suffer this agony. She knew her sister would take it all on herself if she could. There were even tears in her eyes, and that frightened Lorry more than anything. Karen, the stone, almost never cried in public.

Nights were the worst. Lorry lay in the seclusion of quarantine, and struggled with her fears all alone. Thinking she couldn't hear, the staff was less than discreet. Nurses whispered words which rang hollow in her ears. *AIDS. They think I have AIDS.*

Several nurses refused to touch her or even enter the room. Lorry never told Karen about these little incidents, knowing her sister would turn into a one-woman army, and attack.

One nurse, however, was an angel sent by God. Of this, Lorry was certain.

It was her second night in the hospital. She'd gone through a barrage of tests that day, the worst one being the MRI which was loud and frightening.

Another nurse refused to enter the room to change her IV, and Lorry had to consciously regulate her breathing. Panic breathing not only made her dizzy, it was painful.

She lay in the lonely isolation ward and wondered how long she had to live. "Am I going to die tonight, all alone in this room? Is this how I'm going to go?" She was so frightened. She needed someone to comfort her.

"Please," she prayed, "Please don't let me start screaming. I'm so scared. I hurt so bad. I miss my babies."

A nurse came in just then. An answer to her prayer. A beautiful, compassionate angel in a size sixteen. She was soft and kind, motherly and comforting, and she sat on the bed next to Lorry, holding her for half-an-hour. Lorry wrapped her arms around her and started sobbing. Years of sorrow and illness and months of pain all poured out over a starched white collar, smelling of lavender and strong soap. It was as if her mother were there, hidden in the body of this angel. Rita had always loved lavender. Lorry cried and cried and cried, and needed a drink of water afterward.

The angel's name was Helen, and Lorry ached every day for her shift to begin. *Helen*. Kindness itself rode in on her shoulders.

After a week, she was moved to a regular room where she could have visitors. This did little to cheer her up.

People's demeanor when they visited, was, for the most part, depressing. Everyone but Karen and Richard thought she was going to die. The verdict was on every pair of lips, every furtive look.

Even Lorry's attorney had tears in his eyes when he brought the divorce papers to the hospital for her to sign.

"If you wish to reconsider, I'm to tell you Mr. Salluzzi is willing to do that."

Vinnie was more than willing, he was eager. Visiting often at the hospital, bringing flowers and gifts, he never failed to mention how much he loved her. Lorry turned away. She had to move forward. The marriage was killing her; her old life was toxic. She realized that now, in the flash of insight one has at death's door. If she wanted to live, she had to be free.

There was a strange sort of comfort in such a limited choice. Change your life or die. An odd frame of mind seized her, and Lorry made her choice. She couldn't let her children grow up with the same old-world, outdated nonsense she had been raised on. Lorry wanted better for them.

Karen was busy. She read old volumes on systemic Lupus, quailing at the dire prognoses of old cases. Once symptoms first appear, the disease killed everybody in five years. Five years of perpetually downward spiraling agony, and Lorry was already so ill ... had been for almost three years.

Time. Time was not on their side. They learned to check the copyright dates in books, but the more recent volumes were only slightly better, from seven to ten years after diagnosis.

The knowledge about Lupus could be strained into a thimble. Nobody knew much of anything, and there wasn't a clue as to a cure.

After eleven days, Lorry's test results came back. Alguta's diagnosis was confirmed. He prescribed Plaquenil, Procardia, and Prednisone, then sent her home.

Weeks passed without any improvement. Her hair started falling out. Her feet couldn't bear hard floors. Her hands turned black with Reynaud's Syndrome if she so much as reached in the refrigerator for a soda. Steroids weakened her bones, and she developed osteoporosis. Some teeth were lost.

Lorry was unable to hold her daughters for any length of time, if at all, so she devised play areas for them to entertain themselves. The bottom of the china hutch held unbreakable pots, pans and toys. Rita and Toni banged noisily in the dining room while Lorry lay on the couch.

Great dark shapes began plaguing her in the night. Similar to those she'd seen by her father's deathbed, these swooping figures and ragged goblins danced on the ceiling and swam above her nose. Half-paralyzed because of the pain in her body, Lorry watched them with wide eyes, wondering if they were real. *Is this the medication he's got me on or am I going nuts now?*

Finally, the black humor of the situation kicked in, and she laughed. "I've been through hell all my life, now I'm probably going to die, and you think this will scare me? Get outta here!" She treated her demons with wit and contempt, and they slunk away in sullen disappointment.

Lorry began dating. As soon as she could walk, she dropped the children off at Karen and Richard's and went out. "I need a man. I need someone to prove to me, I'm still alive." Lorry needed affirmation that she was attractive despite her illness, that a man would still want her. That was important. Appearance had always been such a large part of her upbringing. *A woman isn't complete without a man.*

But Lorry wanted more than just another husband. She was searching, desperately, for a soul mate. Someone to fill the void in her life and make her complete. It had not yet occurred to her that she, herself, was the person to do that. Only the man of her dreams could make her whole.

So she searched, endlessly disappointed. Still ruled by the need to serve, Lorry never learned to view men as equals. They came to her, wounded and empty, and left whole, with a piece of her heart in their pockets. Every wound she had was still fresh. To Lorry, shackled by her insecurity, the only soul mate somebody as worthless as she deserved, had to be needy, greedy, and damaged, so she could mother him. He had to be worse off than she. Then she could save him, heart and soul, and in his gratitude, he'd love Lorry best, above all else. That was her real dream, her secret passion. This was all hidden inside, behind doors her conscious mind didn't want to enter.

Confused and upset as well as worried, Karen planted her feet and stood as a rock for her sister to cling to, knowing that, time after time, Lorry was going to dash herself against the tide and get swept away by yet another unworthy man. When she was involved with someone, Lorry slid away from Karen, ignoring heartfelt advice, disregarding the warnings about her latest love.

"I don't understand her, Richard. She always asks me to tell the truth about how I feel, then ignores every word I say. Why ask if you don't want to know?"

The answer was denial. Lorry viewed Karen's concern as an unfair and biased judgment, but didn't say this out loud. If she did, Karen would want to argue the point, and Lorry hated confrontation, preferring her make-believe world of blind devotion rather than seeing with open eyes.

Eventually the boyfriend would show his true colors, and Lorry would be alone again. Sick with self-disgust and resentment, her guilt training took over, making her apologetic and needy with her sister.

A few months would go by, she'd begin dating again, and the cycle would start all over.

Karen was always eager to baby-sit Rita and Toni, to keep them separate from Lorry's doomed relationships. Karen tried not to judge her sister's choices, but if one of her nieces came to her with a story of cruel behavior, Karen spoke up. Over-protective because of their own past exposure to Bill Kelly, she was determined to protect the girls from a similar fate. With Lorry's tenuous health, clarity of thought and barely transparent figure in the coffin, Karen couldn't help worrying.

Lupus can curtail a person's lifestyle very quickly. When even the smallest exertions can cause staggering exhaustion, a positive attitude is often difficult.

Doctor Alguta sent Lorry to a psychotherapist named Rand.

An overweight, chain-smoking man in his early sixties who suffered from crippling arthritis, Rand had created a whole series of inventions to cope with his twisted joints. Using a strong imagination to compensate for what his body could no longer do, he had a plethora of ingenious toys to help him. Grabbing tools that reached overhead for things, pincers that gripped small objects; even a device that tied his shoes. He refused to be limited by a disease.

"I can't do things like I used to, Mrs. Salluzzi. But that doesn't mean I can't do them at all. I just plan them differently. The only way arthritis will get the better of me is if I let it."

This was the lesson that Doctor Alguta had really sent Lorry for. Limits exist only in the mind. *Harness your imagination, and create a way.* Watching this man, bent but unbroken, she decided to give it a try.

Unable to drive or walk any kind of distance, Lorry started planning alternative ways to get around town. She focused on smaller shops instead of enormous malls or supermarkets. Parking was often close to the door so she wouldn't have to walk as far.

Unearthing an old-fashioned scooter from the garage, she rested her weight on the base with one foot and slowly pushed with the other. It became an odd sight, a grown woman going around town on a child's scooter, but Lorry didn't mind. Rita and Toni liked to ride on it with her, and friendly neighbors made the 'thumbs up' sign as they tooled past.

* * *

Karen discovered she was pregnant soon after Lorry's diagnosis. She was twenty-four. It wasn't negligence that caused the unplanned pregnancy; Karen and Richard were always strict about contraception. Unable to endure birth control pills, her latest prophylactic of choice was the sponge. It didn't work.

The pre-marital pregnancy was the last straw for the Lorenzos. "Now Karen's going to have a bastard. God help us all." Grandma Lorenzo chastised at every opportunity. Uncle Marco simply shook his head, asking why everyone was so surprised. His wife Anna told everybody to relax and leave Karen alone.

Aunt Emily, always the rabble-rouser, also defended Karen. She lamented the fact that her niece wasn't married, but Emily loved her unconditionally and refused to shun her.

For days, Karen carried the fetus in indecision, weighing the hated concept of abortion against an unplanned pregnancy with a man she was still unsure of. She loved Richard, but wasn't certain about marriage.

The bleeding started in the Post Office, less than a month after she discovered she was pregnant.

She was waiting in line to mail a parcel. Suddenly, there was a warm gush, and for one horrified moment, Karen thought she'd wet her pants. Then the pain hit. Hobbling, close-legged, to her car, she drove home and called Richard.

The doctor told them that she was miscarrying. "If you don't want to lose this baby, you have to go to the hospital right now."

"No," Karen said. "No hospital. I want to go home."

After a long debate failed to change her mind, the doctor shook his head and said, "If that's your decision, I'll have to accept it. But you must lie down. You have to rest, and try to elevate your feet. Stay quiet. If something falls out, save it in a cloth or some paper towels and bring it with you to the emergency room."

The instructions appalled her.

Now, when it seemed too late, Karen realized that she wanted this baby. Desperately. Her own indecision and regret were hurting this unborn child. Of that, she was certain.

She called Lorry. "I didn't want it. I didn't want this baby, and now my body is destroying it. It's reacting this way because I couldn't make a decision!"

Lorry chewed a lip in rapid thought.

"Karen," she said gently, "Why don't you talk to it? Why don't you just talk to the baby? Tell it how you feel now. How much you love it."

Karen focused on this suggestion with the same passion and intensity she'd had when Grandma Lorenzo suggested prayer to the Virgin Mary, all those years ago. She prayed to her child, to the threatened life inside her, and the prayers were continuous.

For eight hours, she bled. Her hands, gentle and loving, smoothed over her belly, soothing the tiny child.

"I love you, my baby," she said. "I love you, my sweetheart. Nothing will ever harm you, again. Even if we're alone, even if we don't have anybody else in the whole world, we'll be together. I love you, my little one. Heal yourself. Mommy will help you. Mommy loves you."

Karen talked this way for hours. She dreamt love and comfort in her sleep, poured adoration and warmth on that tiny unseen fetus with every breath she took. Her ferocious will focused entirely on her womb, and after eight hours, she stopped bleeding.

Richard breathed a sigh of relief. This was an uncommon experience for him, such a terror. Not only for his unborn baby, but for this woman he adored. *I should have known better. Nothing can beat Karen. Nothing ever has.*

The obstetrician had no answer as to why she'd started bleeding in the first place. All he knew was that she had stopped, and the baby was fine.

Worry about the baby brought on a Lupus flare, and Lorry's symptoms worsened. Face was covered with the Lupus "butterfly" rash, no longer able to tolerate the sun for any length of time, she had flares of the disease that robbed her of speech. Her throat simply swelled up, and she couldn't talk. Blue jeans were impossible because of the heavy stitching; wherever a seam touched her skin, lesions appeared and bled.

Vinnie's mother came to visit her. A cold, superstitious woman, harsh in her beliefs, she had cursed Lorry with suffering after the divorce. She came to apologize.

"I wanted you to suffer, Lorry, but not this much. How terrible this is. You're dying. I can see it."

Lorry established a backup system for whenever she went out. Privacy was a thing of the past. In case she got stuck in the car or the driveway, her neighbors were there to help. Lorry never failed to call them when she was on her way home, so they could be on the lookout.

Reynaud's Syndrome, one of the many symptoms of Lupus, became a source of inane fascination to Lorry. She was mesmerized by the rapid color change in her hands whenever temperature was even slightly varied. Like a human cuttlefish, Lorry streamed through a kaleidoscope of black, blue, raspberry and olive, waving her hand in front of the air conditioner to watch it change colors.

Any research of the disease was overwhelmingly depressing. Karen brought her books from the library. Medical textbooks and conventional journals left her feeling hopeless with their cold and negative descriptions and somber prognoses. She floundered about for a new avenue of study.

The idea of tapping into the mind and spirit to heal was one that had always fascinated Lorry. She pored over books and tapes her mother had discarded long ago, books about self-healing and positive thinking, tapes about guided imagery. This was an alternative avenue Lorry was eager to explore.

She went to a psychic fair after reading an ad in the local health food store. It was the first in a series of changes Lorry was attempting in an effort to save her own life. She could find no answers in conventional medicine. Eventually, the medications were going to kill her. She must look elsewhere. She was now fishing around in left-field thinking, and the experience was unsettling.

The psychic fair was full of both the bizarre and intriguing. Lorry stumbled about, leaning on her mother's acrylic cane. As she wandered from stall to stall, a lean, sharp-faced woman named Norma caught her attention.

Surrounded by a large audience, many of whom were openly weeping, Norma said she was a psychic and practicing medium. She also claimed to be channeling the archangel Michael.

"Oh, brother," Lorry muttered under her breath, but the ensuing show caught her attention anyway.

Norma was obviously unconcerned about the feelings of her subjects. She relayed horrors and death with a total disregard for the contents of her channeling or the emotional response it received. People in the crowd whispered at her uncanny accuracy.

Lorry was impressed by this crabby, unfeeling creature. *This woman tells it like it is, with no padding. If I'm going to die, I want to know, and she'll tell me.*

She paid the required fee then sat down, her fingers raspberry-dipped and aching from the Reynaud's. She was shaking.

Norma stared at Lorry's battered face and bent form.

"What do you want to know?"

Lorry was so frightened, and irritated for being so. *What's the matter with me? This doesn't mean anything. It's just something to do. I'm just looking.*

"Am I going to die?"

There it was, hanging in the air above their heads.

"No, no, you're going to be fine."

Lorry blinked once, twice, and wondered at her hearing.

"Fine? Is that what you said?"

"Yeah, fine. Don't worry about it."

Everybody, even the doctors, think I'm going to die. This is the first woman the whole time I've been sick who says I'm going to be fine.

She laughed, and the moment was a revelation.

"I'm going to be fine! Lady, I'll follow you anywhere!"

Norma fixed her with a razor glare. "I think you should go to a rebirthing session, though."

Huh?

"I'm having a rebirth session this Saturday. Come to it."

"What's a rebirth session?"

"Something you need," Norma snapped. "Here's my address. Eleven o'clock."

Lorry took the card, nodded blindly, and left.

When she got home and had time to think about it, skepticism returned.

"Oh, brother," she muttered. "What a sucker I am. This rebirthing thing is thirty-five dollars and after a baby-sitter, I'm gonna be milked for at least fifty. What an idiot."

Every conservative argument she could throw at herself notwithstanding, Lorry found her feet planted on Norma's front walk Saturday morning.

The rebirth room was upstairs. Eying the long staircase with trepidation, Lorry cursed herself for a fool.

The climb seemed endless. By the time she got to the room, all Lorry wanted to do was lie down. *I'll only stay a minute and catch my breath. If I don't like it, I'll just leave.*

The room was a sea of people lying on mats. Some were in lotus position, others were stretching, still others had arranged little crystals all over themselves. Lorry mentally rolled her eyes. *Welcome to Freakville.*

Then she spied the horror of horrors. Each mat had a box of tissues in front of it. Norma had mentioned that this would be an emotional experience.

"Oh, crap," Lorry whispered.

A fairylike woman guided her to an empty mat. Lorry sank down with little grace, fatigue giving way to gravity in a tumble of limbs. Lorry lay on her back and gasped.

I hope they don't kill a live chicken or some other stupid ritual for at least five minutes, until I can catch my breath. Her blood felt thick and heavy, pooling in her back as her limbs relaxed.

Norma came in, gave a cursory greeting, settled down with a sheaf of papers on her lap, and without preamble, began reading from a prepared text. Speaking about the inner child, she described injuries people still carried, unhealed, inside.

Then, the meditation began.

Lorry had never meditated in her life. She thought vaguely of yogis in pretzel-shaped circus freak positions, chanting mantras and burning incense. Norma did none of this and asked it of no one. She put on some soothing music, told them to close their eyes, and started talking. Breathe in, breathe out, relax your face, relax your ears; every part of the body was touched upon.

Slowly responding despite a brick wall of resistance, Lorry felt herself flowing into the mat. She turned and curled up into a fetal position.

Norma's voice grew odd and hollow-sounding as if she spoke from the end of a long tunnel. She talked about the inside of a mother's womb, where all was wet and warm and safe from the outside world. Traveling toward the birth canal, ready to be loved. Then thrust out into the cold harsh world, where the light was too bright and the sounds too sharp.

Lorry never did see the birth canal she was supposed to visualize. She just listened to Norma's voice, like a child hearing a bedtime story.

Then, Norma started mentioning child abuse, sexual abuse, and domestic violence. Fists and knives and cracks with the belt, jagged words and vicious wit were all touched upon. Children being harmed again and again until they were children no more, but damaged, wounded animals, limping through life with no hope of joy or completeness, full of gaping holes they tried to fill, be it with food, drugs, sex, or even more violence.

Norma droned on, telling tales of change, of free will, of pessimism and exhaustion changing to optimism and life. The room started weeping.

Lorry lay curled up, listening to the sobs and sniffles around her with a sympathy and discomfort she was helpless to stop. One woman in particular was sobbing hysterically; terrible, gut-wrenching cries torn straight from the soul. Lorry wished someone would go over and help her. God, what a terrible sound. Somebody please help her. Help that pitiful, sad creature.

A gentle touch on her shoulder jerked Lorry from her trance. Norma's fairy-tale assistant was kneeling beside her. She dried Lorry's face with a tissue, stroking her hair, comforting her, and Lorry realized, to her horror, that the hysterical woman was herself.

The freedom to cry without shame, after all these years, was a treasure Lorry never expected to experience. The loss of a father who never loved her, a mother who almost destroyed her, a sister who terrified her, a brother-in-law who raped and abused her, an uncle who ignored her, and a failed marriage. All of the people she trusted and looked up to. All those whose job it was to nurture and protect her, a responsibility so dreadfully failed, so twisted and tortured and diseased as it was. Vampires. Cannibals, all. They had feasted on her, and Lorry had learned to serve herself up as both entree and appetizer, supping on their gluttony as they ate her alive. And she had been grateful for their attention.

"Oh, God, my life," she cried. "I'm not alive. I'm already dead. I've always been dead. I have to take a breath; I have to start breathing on my own! Please, God, help me. Help me!" The tears from a lifetime of sorrow and pain poured out for endless, drenching minutes. For half-an-hour, they wracked her.

The girl kneeled over her the entire time, passing her hands over Lorry's body, stroking away the pain with a touch that was feather-light.

When the deluge was over, Lorry stood up, spent and angry. A shaky hand dove for the compact in her purse, and the little round mirror revealed a ridiculous clown in running mascara. Lorry was very, very angry. She looked like a freak from the circus, everything hurt worse than ever, and she was down fifty dollars.

 Storming out as fast as her tortured limbs could carry her, she got in the car, and drove home, not noticing her foot was a lead weight on the gas pedal, and not caring. All she wanted was her bed and her electric blanket, and a sleeping pill.

Lorry got home, tumbled into bed and was asleep in moments.

She forgot her pill.

The next morning, still irritated, she threw back the covers, and got up. Halfway to the bathroom, she stopped in her tracks, realizing what she'd just done. For over two-and-a-half years now, Lorry had not been able to rise from bed without pain. She could barely make it to the toilet without an accident en route. Today, she'd just gotten up.

Glancing back at the bed, fully expecting to see her own corpse lying there, she was surprised to see the bed was empty.

Lorry went into Rita and Toni's room.

"Can you see me?" she asked stupidly. They giggled and demanded breakfast.

"They see me." Covering her delighted grin with a hand, Lorry turned away and went into the kitchen, where she called Karen.

Swollen and pregnant, Karen was delighted at Lorry's lack of pain, but worried about this latest obsession. She didn't want her sister diving into another doomed relationship, be it man or movement.

"This meditation group sounds weird, Lorry. Are you sure it's legitimate? Sounds like a cult."

"I'll leave you the number in case I disappear, so you'll know who killed me," Lorry said sarcastically.

"Just asking questions, Lorry. You know me. I'm just curious as to how this class made you feel so much better."

"I don't know, myself. But I'm going to find out."

Lorry started taking a psychic awareness class once a week for twenty dollars a pop. It was money she could ill afford, but the bit was between her teeth now, and she felt as if she were onto something. Karen and Richard baby-sat.

***

Shortly before dawn, after hours of intense labor, Matthew Kikel Farley was born. It was January 26, 1989. Coincidentally, it was also his father's birthday. Richard, bursting with pride, stroked his son's head, chin resting on Karen's tossled hair.

As she gazed down at the baby in her arms, Karen felt a rush of love more overpowering than anything she'd ever experienced. This baby was the most beautiful human being she'd ever seen. The love was instantaneous. She knew she'd die to keep him safe.

With the scandal of a great-grandson born out of wedlock, Mary Lorenzo pushed for a quick marriage in the days that followed Matt's birth.

"It's a sin, Karen. It's a sin!" she kept ranting. "People are calling your baby a bastard and you a whore."

"What people? Who's saying it?" Karen demanded.

"That doesn't matter!"

"Who? Tell me."

"I can't say. Don't ask me."

"Would they rather I'd gotten an abortion instead of having the baby? Would that have been a better choice? Then nobody would have known."

Mary grew flustered. "This is a disgrace! A disgrace for the whole family!"

"Who do you think we are?" Karen asked, "The Kennedys? Who gives a shit? Am I supposed to feel honored that they give that much thought?"

"I can never get through to you, Karen. You never listen, you always know what's best."

"At least I know I don't live under a microscope like you do. I don't care what people think of me anymore, Grandma. If they want to judge me, let them. They don't know me, they don't care about me, and they certainly never loved me. At least I'm honest."

Mary Lorenzo was howling by now. She clasped her hands in front of her, pleading.

"Marry Richard, Karen. Marry him! The baby's innocent. Let him live in God's name, poor little boy. Do it for him. It's a sin. Everybody's talking about it. It's a sin. It's a sin!" Mary's voice grew conspiratorial. "I have five hundred dollars that I've saved for you, for when you get married. I gave the same to Patty and Lorry. Marry Richard, and I'll give you the money."

Karen sighed.

"Grandma, if and when Richard and I decide to get married, you'll be the first to know."

"If only Rita were here," Mary sobbed, slipping into her martyr role like a comfortable old glove, "things would be different. My Rita, my Rita, my darling Rita. I miss you, my darling. My life isn't worth anything anymore without my Rita! Ohh."

Karen kissed Mary good-bye, and left her in a Rita-mojo, rocking back and forth and whimpering. These bouts of weeping never lasted long. As soon as her favorite soap opera came on, Mary would settle into her chair and be at peace.

Richard and Karen decided to marry soon after Matthew was born. Their relationship had grown strong enough during her pregnancy to convince Karen, and they set the date.

It was to be a quiet ceremony. There was no money for a big wedding as there had been for Patty and Lorry. Almost all of Rita's savings had gone to the Antineoplaston and living expenses in Texas.

Karen didn't begrudge that she never had a wedding celebration; she would have spent even more to save her mother's life.

Still, she was determined to have something grand to remember, and in typical Karen fashion, went after it herself with imagination and brass.

She marched into a bridal store and wrangled a rented gown before there was such a practice. The gown was simple elegance, with beading around the collar, but it was a real wedding gown.

Karen stopped at Emily's house before the ceremony to show her the dress. Aunt Emily lovingly tucked an envelope containing three hundred dollars into Karen's hand. Neither she or the Lorenzos would be attending the wedding.

When Patty, Lorry and Karen were growing up, Mary Lorenzo used to love to tell them about their wedding money. She had saved five hundred dollars apiece for each of the girls when they got married. It was the only gift Karen was looking forward to. More than the money, it was the tradition that captivated her. She could do without the bridal shower, or the engagement party, or a large wedding and reception, but she ached for the traditional five hundred dollars from her grandma. Through the gift that would now be given to all three of them, Karen could feel a common link between her and her sisters. Even Patty and she would be united through this.

She left her aunt's house clutching only Emily's gift.

They were married on a weekday at a little church in Bellmore. There were no decorations, no cake, no table of gifts, no cards. The whole family was invited to the ceremony, but only Richard's sister, Brigid, and Karen's sister, Lorry, attended. All other family members were working or busy. An overnight stay at a hotel, paid for by Lorry, was their honeymoon, her wedding present to them. Richard went back to work the next morning.

A few days went by before Karen went over to the Lorenzos' to tell Mary about the wedding. Her grandmother was alone in the house, sitting at the kitchen table. An envelope sat beside her coffee cup. Handing it to Karen, she grinned with all the flourish of a poor woman giving a thousand dollars.

Radiant with joy, Karen laughed.

"I appreciate this more than anything else, Grandma," she said, eyes shining. "Now I'm like Patty and Lorry. I feel as important to you as they were. Mom would be so happy today."

Almost choking with emotion, she opened the envelope.

Inside was a single hundred-dollar bill.

Karen stood staring down at it, confused. She looked up at her grandmother. Mary's eyes skittered away.

"I can't afford to give you anymore right now. Come back in a few weeks, and I'll give you a few more dollars."

"Are you *trying* to hurt me?" Karen demanded. "You always talked about our wedding money. Five hundred dollars each. Patty got five hundred dollars. Lorry got five hundred dollars. You spend money like water on other people ... if I honestly thought you couldn't afford it, Grandma, then it wouldn't matter to me." Karen twisted the hundred-dollar bill and held it up in the air.

"But this? Why?"

"Karen, you ... when I have a few more dollars, I'll give it to you."

Karen saw her expression. Mary wasn't meeting her eyes. Her gaze kept shifting. She was lying. What statement was she making through this insulting gift?

Karen knew how the Lorenzos talked about her. She knew their opinion about her son being born out of wedlock. She glanced over at the family photos—Rita and Norbert, Patty and Bill, Lorry and Vinnie. Marco, smiling in a turtleneck sweater, his eyes stared steadfastly at her from the picture, and Karen knew. This wasn't about finances. This was a punishment.

Long and hard, Karen stared at the money, then laid it down on the table. Straightening up, she faced her grandmother, the matriarch of these people who dared insult her beloved son.

"You keep it," she said. "You need it more than me."

She bent and picked up her pocketbook, swinging it over a shoulder. "I don't need your gift. I don't need anything from you, ever again. How dare you hurt your own daughter's child like this? If my mother were alive, you'd never have treated me this way. My son is beautiful, and I love him very, very much. How dare you try to hurt him, hurt me, with this cruel gift?"

She stared Mary down, and for the first time in memory, the old woman was speechless for one self-conscious moment. Then, she became hysterical, trying to shove the money into Karen's hand as she walked out. Karen closed her fist, refusing to accept it.

"I don't want it, Grandma. Not anymore. It's over. Everything your gift meant is gone. You keep it."

She walked out.

A life-threatening asthma attack hit Karen soon after that. She was hospitalized for two weeks.

Doctor Alguta recommended a new doctor who'd been handling her more mild asthma attacks: a pulmonologist/general practitioner named *Weil*. The man would help change Karen's life.

Restless and depressed during her stay, Karen struggled to keep her spirits up as hard as she struggled for breath.

The children were instrumental in her recovery. Rita, Toni, and her stepson Kyle came to visit. Best of all, Richard and Lorry snuck baby Matt into the ward to see his mother. Richard passed the baby through Karen's hospital window, and Lorry handed him to his mother. She recovered quickly after that.

Months passed, and Karen's asthma dwindled to the point of non-existence. She relished her new role as wife and mother, lavishing attention on her son.

Richard was working long hours establishing a law practice, but he always took time to be a father and husband.

Karen was a doting (some said overprotective) mother. She rarely left little Matt's side. There was reason behind her obsessive care of her son. The visions were acting up again.

They came to her one morning when Matt was three-months-old. She was feeding him a bottle when he gave a tiny, hiccuping cough. Instantly, she saw him in her mind's eye, sitting in a high chair, turning blue. He was choking to death. His arm waved frantically. Then he fell face down into his plate. He wasn't breathing.

Karen snapped back from the nightmarish vision, and her eyes flew to the smiling infant in her arms.

"Oh, my God! Why am I seeing this? What happens to my baby?"

It wasn't her voices, but an intuitive knowing, that gave Karen her answer.

"If I'm not with him when this happens, he's going to die."

She knew it.

That was enough. Dinner parties, social engagements, doctor's appointments; Matty was always with her, no matter where she went. Every night, he slept in their bed, in an upright position, between his mother and father. A crib was out of the question. When he was flat, the baby seemed to have difficulty breathing.

Karen feared that Matty might be a Sudden Infant Death Syndrome, or SIDS, baby. She wouldn't allow it. Richard was impatient with her at times, but he knew enough about her visions to trust their warnings.

Ever vigilant, Karen welcomed any distraction from her fear over Matt. She called Scott De Simone, her old friend from the Roman Garden, hoping for a shot of past camaraderie.

Scott gave it in droves, delighted to hear her voice. They hadn't spoken for several years. Studying for his law degree, he'd begun scouting around for a job.

Richard put him to work in his office at the house, and Scott was delighted to see Karen almost every day.

They talked about their buddies from the Roman Garden, now scattered to the four winds.

Not wanting her old friend to judge her too harshly, Karen never told Scott anything about her strange abilities and prophetic visions. Exchanging normal, commonplace stories with Scott relaxed her, and softened her fears for her son.

***

Matty had his first cereal, and his first asthma attack on the same day in April, only a handful of weeks since Karen's vision of him in the high chair.

Based on Karen's own history with the disease, the pediatrician diagnosed severe asthma.

Matt was sent home with a provental asthmatic medication, but he only seemed to get worse as time went on.

With a constant stream of earaches and infections, aspirating fevers and projectile vomiting, he was eventually prescribed a nebulizer, as well.

Choking if he lay in a prone position, Matt still slept upright in the bed at night between his parents, propped up in his kangaroo rocker.

Instead of improving as he grew older, his asthma grew worse. They needed special monitors and oxygen in the house by the time Matt was thirteen months old. He didn't walk until he was almost a year-and-a-half.

Despite being so ill, Matt was a happy child, always filling the air with a little silver bell of a baby laugh. So full of life; so adorable.

"The vision can't be right," Karen said. "He's just too precious."

But, like every other time she doubted their input, Karen was to be proven wrong. Her visions were warnings to be heeded, glimpses of things to come.

In early February, 1990, Matty stopped breathing in his high chair.

Karen was at the kitchen stove. She heard the thump as his little head fell forward into his plate, and screamed.

"No! Matty, no!"

She grabbed his limp body out of the chair. Not breathing, his face turning blue, there was a thin smear of vomit on his chin. Karen flipped him over, no time for 911, and began slapping him on the back. No response.

"Oh my God, oh my God, oh my God, help me! What do I do? What?" Matty lay face down over her arm, his head lolling.

"Mom!" Karen called to Rita's spirit. "Mom, please, tell me what to do. I don't know what to do! Please help me! Please, please ... " She hit Matt on the back again.

On the fifth blow, he took a shallow breath. The color started coming back to his face, and his breathing was reedy.

Karen raced to the phone and dialed 911. The operator stayed on the line while they waited for the ambulance, asking Karen numerous questions about Matt's breathing.

"Now, I'm not saying you'll have to do this, Mrs. Farley, but let's be prepared just in case. You may have to do a tracheotomy yourself. Do you have a ball-point pen that you can pop the ink cartridge out of?"

Karen looked around. "Yes."

"Do you have a sharp object, like a really sharp knife?"

"Yes." A thread of sound.

"Good. Just keep everything out; keep it all there in case he stops breathing. As long as he's breathing, we'll just leave it the way it is. You have to let me know if anything changes, right away."

"Okay."

The ambulance arrived, and the paramedics tried to take him from her. Karen would have killed them if they pursued it, and they knew it. Together, they scrambled into the ambulance, then worked on the baby in her arms as they drove the fifteen minutes to the Medical Center in East Meadow.

Matt was fading. Karen never stopped talking, never allowed him to feel abandoned. She prayed for his life; she offered her own. Matt turned bright blue, and he stopped breathing again.

The emergency room staff wanted her to remain in the waiting room, and Karen showed them the folly of that.

"No. I have to be with him. He'll respond to me. You work on him in my lap. He knows my voice. He needs me now. Work on him in my lap."

Matt stopped breathing again, and this time, Karen felt him leave in a rush across her soul.

"No, Matty! Mommy's here! Come back, baby, come back! Mommy's here! Don't go! Come back!" There was a tiny cough, a thread of vomit, and his breathing returned.

For over an hour, Matt faded in and out of life as his mother looked on. Karen called to him, felt him leave, dragged him back with the sheer power of her will and love.

"Matty, it's Mommy! Come back to me, Matty, Mommy loves you! It's okay, baby, you're going to be okay. Mommy loves you."

She chanted the words over the doctors' grave shouts and the nurses' pleas, and after Matty stopped breathing a third time, they lost the left lung. The doctors shook their heads, voicing their concern, and Karen was chilled by their words. She knew they were at an end as to what to do, or why this was happening.

"Mrs. Farley, please. You have to step out while we intebate his left lung. It's not something that you should see. We have to do our job. If we don't get this lung reinflated, your son is going to die."

Karen looked in their eyes, and her intuition flared. The knowing came to her again, saying *pull back, let them.* She nodded. If she stayed at that precise moment, she was going to lose her son.

Richard got a call at work, and the news hit him like a brick. He asked the hospital if his son was going to be all right and heard the worst words in the English language.

"We're doing all we can."

Flying to his car, he didn't remember the drive to the hospital, to the same emergency room where Patty had been pronounced dead. Karen stood alone in the same corridor. She was sobbing. His heart hit the floor.

They stood together outside the emergency doors, trying to see something, anything as the doctors aspirated their son. The lung was reinflated successfully, and the inserted tube was filled with cereal and spinach. The doctor nodded.

"His air passage was blocked. Look at this."

He put Matt on the drug *Reglan*, and placed him in an oxygen tent.

Matt developed double pneumonia and moved to the pediatric ICU. He was given an injection that paralyzed him, so he wouldn't pull out the various tubing connected to his little body.

Karen spent the night in the chair by his bed. Watching his chest rise and fall as he struggled to breathe, she never stopped talking to him. "Mommy's here, Matt. Mommy's here." He was unable to move or open his eyes due to the muscle relaxant. Karen kept up a steady stream of talk to reaffirm that she was with him; that she wouldn't leave him. She reached a hand under the oxygen tent and stroked Matty's arm, her voice soft and constant. A tear slid down the side of his face.

It was that glistening tear that tore a hole in Karen's heart. The pain hit like a car wreck, and she doubled over with it. Astonishing, the amount of physical pain a mother could feel when witnessing her only child's suffering.

"Dear God," Karen whispered, her eyes riveted on Matt's white face, "I cannot leave here alone. I cannot leave without my son. If he dies, please take me, too. I will not live without my son. My life will end without him. We'll be together here, or we'll be together with you, Lord. There would be no reason to stay here without him. Please take me instead of Matty. Please take me instead of him."

The vision came without warning, circling her, surrounding her, shaking her free of the outside world for one terrifying moment. Matty. Matty lay in a coffin, before her eyes. She stared, willed the wooden box to fade and let her see inside. The walls of the coffin grew dim.

Matty was transparent.

The knowing flowed into her; the intuition of future knowledge. It was a warning. If Karen stayed with him, if she was careful, he could be saved. But a warning was a warning. She had to stay on her guard and never leave his side. The vision gave her focus, filled her with determination, warned her against giving up control to someone else. She had to be present for the healing of her son.

Lorry came immediately. She'd never seen fear on her brother-in-law's face before, but Richard was ashen with it. Slipping on a persona of comfort, she set about being positive and optimistic. The room was empty of both.

Richard scarcely heard her, for fear of losing his beloved little boy, laying so pale and seemingly lifeless in the oxygen tent.

"Matty's going to be fine, Richard," Lorry said. "Karen would never let anything happen to him. Don't worry. He's going to be all right."

Karen registered her sister's presence but paid no attention. Everything was concentrated on her son.

For thirty-six hours, she never left Matt's side. A constant stream of stories, jokes, songs, little cooing phrases reserved for babies; Karen never stopped talking.

During visiting hours, Richard sat with her. Lorry came when she could, and practiced sending healing energy to the paralyzed boy, a technique she was learning in her psychic awareness class. Stress brought on a Lupus flare, and she cursed her own body.

Some of the staff in ICU called Karen *the pain in the ass*. She was there for every test, every procedure, every fifteen-minute check. "You can't sleep here, Mrs. Farley." Karen just laughed at their stupidity.

"What are you telling me, I can't sleep here?" she asked. "Well, I am. My son needs me. Deal with it."

Then she wasted no more time with them. At first the nurses were gentle, trying a soft coax to get her out of their hair. When that failed, they became abrasive.

"Well, you'll have to sleep in that chair."

"Fine."

Some staff members were kinder than others and brought Karen a chair that folded out so she could stretch her legs and get the weight off her back. She was having pain in her lower abdomen, and the strength of it worried her. One look at Matt's still figure, however, and her thoughts turned back to him. Nothing else mattered.

Karen was the only parent who stayed the entire time in the hospital with her child. It was almost unheard of, a parent staying in ICU, refusing to leave, with only a chair to sleep on. Normal routine was visiting hours; then the parents went home. Remembering her vision, Karen remained glued to her son's side.

The next day, she told a nurse about her pain and where it was located. When they did some preliminary tests, the results were a complete surprise.

She was pregnant.

Karen felt little joy at the news, even though she wanted another baby. All her attention belonged to Matt. He was the child who needed help now. He was already here, born, and in danger. She'd think about the baby later.

When Richard was told, he ran a hand through his hair in bewilderment. He too could think only of Matt.

Karen described the pain nonchalantly as the reason for the test in the first place. Suspecting something far worse than mere pregnancy discomfort, she pushed that thought to the back of her mind. *I don't want Richard worrying about anything else. He's got enough on his plate. It's probably just bad cramps from sitting so long.* Her mind whispered other answers, but Karen wouldn't listen.

Lorry sat at home, nursing the flare. Hands purple, body covered with lesions and crippled with pain, she swam in guilt for not being there.

Matt spent seven days in ICU before his condition stabilized. The doctor ordered he be taken off the monitors and given regular food. "Your son is doing well, Mister and Mrs. Farley. You'll be able to take him home in a few days."

Richard and Karen looked at him as if he'd grown two heads. Karen knew it was a mistake. Matt was still in danger. She saw it.

"Listen, you take him off the monitors and give him food, he's going to reflux solids back into his lungs, and it'll kill him," she said. "You can't do that."

"Mrs. Farley, your son is stabilized. His pneumonia will be watched very carefully. The danger of aspirating has passed. He'll be fine. He hasn't had an episode in seven days. Maybe the medicine is all he needed."

"How can you say that? You haven't given him solid food for seven days. He's been on a liquid diet. How do you know he won't aspirate once, twice, God knows how many more times? What if it happens in the middle of the night?"

"I can't be one hundred percent sure, but in my professional opinion, I think the danger's over."

"Listen, doctor," Richard said, "I think you should keep him here, do some more tests, and under no circumstances, take him off the monitors at this time. My wife knows what she's talking about."

Despite heavy protests, the monitors were removed, and Matt was moved to a room on the pediatric ward. Karen and Richard noted, with disgust, that it was eleven doors away from the nurse's station.

"Richard, why don't you go home and get some sleep? I'll watch him."

"No, I'll stay." He looked around for another chair.

"There's no reason for us both to lose sleep. You've got a case in the morning. Come afterward."

Reluctantly agreeing, Richard kissed her, placed a loving palm on his son's forehead, and left. "I'll be back around lunch. Call me if you need me."

"I will."

Karen arched her back, wincing as her abdomen protested. Settling back in the impossibly uncomfortable chair, she prepared for another sleepless night.

Most of the staff on pediatrics were no friendlier than in ICU, and Karen once, again, had to show these strangers that she was not leaving her son. Period. Something was coming. She saw it all in her mind, and she had to be there to protect him.

The nurses advised her to go home. "Get some rest, Mrs. Farley. Your son'll be fine."

They assumed she was just a controlling, overprotective mother, but Karen Farley was far more than that. She knew, without a doubt, that if she followed their advice, if she went home to sleep, there would be a call in the middle of the night. *Mrs. Farley, we're sorry to inform you, your son passed away during the night.* If the years of sickness and death had taught her anything, it was to expect screwups in hospitals. Human beings aren't perfect in any profession, and doctors and nurses are human.

The head IV nurse came in and saw Karen sprawled in her purgatorial chair. She'd heard about this Farley woman. Taking pity, she brought Karen a reclining chair, pillow and blanket.

As the ward was dimmed for the night shift, Karen slid a hand through the bars of Matt's bed. She talked softly to him for several hours, until her head drooped, and she dozed off.

It was not the strange, subdued little cough that woke her, but rather, the cessation of sound.

Her head snapped up; her eyes cleared instantly and she stared at Matty. He was not breathing.

"No! Matty! Matty, wake up! No! *Nurse!*"

She tore the covers off him, grabbed him up, and ran down the hall, rubbing his back and screaming. She held him face down along her forearm, shrieking, and the entire ward exploded.

"Nurse! Nurse! Help me! He's not breathing! Hurry!"

The nurses leapt into action, but their movements seemed like treacle to Karen, sluggish and ancient, and she hated them. They ran together back to his room, where the code team worked on him, over an hour this time.

Matty stopped breathing, yet again. His body fell limp, he was bright blue and then mottled. Karen screamed his name, calling him back, searching for his little spirit, trying to catch a tip of it and pull it down into her.

Again, food was suctioned from his bronchial tubes. The airways were cleared, and Matt stabilized. The monitors were reattached, and they had to start from scratch.

He was sent back to ICU.

Karen settled once again into the hated chair by the side of the bed, and set up watch over her son. During the time she was with him, only one friend, a woman named Laura, was able to stay with him all night so Karen could get some rest. This was a gift she never forgot. It was the only time in the whole three months of Matty's illness that Karen slept through the night.

Richard took over everything outside of the hospital. Now the sole breadwinner for the family, he paid all the bills and shouldered all the financial responsibilities so Karen could be free to stay with their son. It was difficult for Richard to perform at work, day in and day out, and not be able to be with them, but he knew the necessity of it. Every moment he could spare, he was by their side.

Karen started taking over. Determined to protect her son at all costs, she charted his meds along with the nurses. She kept track of what foods he ate, how much he ate, what tests were scheduled for each day. Bowel movements, temperature and blood pressure variances, readings on the oximeter; everything was recorded in a spiral notebook by her side. With Matty's veins so compromised, she even knew when it was time to change the IV.

The head of the IC unit told Richard and Karen that the answer might have to be surgery.

"It appears as though your son has a reflux problem. He may grow out of it, or he may need surgery. We won't know for sure, unless he has a certain test done which this hospital doesn't have the facilities to perform."

Karen stared in astonished contempt.

"You've got to be kidding me," she said. "You mean, you want me to have my son transported from this IC unit to another IC unit of another hospital to have this test done? Why can't you bring someone in to perform the procedure here? It's too dangerous to transport him. What if he aspirates on the way? Another facility isn't familiar with my son's case. What if he has another episode? At least here, you all know what to do for him if he stops breathing. They'd be coming in green."

"Well, Mrs. Farley, we just don't have the facilities to help you out with this particular test. We've done all we can."

"Great." Karen threw up her hands. "I must be in a nightmare, a fucking nightmare. You're telling me that you can't provide me with someone who had the expertise to perform this test here, so my son doesn't have to be moved and put at risk, traveling to another hospital? I can't believe it."

"I'm sorry, Mrs. Farley."

"Fine. Fine. Let's get it done as soon as possible. The minute he's ready to move, I want to know what's involved."

Karen turned to Richard. "You know what, Rich? This is a message for us. We're supposed to get him out of this hospital. They can't help him, anymore."

The Farleys had had enough of that place. As soon as Matt stabilized (this time it took a week), they moved their son by ambulance to another hospital in Mineola, where the test for Gastroesophageal Reflux Disease (GERD) would be performed.

Karen's pediatrician recommended the doctor who could do the procedure. Karen and Richard disliked him immediately. He was the only one, however, who could perform this unusual test in that hospital. Pompous and distant, he didn't listen to a word the Farleys said.

The doctor examined Matt very carefully, straightened, and said, "This child is fine. He doesn't need this test. It's a very unpleasant experience. Just take him home; he'll be fine. If he has a problem again, bring him back and we'll do it then."

Another madman.

"I can't be hearing right," Karen said, "Didn't you review his records? We brought him here to do this test."

"The child hasn't had an episode for over a week, Mrs. Farley. He may just grow out of it. I don't think this test is necessary."

"Do you realize we transported our son from ICU there to ICU here specifically for this test? I'm not asking for your opinion. Do you think I'm going to take my son out of the intensive care unit and take him home, with no way to suction him or bring him back if he refluxes again, just because you think that he doesn't need this test? Are you out of your mind?"

"Mrs. Farley, I think you're getting a little carried away. Your son is fine. I don't think he needs this test. And I'm not performing it."

"That's right. You're not performing it."

"What?"

Karen fired him.

"I don't need you to do it. I'll find someone else. As a matter of fact, I don't want you to do it."

"My dear young woman, you can't simply—"

"Watch me."

At a loss for words, the disgruntled physician stormed out the door. Richard went to his wife, and together, he and Karen looked at the still figure of Matty in the bed.

They searched through their insurance forms, made endless phone calls, and basically bullied the insurance company into covering the procedure by the doctor of their choice. *No* wasn't an option for Karen or Richard Farley.

They found a doctor from Northshore, a family man with a pile of children of his own.

A tube was inserted down Matt's throat, and remained there for twenty-four hours. Its purpose was to count how many times Matt refluxed in a day with normal eating and drinking.

It counted twenty-two episodes, an absolutely enormous amount. The test confirmed GERD.

Another little boy down the hall had the same thing but didn't survive. He was one of many young children in the hospital without parents for most of their stay, and the day he died neither his mother or his father was there. Karen thought about the boy and all the other young patients in ICU. She thought that ill children needed something other than the parents and the medical staff to help them through these long days and nights of fear and sickness; something else was needed, a support system of some kind, something that could be there for them always. The rest of the day, she couldn't stop crying for that little lost boy.

By this time, Matt had been in one hospital or another for almost three months. For the surgery, he was moved to yet another hospital, this time in Manhassett. His body had been poked and prodded so much from so many tests and endless intravenous needles, that the doctors couldn't find a normal spot to slide an IV in. They had to put them in his leg, his feet, even his neck.

Karen and Richard weren't encouraged to be in the room when Matt's IV was changed. "It's going to be very painful for him, and he's too young to understand," the doctors said. "Parents shouldn't be associated with such a traumatic memory." They stood outside and listened to Matt scream as the IV was changed. He called over and over again for his mommy, and Karen's knees almost buckled.

The IV had to be changed every four to five days.

The day of the surgery, Karen waited alone. Richard had a case in court, Lorry had a flare-up.

She went down with the surgical team to help prepare Matt for the operation, praying for a sign that he wouldn't be alone. Karen felt real despair that she couldn't be in the room with him.

The OR doors opened, and one of the surgical nurses came out. She wore a pair of scrubs and had not yet donned her mask. Karen couldn't believe her eyes. The nurse recognized her, too.

It was Kathy, an old friend from the Roman Garden. Her brothers had been waiters there. "I'll be with your son every step of the way, Karen. Don't worry. This surgeon is the best. We'll take care of him."

Her words were a gift of such magnitude that Karen Kikel Farley, the Stone, started crying in public. Tears spilled over and ran down her face, salting the corner of her lip. She drew in a breath shaky with gratitude. "Thank you, Kathy. Thank you so much."

Kathy smiled, patted her arm, and went back in.

Time became glacial. The clock in the waiting room became her enemy. Karen glared at it.

The surgery was a success. A section of Matt's intestine was wrapped, preventing food from rising up, and the doctor came out to Karen with a smile and a handshake. "It went fine, Mrs. Farley. He'll have a feeding tube in his side for a few months, and he won't ever be able to vomit, but I don't think he'll miss that much. Oh, and he won't be able to belch, either."

The years would prove him wrong on both counts, but for now, Karen was giddy with relief.

Matt was moved from recovery to his private room, and his mother felt her whole body slide into one enormous sag of relief. She couldn't stop smiling. A frisson of fear tapped on the back of her mind, and she turned, looking for a coffin with her little boy in it. She searched for the vision, for a clue of some as yet unforeseen new danger for her son, but nothing happened. There was only an empty coffin. Matty would live.

She settled down for the night in her recliner, relaxing into her borrowed pillow and warm blanket, smiling at the thought of her first real sleep in three months.

A few hours later, Karen woke up in agony, sudden and intense, like a gunshot wound. She clamped her teeth down on her bottom lip to keep from screaming. The pain was back, saying hello in a silent voice all its own, torturing her with new fear and lacerating torment. *My God, am I losing the baby?*

She sat for an hour in the dark with Matt, willing herself to stay conscious. She vomited, and it didn't help. Karen has a very high threshold for pain, and it was put to the test that night. Sweat rolled down her forehead and slipped into her shirt, staining the collar and soaking her by the time it started to subside. Another fifteen minutes, and she took a shaky, shallow breath, sighing in relief. The pain was still there, but now it was endurable. "Not now," she told it. She wasn't ready yet. This wasn't the time.

They did a sonogram of her pelvis the next day. Uncomfortable at leaving Matt, she reassured herself that the danger was past with him. She could leave him for an hour.

The sonogram took longer than usual, then the radiologist ordered another series of tests.

Nervous by this time, Karen asked, "Is there something I should know about?"

The radiologist looked at her. "I don't normally discuss our findings with the patients."

"But, I want to know." Karen persisted, not to be put off. The radiologist sighed.

"There's a little mass showing up. Could be bile; we don't know exactly."

"What do you think it is? What else could it be?"

"Don't worry about it, Mrs. Farley. We're going to tell your doctor what we found, then he'll talk to you about it."

Karen called Lorry as soon as she left the examining room. "Lorry, they found a mass in my pelvic region. What do you think it is? They said it could be bile. What do you think, psychically?"

Lorry couldn't breathe. "I think it's going to be fine." Her voice was convincing but her hand shook. She was glad Karen couldn't see it.

"Tell me the truth. Do you think I might have cancer?"

Karen heard a catch, then a deep pull of breath on the phone, released in a rush of air. "Noo! No, no. Why, do you think you have cancer?"

"I've always had this feeling that I was going to get it. Don't know why, though."

Karen met with her obstetrician a few hours later. He was a witty man who could always make her laugh. Calmed by his nonchalance, she asked, "So, what's the verdict?"

"There's a small mass showing up on the pelvic sonogram. Probably just bile."

The *knowing* swirled around her, and Karen understood what it was. The mass wasn't bile.

"Oh my God. I have cancer."

He laughed. "Don't think that way. Talk to me in twenty years, maybe then."

"But I've had a lot of pain, and there's cancer in my family. Both my parents died from it."

"I don't think it's necessary, but if you want, we can do further testing."

"Will it harm the baby?"

"Depends on how far we go. Most tests to determine cancerous masses involve heavy X-rays and radiation, and the baby could be harmed. Of course, if something *is* found, and further action is needed, it might be necessary to terminate this pregnancy."

"That's out of the question."

"I'm sure it's nothing to worry about, anyway, Mrs. Farley. It's probably just bile."

Now that Matt was recovering, Karen was able to spare a moment of thought for anyone else. She turned her mind to Lorry. Still bedridden with the Lupus flare, Lorry hadn't been to the hospital since before Matt's surgery.

That evening, Karen closed her eyes in the quiet ward. She wanted to check Lorry's progress in her visions. She concentrated, and the coffin appeared.

It was different this time. Lorry wasn't in the coffin. Karen was.

The great stone was suddenly there, before her inner eye, and the numbers she'd seen carved in it years ago were there, as well. Her stomach quailed as she reread them, and realized her mistake.

The number wasn't twenty-one. It was twenty-seven. The age she would be in seven months.

Her eyes snapped open, and pain kicked her under the ribs. It was a fresh, new pain, one she hadn't felt before, a herald of things to come.

"No," she hissed. "Not yet. Not now. Go *away!*"

The pain reared up in her, sliding a sinewy net of agony along her spine, curling around her stomach until she could feel its shape.

"No! I'm telling you, no!"

It slunk away without haste, giving a last flick of a barbed tail as it disappeared. Karen remembered the prophecy of her childhood vision. Cancer. *Goddammit.* She couldn't even feel fear. All she could register was anger at the timing. Thoughts of the sonogram, the doctor's nonchalant talk of a mass, and she knew the truth.

Who can I tell? I've got to talk to someone. She couldn't call Lorry, who was already overburdened with her own terrible illness. Richard couldn't possibly imagine anything so horrific; he'd just refuse to believe it. Karen could feel his anxiety over Matt. Burdening him with another disaster was out of the question.

The only person she could turn to was Lynn. A cancer survivor twice over, Lynn would know if Karen's dread was unfounded or not. Her intuition was always strongest in regards to a subject's health.

There was a pay phone near the hospital cafeteria. Dialing the number, Karen waited. Lynn knew who it was on the line before she could say a word.

Hiding nothing, Karen told Lynn about her visions, the malignant prophesy, what they'd found on the sonogram.

"I know what this all means, I'm just afraid to say it. They told me. The voices told me, years ago. I have cancer, don't I?"

Lynn paused, then said gently, "Yeah, honey. I think you do."

"Is my son going to be okay?"

"Yeah. He's going to be fine."

"Do you see him as a grown man?"

"Yes."

"Do you think that I'll live through this pregnancy?"

"Yes, I do."

"Is the baby going to be okay?"

"Yes, I think the baby will be fine."

Karen swallowed the lump in her throat. "Do you think that I'm going to die soon?"

"Oh, honey, no. I think you're going to be very sick, but I feel that you're going to be okay."

"Well," Karen laughed, unsteady. "That's good. Thank God." She grew serious. "I'm not going to do anything about it now, Lynn. Until my son is one hundred percent, and this baby's born, nobody knows about this.

I made a deal with God, Lynn. When Matthew first collapsed, I asked him to take me, and not him. Maybe now ... "

"No, honey. You have a purpose here, and you haven't fulfilled it, yet. My guides tell me, you're going to be fine. There's no death around you. Now, it won't be easy. You're going to have a tough time. Just never forget that you can always renegotiate your contract."

That caught Karen sideways. "What?"

"With God," Lynn said. "Your contract with God. The time you're alloted, here on earth. When they first diagnosed me with cancer, my kids were little. Five years before they'd graduate and be out on their own. So, I asked God for five years. Then, when the doctors found another lump, I renegotiated for another five years, and got it. As far as contracts with the Lord are concerned, I figure to keep this up until I'm too old to care anymore."

Karen burst out laughing. "Thanks, Lynn. I gotta get back to Matt."

"Good-bye, honey, and take care. Remember, I'm here for you. I love you."

"Love you, too. Bye."

Matt was nearing the day when he could go home. Lorry was up and about again and always at the hospital now. Karen shared bits and pieces of her visions with her, but shied away from telling Lorry too much. She was afraid of bringing on another Lupus flare.

Karen, Richard, and Lorry enrolled in a one day crash course in CPR while Matt was recovering from the surgery. They were taking no chances, after all this danger. If anything went wrong, if Matt stopped breathing again, at least with training, they would know what to do.

Lorry held the little rubber baby doll they were practicing with, picturing it as Matt. *This is my nephew. This could be Rita or Toni.* Her hands turned bright raspberry at the thought. Pressing them together for warmth, she finished the course.

Chapter 9:

Lymphoma

I am never going to get this. Not in a million years.

Lorry was frustrated. She was frustrated, embarrassed, and ashamed. Everybody else in the class was talking about seeing visions of Buddha or angels, great rolling fields of grass and wildflowers, or entire star charts under their fingertips. Lorry, even after a couple months of classes, and endless hours of trying, still saw nothing. Zilch. Zero.

It was the meditating. To ask a person with attention deficit disorder to sit quietly and relax for twenty minutes before they even started *doing* anything was pure agony. Three minutes into the meditation, Lorry was rocking back and forth, gritting her teeth, crease mark in her forehead. *All right, all right, I'm relaxed already, let's get on with it!*

Lorry was the only one who couldn't do it. She couldn't see energy and she hadn't found her guide yet. There were no discernible changes of temperature in her palms from various energy patterns, and her third eye wasn't open. "I don't even have a third eye!" she'd rage silently. Her legs throbbed from sitting in one spot for so long. Forget the lotus position. Lorry was lucky if she could get down on the floor. Without a doubt, she was the lousiest student in the class.

So it came as a complete surprise one day, halfway through the opening meditation, that Lorry discovered she could see the room with her eyes closed. Her eyelids flew up, startled, and she saw a filmy purple glow rising out of the floor in front of her.

They didn't tell me Plaquenil is a hallucinogen. Feels like I'm in a Jimmy Hendrix song. That was her first thought. A pulling began in her chest and head, a gentle tugging that felt like the handbook's description of an out-of-body experience. *Maybe it's not the medication.*

She just went with it without thought or effort. Closing her eyes, Lorry began to dream, all the time aware of her surroundings and the steady voice of the instructor.

She was on a hill. A man was waiting at the top. Lorry started to run. Somehow, she knew him. They embraced, and she felt as if she were coming home.

Lorry had found her guide.

After that, things happened fast. The clouds of colored light were energy patterns. Her teacher explained the meaning behind the different colors, pointing directly at each individual cloud. Any lingering skepticism that Lorry had, flew out the window. It wasn't her medication. She really was seeing them. Excited, she drove over to Karen's after class.

They went into the living room. Concerned, Lorry watched as her sister maneuvered awkwardly around the room.

Karen, sweat beading her forehead, was into the second trimester of her pregnancy, and the baby was heavy. Pain was with her all the time now. Sometimes throbbing, sometimes a dull ache, but always there. Karen knew it wasn't the baby.

Lorry's instructor was teaching them how to heal psychically by observing disturbances in a person's energy pattern. Lorry looked at her sister and decided to try it. Karen was suffering; anybody could see that. Maybe she could help. After an initial protest, Karen finally agreed to play guinea pig, and stretched out on the floor.

Lorry knelt beside her, workbook nearby, and closed her eyes. Passing her hands over Karen's body, fingers together, eyes closed, Lorry struggled to see an energy pattern.

Gradually, a picture came into focus in her mind's eye. A gray mist, like fog in twilight, hovered all around Karen's shape. This fit the description her instructor told her to look for.

"It's working. Karen, I see it!"

"You always did need a lot of attention." The words were affectionate.

Lorry began working her hands down the body, and Karen fell silent. The idea was to smooth out any bright or *hot* spots, watching for holes in the aura. Matt was asleep, Richard was in court, and the only sounds in the house were Lorry's soft words, and Karen's steady breathing.

Despite Lorry's headlong dive off the deep end lately, Karen had to admit her sister's hands felt good, like a delicious hot water bottle. Nothing could ever compare to the touch of a loved one, and Karen sighed with pleasure. Her pain actually was a little better.

What is that? Lorry frowned in confusion as her hands passed over the abdomen. The whole area was bright white, speckled with little gold nuggets, like a miner's sluice pan. The baby kicked her palms, the softest of flutters. There were more concentrations of nuggets down below the stomach.

"What is that?" Lorry asked.

She grabbed her Psychic Healing Workbook and flipped through the pages, trying to find a reference to gold nuggets. In chapter five, she found them.

Gold nodules meant disease.

"Oh, God!"

Panic ate her for breakfast.

Striving to keep her voice calm, Lorry said, "Karen ... do you have any appointments with the doctor soon? I see something, and I don't understand what I'm seeing."

"What's the matter with you?"

"I see gold nodules. The book says gold nodules mean disease. You should go to the doctor."

"I see the obstetrician every week, now."

"No, I mean tests for disease." Lorry couldn't say the word *cancer*.

"They can't do any tests, now. It'd hurt the baby."

"Well then ... just try to take it easy more."

"I haven't been feeling well lately; it's true. But Lorry, think about it. What am I supposed to say? *Well, doctor, I came here for tests because my sister saw gold nuggets in my aura?* You've got to be kidding!"

They both laughed.

"Well, I've got to get home. Thanks for watching the kids."

"Anytime."

Karen sat on the couch after Lorry left, thinking about the age of twenty-seven. She spread a hand over her belly. The baby whispered a greeting with a butterfly quaver deep in her womb, making her smile.

The pain shoved its head into her gut, and the smile vanished. Gorge rising, fear pushing at the back of her throat, she beat down the panic.

"No. I don't have time for this. Go away!"

Pain, regardless of the cause, was of no importance in Karen's scheme of things. She had one goal, and that was to protect Matt and this unborn child. Once again, family before self, but with a twist. This time, she was protecting innocents.

The pain receded. Karen went to the bathroom and washed the sweat from her face. She knew she was ill, but it didn't matter. She didn't matter. Only duty and obligation were important.

Pulling the vacuum cleaner out of the closet, Karen plugged it in and started sweeping the rug. By the time Richard got home, hours later, the house was spotless. Work hard enough, and a person doesn't have to think.

Since the age of twelve, Karen had always overdone. It was one way to escape problems. Rita taught all her girls that.

As Karen grew older, her plate was perpetually overflowing with projects. Helping Richard in the office, tending to Matt, babysitting her nieces, Kyle on the weekends and cooking for scores of parties. Social and community obligations were numerous, and the charity drives, endless. Richard and Karen were both generous with their time, and few projects were refused. She overworked, but Karen had always overworked; now was no different.

* * *

Lorry still attended her classes with Norma. Karen questioned her sister about this dive into the paranormal. In earlier years, they'd both gone to mediums and psychics for kicks, getting their palms read, enjoying a good show. Karen rarely believed their authenticity, but Lorry was far more likely to accept without question. Her loyalty was more easily won than Karen's. Karen would test the patience of a saint with her incessant probing.

Perhaps it was her own unwanted abilities that made her such a skeptic. She herself was very powerful, and she didn't like it. "Ah, gee, God, thanks for the gift," Karen joked. "How's about you let me see next week's lotto numbers, instead of who's going to die next? Then, I'll consider it a plus."

Glimpses of the future started coming to Lorry in her sleep, jerking her awake with a scream. These nightmares worried her. She dreamt of Karen, lying dead in a pool of blood. This was far worse than any dark shape in the corner, any ghostly vision that tried to communicate. All these things were becoming commonplace. Even worse, Richard's sister Brigid was having the same dream. Karen, cold and lifeless, soaked in blood.

The answer was simple. Norma. She'd brought Lorry back from the brink of despair with her blunt assurances. She'd do the same for Karen.

Norma was having a seance the next week, and Lorry signed them up.

Arriving at Karen's doorstep on a bright autumn day, shiny as a new penny and freshly washed by morning rain, Lorry felt buoyant. The leaves were just touched with gold and scarlet in the early October sunshine, and the beauty of the day cheered them both. Tonight was going to be fun.

They made their plans. Lorry had to run some last minute errands, and she'd be back at seven.

They got to Norma's house around seven-thirty. A woman named Margaret greeted them at the door, asking them to take off their shoes.

Large pillows were scattered on the floor, with several loveseats pushed up against the wall. A single chair sat at the far end of the room. People milled about or lounged on the cushions—about twenty in all. Norma was nowhere in sight.

Margaret asked everyone to take a seat. Karen leaned over to Lorry and whispered, "Why did I let you talk me into this?"

Lorry grinned.

The door opened, and Norma entered the room. She was as austere as ever, dressed in jeans and a shirt. Tonight, for the seance, she was functioning as a medium.

Norma sat in the chair, braced her hands on wide spread knees, and began to sway back and forth, her head bobbing and snapping, like a bird listening for insects. Her breath whistled deep and slow through her nostrils. Karen rolled her eyes. "Why the hell did you bring me here? What a freak."

Lorry stifled a giggle.

Eyes closed, Norma started calling out names. "Susan wants to speak to Joe."

A woman raised her hand, went up, and talked to Joe.

This went on for forty minutes, with roughly ten-minute sessions per person. Sometimes the people talked to Norma from where they sat, sometimes the medium had them sit beside her.

This last bit made Karen nervous. "Oh, shit, Lorry. What if she calls me? I don't want to go up there."

At that moment, Norma called out a name. "Little Flower wants to talk to Innocenza. Lorry. Lorry?"

Florindo was Grandpa Lorenzo's name. It meant "little flower" in Italian. *Innocenza* was Grandma Lorenzo's name in Calabria, before the American immigration board changed it to "Mary."

Lorry raised her hand. "I'm here."

Norma rocked in her chair, a gentle sway. She didn't look at Lorry, seeming to stare somewhere over her shoulder. "You tell Innocenza that I am working hard, Lorry, and everything is almost ready. The house has been prepared, and I am cooking sausages. There is a garden, too. I'll come for her soon. Don't be afraid."

"But, Grandma's not sick," Lorry said. "When will you come for her?"

"In three months."

Norma opened her eyes and asked, "What are you here for? What do you need to know?"

"I'm very concerned about my sister."

"Okay."

Norma began swaying and bobbing again. "Ri ... Rita ... "

Karen and Lorry both froze.

"Rita ... Reet? Reet Petite wants to talk to Karen."

Karen felt her stomach hit her toes. *Reet Petite*. Uncle Marco's nickname for her mother. She raised her hand.

"Karen? Come up and sit beside me."

"I'd rather stay here."

"Are you shy?"

The room laughed softly.

"Come. Come up here."

Karen got up and sat in the chair next to the medium. Norma smiled at her.

"You are with child, yes?"

Can't get more obvious than that. I'm as big as a whale.

"Yes."

"Do you know you have a little girl inside?"

Karen smiled back, uncertain. "No, I didn't know."

"Well, you do. Why do you hold so much pain?"

"I didn't realize I did."

"Why do you feel so guilty? You've got to let go of all that guilt. Your mother's death isn't your fault. You did everything you could to save her. She's here with you. She loves you very much, and she's very proud of you. What do you think of that, Karen?"

"Great." Karen wasn't buying it.

"You don't believe me, do you?"

"No offense. It's just a little hard for me to believe that my mother's here, right now."

"Well, she is. Why aren't you wearing the pendant that she used to wear? It was left to you. There's a face on it, a woman's face. I think it's a religious medal."

"It's broken."

"Have it fixed. Your mother wants you to wear it." Norma paused, then said, "Your mother is very concerned about you."

"Oh really?"

"What I'm about to tell you may be a shock. At the time of your daughter's birth, an organ in your body will burst. You and the fetus will die in a pool of blood."

I am going to kill Lorry.

"Your body is sick."

Fear began to curl up.

"The baby inside has no spirit. It couldn't stay in such a sick body. You have a soulless fetus growing inside you."

Jesus help me.

"Do you believe me?"

This kind of shock, Karen didn't need. All she wanted to do at that moment was get up, grab Lorry, and get out.

"This is a lot to hear right now," she said. "How do you want me to answer that?"

"Your mother loves you, and will not let this terrible thing happen. Her spirit is going to enter your womb to save you and the baby during childbirth. But I have to help your mother go into you. Would you like that?"

"Uh ... I guess so."

"Sit forward."

Karen leaned closer. Norma touched her head, her back, and spoke some soft words. When she was done, she sat back. "Your mother is with you now. How do you feel?"

"Okay."

There was no chill, no wind, no shimmer of awareness. Nothing but the urgent need to get the hell out of there, then kill her sister. Karen got up and left, Lorry close behind.

They rode a tidal wave of recriminations and rage on the way home. Karen was in shock. *What was Norma thinking? Don't I have enough on my plate without some bitch spouting blood prophecies and stillbirth? Is she kidding me?*

"Lorry, I can't believe you brought me here! Oh, great. Now, I'm going to give birth in one month and die in a pool of blood. I'm so glad I paid money for that piece of important information." She stared out the window. "It's not your fault, Lorry. I don't blame you. Good thing I'm not impressionable. That woman could have done some real damage if I was."

Swamped with guilt, Lorry shrank behind the steering wheel. "I'm sorry Norma said all that, but Karen, everything's going to be okay, now. That terrible feeling I was having about you is gone."

"And what was that about *Reet Petite?* Did you tell her about Mommy's nickname?"

"I didn't tell her anything about my family."

"Well, that was freaky." Karen snorted. "At least I'll live now. That's a real load off my mind."

***

Once more, chaos had overtaken the Lorenzo home. Marco's young wife Anna got into a snit with his mother, and the two women were not speaking.

Marco sided with his wife, and Mary was frantic with anguished rage. Bad enough that her own daughter-in-law shunned her, but the grandchildren?

Anna had proven herself fertile. There was a new baby girl to go with Marco Junior.

Asked to intercede, Lorry recruited Karen. "Things are a mess over there. Anna's really awful to Grandma, Karen. She holds a grudge."

"What happened? What started it?"

"Apparently, Anna's sister overheard Grandma complaining about how self-ish Anna is. She was snooping around the corner while Grandma was on the phone with Aunt Emily. Then she went and told a twisted version of the conversation to Anna, who blew her top. Now, she acts like Grandma's dead. Doesn't talk to her, doesn't acknowledge her presence, won't shop for her. Grandma's not even allowed to see the babies unless Uncle Marco brings them to her personally. He's on Anna's side. If you could just talk to Uncle Marco, show him how bad this is hurting Grandma ... "

Karen sighed. "Well, it's ridiculous. Persecuted in her own home. Poor Grandma. I'll talk to him this weekend."

Mary kissed little Matthew's feet as they came in the door Sunday morning. Placing her hands on Karen's belly, she squealed with pleasure when the baby moved.

The family was all there. Lorry brought Rita and Toni, who played with Marco Junior and Matt on the floor. Grandma Lorenzo sat in her chair, her new baby granddaughter beside her. Karen lounged in the recliner, feet up and nine months pregnant. Marco sprawled on the couch. Anna was at work.

The argument began with a nothing: Grandma asked if Karen could take her food shopping that Tuesday, accompanying the request with a sigh.

"I also have a doctor's appointment in two weeks. Since Lorry's feeling bad, I didn't want to ask her, what with her two babies."

"I can probably take you food shopping, Grandma, but I don't know about the doctor. Maybe Anna can take you."

"Ohhoof!" Mary made a gesture of disgust. "I don't ask her anything anymore. I could drop dead and she wouldn't notice."

"What are you talking about, Grandma?"

"If I'd known what would happen to me in my older years! That woman doesn't talk to me, doesn't look at me. What kind of a daughter-in-law is this? What kind of a woman is she?"

Marco interjected. "Ma, you shouldn't talk about my wife when she's not here to defend herself. If you have a complaint, say it to her face."

"How can I? She won't even talk to me."

Karen spoke up. "Why isn't she talking to you?"

"I don't know why she doesn't talk to me. I've been good to her. I've been good to her children."

"Ma!" Marco barked. "You know exactly why Anna isn't talking to you."

"Why?" Karen asked.

He shook his head. "It's not nice to gossip about people when they're not here. I don't want to get into it."

Mary Lorenzo's eyes began to roll, and she gave a snort of derision. "She's full of prunes! I've been good to her, from the first day she came here, I've been good to her and her family."

"So good that you talk about her behind her back?" Marco asked.

"Aah, she's full of *moot!*" Mary's face scrunched in righteous pain.

Marco sat up. "Oh, really? Anna's sister heard you gossiping about her. You hurt her feelings. If you want Anna to talk to you again, you have to apologize."

Mary Lorenzo flared with rage. "You're bullashit. Me? Apologize to her?"

"My wife is very nice to you. You don't appreciate anything she does."

"Marco, she goes for months without knocking on my door, asking if I need a gallon of milk. Nothing! She's mean. She's very mean."

"She's that way because of you. You make her that way. She's not like that with anybody else, only you. And I don't blame her."

Karen watched Mary's eyes, shimmering with tears, and decided to intervene.

"Uncle Marco, Grandma's in her eighties. Anna's in her thirties. Don't you think Anna could be the bigger person and let things go in one ear and out the other?"

"No! If you want respect, you have to treat other people with respect. She," pointing at his mother, "needs to respect my wife more."

"How about your sister-in-law respecting Grandma's privacy? After all, this is Grandma's house. Seems to me, the whole reason your wife is mad is because her meddling sister listened to a private conversation, and in order to make trouble, repeated it to Anna."

Marco turned to his mother. "Ah, so I see you're talking about it to other people!"

"I'm not other people," Karen said. "I'm her granddaughter. A woman has a right to have a conversation with her own sister, in her own home, in private. Anna not talking to her for months is immature and cruel."

"This is not something I want to get into with you," Marco snapped, "but her talking about my wife is not acceptable, and she knows better. Right now, she's getting what she deserves."

"How can you say that? Grandma's an old woman who's lost her husband and daughter. She depends on the two of you. If Anna was thinking straight, she'd realize she doesn't have such a bad deal. Grandma lets the two of you live here. Anna should appreciate that. You can't have one without the other."

"Why is this any business of yours?" Marco asked, "How do you know what goes on here?"

"Do you know how lucky you are? You and Anna have a place to live and someone who cares about you. After my mom died, my whole life changed drastically, for the worse. Because of that, I learned to appreciate things. Anna's older than me; she should know better. This isn't her house. She doesn't own it. Your wife should learn to be grateful, and a little more patient with Grandma."

Marco's face grew red, bristling with rage. "What's this really all about, Karen? Why don't you tell us?"

"You want me to be honest? Fine. You and Anna have a great situation here with Grandma. She spoils you rotten, and it's aggravating to see how she's treated. There's no reason for it. If my mom was here, she'd never allow Anna to talk that way to Grandma. Never."

The fight escalated into a bitter mudslinging of accusations and insults, with Marco standing over Karen in the lounge chair, shouting.

Mary stood in the background, waving her arms and shrieking, "Marco, stop. Stop. She's pregnant!"

Lorry tried to console a sobbing Rita and screaming Toni.

Karen, holding her own distraught son, crying openly herself, finally confronted Marco about cutting her and her sisters out of Mary Lorenzo's will.

Angelina, before she went back to Italy, had told them about Marco's ultimatum to his mother.

Flustered, Marco said, "I had to do something to protect myself. For years after Rita died, you girls were trying to work on my mother. I had to protect my inheritance."

Karen laughed in his face.

"Uncle Marco, you had her cut us out right after Mommy died. I don't give a damn about this house, but the principle of it's disgusting. I was eighteen-years-old; we'd just lost our mother, and I had nowhere to go."

"You could have stayed with Aunt Emily."

"You know I couldn't stay with Bill Kelly."

"You chose to leave. That was your doing."

Karen's shock brought a fresh wave of tears. "I had no choice."

"I had my mother change her will because the house is rightfully mine," Marco shouted. "I'm her only living child. So I acted to protect myself and my family."

"That's bullshit, and you know it. She changed her will a few weeks after we got back from Texas."

"That's a lie. I did it years later. You girls worked on my mother for years."

"Why would we want the will changed?" Karen asked, exasperated. "The way it was written actually protected us. No, Uncle Marco. We didn't want the will changed. You did. Don't you dare put that on us."

"You're wrong. I did it years later."

"Call her lawyer. Get the date. Only weeks after my mother died, and all you could think about was making sure we were cut out of the will. If you loved your sister as much as you say, how could you treat her children like that? Don't you think she would have expected you to care for us in some way?"

Uncle Marco jabbed a finger and yelled, "What are you, jealous that I have a mother and you don't? Is that the problem here? Well, she's my mother, not yours. When your mother died, you were negated."

Stunned silence greeted his words as the whole room absorbed the shock. The children snuffled, but the adults were speechless.

His blow hit home, but not in a way Marco anticipated. Karen's heart flared with such an offense, feeling nothing but contempt for his statement and the small mind that made it. Her eyes stared up at him, rain-washed and disbelieving. Any love she'd ever had for Marco was gone in that moment.

She struggled up out of the lounger, grabbed the diaper bag, shifted Matty to her other hip, and walked out. Lorry and her daughters followed.

Feeling the disdain in that cold look, in the silent language of her body as she turned and walked away from him, Marco hated her. He hated her strength, her opinions, her overwhelming presence. Karen was nothing that a woman should be. He hated her ability to make him feel small. He was the heir to the Lorenzo family. She was just his niece, a stupid girl with no parents. Maddening.

Karen cut him out of her heart. She never entered that house again. If Mary wanted to see her, she had to wait at the front door, and they'd go somewhere in the car. She lost another member of her family, but this time from bad blood, not death or disease. Karen recognized the tainted quality of the relationship with her uncle and, like a cancer, cut it from her life. Burdened enough by life's circumstances, she didn't need mental anguish as a chaser.

Lorry was torn. That awful scene at the Lorenzos left her floundering. She didn't want to lose what family she had left, and they had just divided into two diametrically opposed camps. She wanted to pledge loyalty to both, but was afraid.

Karen talked to her about it. "Look, Lorry, if you want to have a relationship with them, by all means, do it. But it's just not working for me. He's a selfish, self-centered, egocentric disappointment, and I don't want to be attached to that anymore. Uncle Marco claims to have loved our mother so much; if she knew what he did, she'd be disgusted with him. All the bullshit about Texas, too. He could've come. If my sister was dying of cancer in another state, nothing would stop me from being there with her. That excuse about getting divorced was just a cop-out. He used it to get out of the responsibility. When he says he loves Mommy so much, I can't believe him. It's just air. Uncle Marco's love is conditional. As long as you do what he expects, and act the way he thinks you should, he'll love you. Challenge him in any way, and it's over." Karen's eyes were far away, remembering. "Do you remember when he taught me to play chess?"

"I think so."

"He told me the object of the game and showed me how each piece moves on the board. Then we played one game. He beat me." Karen's face grew hard. "I asked if we could try again. He said, *No. You lost. That was your one chance.* I kept at him, begged him to play just one more. He got mad, told me to go away. Do you know how old I was, Lorry?"

Lorry shook her head.

"I was nine. Nine-years-old."

"You're the one in my life I care about, Karen. If I had to choose between them and you, I'd always choose you. It was terrible, what he said. I don't want Rita and Toni to ever see anything like that again."

* * *

Karen gave birth to Dana Farley on November 5, 1990. During the labor, she kept thinking about the pool of blood and the dead baby. *Thanks, Norma.*

Shrieking and healthy, with a headful of golden fluff, Dana was a gorgeous little girl. Her proud parents had her examined from tip to toe. She was perfect.

After the baby was born, Karen's pain grew worse. She shoved it to the back of her mind. Thanksgiving was coming, and she wanted the fantasy, if only for a little while, of a happy family.

The obstetrician fed her dream, brushing away questions about increasing pain with the lackadaisical excuse of a contracting uterus.

Weeks went by, the pain increased, and Karen thought blackly that her uterus must have contracted to the size of a peanut by now. "Maybe it'll just contract until it disappears! Feels like a black hole by now."

Christmas that year was a joyous occasion. Too grateful to mention the hidden fears inside her body, Karen focused on the good. Her children were safe and well. Matt was out of danger, Dana was born, and even Lorry was doing better.

Christmas. By far her favorite holiday, Karen excelled at Christmas. The baking and the decorating, the mess and the fuss, the total transformation of her house into a winter wonderland. Threats of the unknown couldn't touch her in the magic of the holiday.

Over four hundred cupcakes were baked for the local orphanage's Christmas party, and Karen did it alone. The pain of bending over, time and again, to slip trays of cupcakes into the oven, then slide them out again, left her exhausted. It took days to bake and decorate them all. When she was finished, she started on the hundreds of holiday cookies left to make.

Despite the physical pain, this was the happiest Christmas Karen had ever experienced. No mention of her fears or discomfort; Karen kept her mouth shut. She wanted this time, this brief moment without hospitals or funerals, where no one was crying or unhappy, where everything was joy.

New Year's Eve rolled around, and the Farleys stayed home. Karen didn't feel well. Richard went to bed early, but she and Matt stayed up and watched the ball drop on TV, ringing out 1990 and welcoming 1991. They wore hats and blew noisemakers, and Karen almost wept with happiness. The pain was immaterial. She had now, this moment, and was grateful for it.

A few days later, Lorry came over for a healing session. Happy to play guinea pig again, Karen lay on the wooden floor. Lorry put a pillow under her head.

There were more gold nodules than ever. Lorry looked nervously at Karen's face. She was obviously suffering. Working together, trading quips and little jokes that only sisters understood, Lorry slid her hands slowly up and down Karen's body. There were hot patches everywhere. Karen gently mocked her concern.

Richard came home, and they ate dinner. A typical day, nothing special or marked in its lines. They watched TV; Karen complained about a bad cold that was acting up again. "I can't seem to shake it."

Putting Dana to bed, she decided to go to sleep early. Richard stayed up a little longer with Matty. Then he, too, went to bed.

In the middle of the night, Karen woke with a jerk, her abdomen spasming like a great knife wound. Her fantasy world over, she lay curled on her side, fighting the reality. Reality was pain, and fear, and something she didn't want to name yet.

Around two o'clock in the morning, it became too much, and Karen's threshold of pain was breached. She couldn't get any air. Breathing was a torment. She woke Richard.

Taking one look at her white face, he sprang out of bed. "What is it?" Richard watched her hand start to shake, then curl into a fist to hide. He placed his palm on her shoulder. The touch was steady and sure.

He has such big hands.

Breath-stealing in its intensity, Karen called Doctor Weil and told him the pain felt as if she were being stabbed.

"How long have you been having all this pain, Karen?" he asked.

"Since my first trimester."

"What? Why didn't you say anything? Didn't you tell your obstetrician?"

"He told me it's just the uterus contracting after birth. He said it's normal."

This pain—this was not normal.

"Karen, go to the emergency room. I'll meet you there."

Karen took a taxi to the hospital, insisting Richard stay with the children.

An abdominal sonogram was performed, revealing a grossly enlarged spleen.

Doctor Weil will be in soon to see you. The staff made sure she was as comfortable as possible. Ticking away the minutes with constant glances at her watch, she waited.

Someone in the hallway was talking about a spleen the size of Texas. Karen wondered, uncomfortably, if they were talking about her.

Richard came, having made arrangements for a baby-sitter. He'd brought her a thermos of coffee from home, which she couldn't drink. She was cold, so he tucked the blankets around her, then threw his coat on top. They didn't talk much, just quiet tension and murmured endearments. Waiting.

Pushing back the privacy curtain, Doctor Weil stepped in, test results in his hand, and shook his head.

"Karen, your spleen is very enlarged," he said. "I want a CAT scan done immediately. We can admit you, and get it done right away, or we can do it on an outpatient basis. That's fine, too. But I want these tests done right away."

"I want to go home."

She called Lorry and told her to set up another reading with Norma. Despite the debacle of the last time, Karen had questions, and Norma might have answers.

Two days later, she went for the CAT scan, forcing herself to lie still, despite the pain, as the machine took endless five-millimeter photos of her body. By the time they told her to go home and wait for the results, Karen was exhausted.

Since she was still seeing Norma, despite an earlier vow not to, Lorry had no trepidation calling for an appointment. When she told the medium about baby Dana and the successful birth, Norma snapped, "Of course. If your sister hadn't come here, she'd be dead now. I'm having another seance. Bring her to that. Somebody's been asking for her, and he's driving me crazy."

Lorry conveyed the message to Karen, whose first reaction was fear, then acceptance of yet another bizarre page in her life.

Vehemently opposed to her seeing Norma, but unable to change her mind, Richard insisted on going with them.

Norma was as recalcitrant as ever. Names were barked out, and people raised their hands.

Richard kept glancing over at Karen, grimacing in distaste. It was too weird for him.

Then Norma called out again. "Norm? Norb? Norb from Sears ... no ... Sperry's, wants to talk to Karen."

Norb? Did she mean Norbert? Karen leaned forward. Her father had worked at Sperry's.

"I'm here," she said.

"Karen, you're going to be very sick. It'll look bad, but you'll be cured in three months."

"What's wrong with me?"

"You don't need to know yet."

"If you don't tell me, how can I believe?"

"You don't need to know yet."

"If you don't tell me, I can't believe."

"Lymphoma cancer."

Karen reared back, Lorry gasped, and even Richard felt his stomach flip at that one.

Then his disbelief returned, and all he felt was anger. *What was this bitch thinking, telling this garbage to Karen? If she's hurt by this, I'm going to destroy this woman. I'll tear her apart in court. I'll put her in jail.*

Karen was speaking again. "Lymphoma? How bad?"

"It will look very, very bad, but you'll be cured in three months."

Falling silent, Norma sagged in her chair.

"He's gone."

They left soon after.

Furious, it took Richard hours to convince Karen not to buy into any of this junk. Despite his own assurances, he had a hard time relaxing after they went to bed. Gently, so as not to hurt her, he pulled Karen close, wrapped his arms around, and fell asleep, her head on his chest.

Karen waited until Richard's breathing became deep and even, then slid out of bed, careful not to wake him.

She wanted to see her children. Karen tiptoed into their room.

Matt lay spread-eagled on his daybed, mouth hanging open, a peek of a bellybutton where his pajama top had ridden up. Bending to kiss his warm belly, she covered him up.

Dana was face down, bottom in the air, snoring softly. Karen rubbed her hand up and down the little baby back, gliding over the diaper and tiny spine inside her pink fluffy sleeper. Just starting to grow soft, downy curls on her head, Karen wondered if Dana's hair would be blonde as a teenager.

The tears came then, wept silently at the prospect of a future cut short, of children who might not know their mother.

Then, squaring her shoulders, Karen set her jaw and went back to bed. Richard was a big warm comfort to curl up against as she waited for dawn.

Doctor Weil called the next day. The results of the CAT scan were back.

"Karen, I want you to meet me in the emergency room today. Right now, if possible. Ask Richard to come with you."

"Why do I need Richard?"

"I think it'd be better if you didn't come alone."

"What? What is it? Can't you just tell me over the phone?"

"No. Come into emergency, and we'll talk about it."

Richard got the call at his office.

"I'll be right there."

They got Jennifer down the street to come in and baby-sit. Together, they walked through the emergency doors and up to the counter, giving their names. They were shown into an examining room and told to wait.

Karen was visibly trembling, so Richard talked about nonsense in an attempt to calm her fears. Because Karen was terrified. More frightened than he'd ever seen her, even with Matty.

Doctor Weil arrived, striding along the corridor beside Karen's obstetrician, who'd been called from upstairs where he'd just delivered a baby.

Richard and Karen craned their necks for a better view. They could see the doctors through the little window in their door.

Weil was standing in the hallway, talking with the obstetrician. He had Karen's X-rays in one hand, and the results of the scan in the other. The obstetrician watched with a grim, white-faced solemnity.

Weil held the scan up to the light, and his face became stone. Karen and Richard watched every nuance of expression as he studied it. Then, the worst: Weil closed his eyes, a slow, tight press of the lids, and shook his head. His eyes opened and stared at the film, continuing that awful, disbelieving negation. He just stood there and shook his head. For thirty seconds. Then he turned and headed toward their room.

Fear, panic, terror, madness. So afraid. Karen had never felt such mind-numbing panic in all of her mind-numbing years. Like Lorry, she was suddenly confronted with the surprising fact that she wanted to live. Unlike Lupus, however, cancer had a shorter time schedule. It was faster, more impatient.

Doctor Weil came in waving the film. "I have something to tell you."

"Are you going to tell me I'm going to die?"

"No."

"Cancer?"

"Looks like it. Lymphoma, probably."

"How do you know?" Richard asked.

"We don't know for sure, not until a biopsy is performed. There are three large masses. We're going to have to schedule you for what's called a staging surgery. I'd like to do this immediately."

They discussed the procedure, and Doctor Weil suggested a surgeon to perform it. "I want it done in the next couple of days." Then he shook their hands, told her he would set everything up, and gave Karen one last tender glance.

"Everything'll be all right," he said. "Don't worry."

Then he left.

They'd gone into emergency in the early afternoon, and lunch was well past when they finally drove home. In survivor mode and deeply in shock as well, Karen was silent.

Richard's hand worked convulsively on the steering wheel, but other than that, he, too, was completely still.

Lorry's car was parked out front as they pulled into the driveway. Karen sighed. She didn't want to tell her sister yet. She was still trying to cope herself.

As the car pulled up, Lorry felt her stomach lurch. When she'd arrived with coffee and bagels for lunch and found no one there, she knew something was wrong. She couldn't get ahold of Richard, Karen and the babies were gone, and nobody knew where they were.

Jennifer had taken the kids to her own house.

The door opened. Richard and Karen came up the stairs to the living room.

Lorry was waiting. One look at Richard's face confirmed her fears, and everything Norma had said the night before came shrieking back into her head.

Karen mouthed platitudes for the first minute, and Lorry felt like she would scream if they didn't tell her soon.

"Now, don't worry, but I have some bad news," Karen began.

"What?"

"We got the results back from the CAT scan, and they found something."

"No." Lorry breathed the word.

"I'm going to be all right. I'm going to fight it."

"No."

Karen leaned her elbows on her knees and clasped her hands. Richard stood beside her.

"I have cancer, Lorry."

Lorry started screaming. She couldn't help it. Couldn't hold it in. Didn't even try, just screamed and screamed and screamed. The neighbors wondered if someone was being killed.

At the sight of her sister's white face, Lorry rallied herself. Wiping her cheeks, she swallowed her fear and began the all-important business of support. She was a master at it. Lorry poured love and bright future, warm as honey, over Karen's shoulders, and watched as her words took root.

With a brave face she was far from feeling, Karen drew strength from her husband and sister. The courage to fight would come with time, she knew, but right now, it had to be borrowed, and Lorry and Richard were there.

"I'm not afraid for you, Karen," Richard said. "Nothing's ever been able to beat you. You're not going to die. I know it."

Aunt Emily's first reaction was similar to Lorry's. Her new tenants came running to see her toppled over the phone, wailing, beating her heart with a clenched hand. Karen found herself comforting others, exhausted with the responsibility of hiding her own apprehension.

Cancer. This was her nightmare, the thing she had feared since she was nine-years-old. The malignancy which claimed her grandfather and parents had now set its sights on her. Knowing it was almost impossible to beat it, despite her brave words. They were said in false bravado. In reality, Karen had little hope, and no vision in stone could convince her otherwise.

There was one person she could turn to, one flicker of daybreak in a world gone black. Lynn. Karen could tell Lynn exactly what she felt, she'd been through it herself. Not once, but twice. And she was still here. That was a pearl beyond price, and right now, Karen needed a happy ending.

The floodgates opened as soon as Lynn said *hello*, and the whole story came out: Norma, the crass medium, the Texas-sized spleen, the sonogram, and last of all, the CAT scan. Karen finished with a tearful finality. "I've got cancer, Lynn."

"Good. It's what you've always wanted."

This wasn't the response Karen had anticipated.

"What?"

"Sure. You've dreamt about this since you were a child. Guilt's been eating you up. Why? Rita and Norbert Kikel are dead. You didn't save them. The only punishment worthy of such a crime is cancer. You've always wanted it. Now you've got it. The wait is over."

"I'm going to die."

Lynn laughed. "No, you're not. This is what you've always wanted. No more worries about getting cancer. It's arrived. Now, you can get rid of it. Go to it."

Karen laughed, a watery hiccup.

"You've been working at this for a long time, Karen. I hope it makes you feel less guilty, and you can get on with life now."

Lynn Wuest was creature of boundless energy. She always had been. After a loved one died in 1986, Lynn found she was growing more and more fatigued, far more than a rationalization of grief could explain.

Assuming it was fibrous tumors from a difficult menopause, Lynn checked herself into a women's clinic at the end of May, where they found a small malignancy.

Unwilling to accept the recommended surgery, which entailed total removal of the breast, Lynn shopped around. She found a surgeon at North Shore hospital in Manhasset who could take just a wedge, with the warning of a radical mastectomy if needed. The biopsy revealed her to be in second stage already. An aggressive routine of chemotherapy and radiation followed; ten months of chemo, pills every day, and the IV twice a month.

Mindset was all-important in the fight against her disease. Lynn used meditation, visualization, positive thinking, and imagination. Every day she exercised, even if it was only for ten minutes.

Family interaction was important. No negative conversations or drama.

Everyone has a phobia. Her teenage sons were troubled by the idea of her losing her hair.

Imagining she was inside her own scalp, Lynn grabbed the hair by the roots and held it in. This was her visualization during each IV infusion.

Thinking she was using ice packs to prevent the chemo from traveling to the scalp (an old trick, and a dangerous one), the doctors warned her about the perils of vanity during chemotherapy. The chemicals had to traverse every inch of the body, including the scalp.

When she lost only a small portion of hair, the doctors refused to consider it was anything other than pure luck. Lynn shrugged. People believe what they want to believe. She chose to believe in the power of her own mind, in doing her homework, and in good, hard work in this fight for life. Lynn chose to believe she'd be cured.

After several months of chemotherapy, Lynn was tattooed for radiation. She had thirty-eight treatments of radiation, which she found to be worse than chemo, because it hindered her life. Whereas with chemotherapy, she could function freely, if carefully, the radiation took up most of every day. Five days of radiation, two days of rest, five more days of radiation.

"The hardest part was the waiting room with all the other patients sitting, usually in pain, definitely in fear, all around me," Lynn said to Karen. "I always tried to stay positive, but in a closed setting like that, with so many ill people, many of them children, it was hard. Even then, I knew I wasn't alone. Even then, God sent me a gift."

A beautiful blonde woman approached her in the hospital. Lynn was sitting alone. The woman smiled and took her hand, kneeling down in front of her.

"Don't worry, Lynn. I'm going to be here for you. I couldn't believe it when I saw your name on the list. You changed my life, and I'm here for you now."

Lynn had no idea who she was.

Her name was Sarah, and Lynn had psychically read her two years ago.

"I was fat, depressed, and unfulfilled when I first came to you. You looked at me, and you were so funny. You said, *You don't like yourself? Then do something about it. Blondes have more fun. Cut your long hair; dye it blonde; go back to school. Become what you've always wanted. I see you doing it. I see you happy, and soon.*"

Sarah had left, dyed her hair, gone back to school, and lost sixty pounds. She became a radiologist, getting a job at the hospital where Lynn was to undergo her treatment. Full circle.

Other cancer survivors were of immeasurable import. A neighbor was diagnosed three weeks prior to Lynn, and they talked constantly on the phone, trading war stories.

"Do you have sores in your mouth yet?"

"No."

"Well, when you get them, this candy works really well."

Knowledge was power.

All this, Lynn told Karen openly, without fear or regret in her voice. It was simply what had happened.

"Listen to me, Karen. Everyone has a purpose. I don't believe God would have let you suffer so much, all your life, just to let you die now. There's something more here. There's something for you to do."

"What?"

"Don't have a clue. What I do know is, you've got your cancer at last. You saw it coming a long time ago. Now, what are we going to do about it?"

"I don't know."

"Read everything you can get your hands on about cancer survival. Do your homework. Be sure to keep an open mind, not confined by any one way of thinking. If something works, keep it, but don't limit yourself. Mix philosophies. Choose a handful of ideas, not just one or the other. Do them all!"

Giving Karen a list of books, Lynn told her to read them, then go out and find some new ones of her own.

Karen thanked her, and hung up.

Lynn went outside after they'd talked. Watching the sun set over the water, she took a deep breath of fresh air and blew it out slowly.

She'd known both sisters for over a decade now, and Lynn was grateful that it was Karen who got cancer and not Lorry. Both sisters were afraid of the disease, but life had made Lorry vulnerable and easily led, especially by men. Most doctors in the medical profession were still male. It would have been, perhaps, too intimidating for Lorry to question doctors about a disease both sisters quaked in fear about. And who could blame them? That fear might have been enough to shackle Lorry's ability to wage war, because war is what had to be fought. A disease with the effrontery to invade Karen's body was threatening her life. Lorry was facing Lupus admirably. If the disease had been named cancer, she might have buckled under the weight of her mother's fate and been too shattered to face such a battle.

Karen would have no such compunction. She'd dig through piles of bureaucratic dogma, regardless of the anxiety she might feel. Karen had the courage, as a girl of eighteen, to question the authority of the finest doctors in the world. When they'd run out of answers concerning her mother, Karen had not accepted any end-of-the road suggestions.

And her children. Lynn thanked God for Matt and Dana. Karen would fight to prevent their losing their mother; she would fight to stay with her children. Maybe her love for Matt and Dana would help her love herself. Karen was a nurturer, and strong inside, like an oak. She'd be able to stand fast in the maelstrom, and maybe inspire others to do the same. Lynn had always thought of Karen as a being of pure love. She knew she could also be a sword.

$\mathcal{O}$hapter 10: Full Circle

January 1991

She woke with a jerk, consciousness flooding in on a wave of pain. *God, it hurts! Jesus, Mary, and Joseph, it hurts!*

Lorry sat in the waiting room with Richard and prayed. Karen chose this hospital because it's where Grandma Lorenzo was. The old woman had suffered an asthmatic breakdown around the time of Karen's diagnosis. The hospital had an excellent cancer surgeon, and Doctor Weil was here.

The doctors had not been able to pinpoint an exact reason why Mary Lorenzo was dying, but dying she was. The losses of the past decade were too much for the feeble mind of the old woman, and she had collapsed soon after the New Year.

Karen and Lorry had visited every day, but Grandma was in and out of coherency, laughing a thick rope of glee. Her mind was gone. It was only a matter of time for the rest of her to follow. Flore Lorenzo was cooking sausages.

She died a few short hours before Karen went in for her own surgery. They didn't tell her until days later.

Lorry sat in the waiting room, thinking about Karen and her grandmother. *I was always ready to be the next one to go. When I got the Lupus diagnosis, I thought, well, this is it. Time to go.* She shivered. *Now look at me. Am I going to be the only one left? Is my sister even alive right now?*

Karen was not only alive, she was having a conversation with a strange and surreal creature floating above her hospital bed. It hovered over her, drifting effortlessly, spreading long and brilliant feathers of light over her entire body.

Who are you? Karen asked the question in her mind.

It just hovered, soft and gleaming, like headlights in a fog. Karen stared up at it, and the machinery keeping her alive hummed.

Am I dying?

"No."

Why are you here?

"For you."

I don't understand. Why has this happened to me? Why is everything that's ever happened to me been so terrible?

"You have been blessed."

Blessed? Blessed with suffering?

"Blessed with knowledge. You have been given a multitude of experiences and the understanding of them. You have been given a great gift, Karen. With this, you are going to help others. Many others. You are going to help people with cancer. Children, men, women. You are going to teach them how."

How to what?

"How to help themselves. The medicine of the future will be the strengthening of the mind and spirit. They must work as one to truly heal."

I can't do that. I've never been taught. I don't even know how to help myself. How do you expect me to help other people?

"A path will be provided for you. You have to stay on the path. Everything and everyone needed will be provided."

What do you mean, a path?

"People will be put into your life to help you. You have to learn to be open to this. What you need, will be provided. But, you have to stay on the path. Don't deviate."

What are you saying?

Question after question followed, in the silent voices of telepathy. A future undreamt of was laid out before her mind's eye, and Karen struggled to take it all in. Finances, phobias, fears of the unknown, of her own abilities, of public opinion; it answered them all. Visions played before her eyes: a house, a book for children with cancer, another book with Lorry and her picture on the cover—dozens of sights that confused and frightened her. Dates, times, events, people, even a book and CD ROM were mentioned as tools to spread the knowledge. Karen was still reluctant.

"I'm not a religious person. I do believe in God. Over the years, I've developed my own definition of faith. My family didn't practice religion, not really. Why me? I'm certainly not worthy.

"This is why you are here."

I don't see how it'll be possible for me to do all this. I don't even know if I'll be here in a month.

"You will. You will heal. Not just the physical. You will heal the spirit as well. If you don't heal the spirit and mind, your physical can never truly heal. They all must be united. If not, disease will enter again. We will help you."

Heat was radiating out of the entity, spreading like warm oil throughout her limbs, burning when it touched her torso. She panicked.

What are you doing?

"I'm healing you."

Why? Why would you choose to help me? I'm nothing. If I died, I'd be forgotten. I can't do everything you want me to. I'll probably fail.

"Everything happens for a reason. This is your reason."

I don't even have the education or influence to do this. How can I possibly do any of the things you're saying?

"You will. You have been learning since you were born."

Learning? Learning what? How to be miserable?

"How to understand pain and suffering. It's only then that your spirit is forced to grow. You must stay on the path. We have always been with you. We will continue to always be with you. If you stay on the path, everything you need will be provided."

What path?

"Your path. No one else's. Your path. Everyone has one."

It was comforting, this strange vision, soothing her with smooth colors and warmth. Even its words were a solace, unlikely as they were. The apparition seemed somehow ancient in its deep tones. She looked at it and thought, *I must be hallucinating. I'm just seeing and hearing what I want. I'm so desperate for help, any help, that I've created this in my mind. It can't possibly be real.*

This was the same Doubting Thomas philosophy that had always plagued and supported Karen. She felt the pain being pulled out like one giant, aching tooth. The entity didn't answer her skepticism verbally; it simply began showing her her entire life. Past, present, and future passed before her eyes in one suddenly clear montage of cause and effect, and Karen could see the lessons hard learned.

I never would've thought to say this. Maybe there's something to it, after all. Maybe this isn't a hallucination.

Comforted by the idea, she relaxed further into the bed, her pain much better. If her lips had been free, a smile would have touched them.

She slept.

The next time she woke, Lorry and Richard were with her. Her hand made a writing motion, and Lorry fetched pen and paper.

Will one of you please stay with me tonight? I'm afraid to be alone.

They took shifts. Lorry stayed the first night, Richard was there the second. She told them about the vision, and the entity's words. Truth is stranger than fiction. They believed her.

The test results came back, confirming Doctor Weil's worst fears. He read the sheets, pinched his nose, sniffed, and read them again. Sighing, he steeled himself, and went to tell the Farleys.

Surrounded by get-well cards, Karen was lying in her hospital bed, talking to Richard. Doctor Weil smiled at them, banishing his trepidation, and began a soft flow of conversation. Then he told them.

"The test results are back, and they do show malignant growth."

"They couldn't cut it all out?"

"No."

Weil felt as if he'd just struck a child. The color leeched from her face.

"What kind of cancer is it?"

"It appears to be Hodgkin's Lymphoma. There's also some mixed cellularity, which indicates possible Non-Hodgkin's as well. I'm afraid it's advanced. Fourth stage."

"Fourth stage?" Richard didn't know what that meant. Karen did.

"There are four stages of cancer. The higher the number, the more advanced the disease. Karen has 4B Lymphoma."

Richard felt his body go numb. *Not Karen. Karen can't die. She's too strong.*

All the nightmares, all the waiting; now it was happening. Twenty-seven, cut into a stone.

Recommending an oncologist, Weil made arrangements for her to come up and see Karen that day. As he was leaving, Karen asked, "Doctor Weil, about the surgery. Was I on any hallucinogenic drugs?"

"Why? Did you see something after you woke up?"

"I was just wondering."

"I'll look into it if you want."

"No. No, that's okay."

Later, puzzled by something, the surgeon came to ask Karen a few questions.

"Mrs. Farley, the lab results showed your spleen to be ninety-eight percent covered with tumor. We had to take it out. There was no other choice. What I'm confused about, is your recent pregnancy. You just had natural childbirth, right? How old is the baby? Two-and-a-half months?" He pursed his lips. "You know, it's amazing that you had no complications. Miraculous, actually. Someone whose spleen is diseased to that extent ... even driving over a bump in the road could make it rupture. And you had natural childbirth? That's extraordinary."

You and your child will die in a pool of blood.

Richard's fingers touched her shoulder. He was staring at the surgeon.

Karen let out a deep breath. "I guess I've already started beating the odds, huh?"

"You have at that. Certainly impressed me. Good luck to you."

It wasn't Norma's frightening prophesy that filled Karen's mind at that moment. As she watched the surgeon leave, she could only think of the other one. *You will be cured in three months.*

Now I've got something to hang onto. Thank you, Lorry. Thank you for bringing me to Norma.

Lorry was at their grandmother's wake. A small crowd gathered around her, curiosity steering their feet. Where was Karen? That's what they all wanted to know. How could she not be here? Didn't she know how much her grandmother loved her?

Lorry's answer was blunt. "She's just been diagnosed with fourth stage Lymphoma. She's in the hospital. The surgery didn't get everything."

Disinterested in the ripple effect she'd just caused, Lorry returned to her sister. She played the clown, telling funny stories of odd students in her psychic awareness class, doing everything possible to ease her sister's suffering through laughter.

Karen found herself laughing a lot during her two-week stay in the hospital. Whenever she began to lose heart, Lorry reminded her of the message from Norbert.

"Remember, you're going to be cured in three months."

Also supportive, Richard bolstered her courage with his unshakable certainty that she was going to live. If she needed anything, Lorry or Richard got it for her.

Knowledge is power. She asked Lorry to go to the library and find books on how terminal cancer patients survive.

Lorry brought her a Walkman, but the New Age tapes she provided were too unorthodox for Karen.

"I need something more down to earth, Lorry. Something written by a doctor or a scientist, or somebody who's actually had cancer and survived."

Lorry found a small selection of tapes; one by Doctor Bernie Siegel and another by Louise Hay. These were far more to Karen's liking.

Louise Hay was a cancer survivor who'd used the power of the mind to heal herself. She never took any medication and never needed surgery.

If she can do it, why can't I?

Her favorite among all the books she read was *Getting Well Again,* by Doctor Carl O. Simonton and Doctor Stephanie Simonton. It cited documented cases of people helping themselves with such simple ideas as positive thinking and diet. Karen read and re-read her copy until it was dog-eared and feathery around the edges.

And Richard? He was her rock, her anchor. Karen's room was festooned with flowers, candy, magazines, photos of their children; whatever she wanted, he brought it. Anything to give a loved one pleasure, he tried to think of, even bringing chocolate and cookies for the hospital staff.

When he sat beside her bed, Richard was surprised to find himself unable to stop touching her. Her hand, her hair, a soft kiss. Karen fed on these simple pleasures. To Richard, they reaffirmed that she was alive. He wasn't repulsed by all the machinery, the bloat or the checkerboard scars on her abdomen. This was his Karen, fighting for her life. That was enough. He knew she'd live.

The doctors had a different opinion. They looked at Karen's chart, then up at her, startled, and their faces closed over. Each new test was met with a similar wall of reserve as soon as they clapped eyes on her. One thoughtless technician went so far as to chastise her for even having children.

"If I had a genetic history like yours, I never would have had children," he said. "I think it's irresponsible and selfish. Why did you?"

Too shocked to answer and too frightened by the test to respond, Karen lay stunned by his callous statement while he finished the procedure. At first, she wasn't sure she'd even heard him correctly. If someone had dared say something like that to her mother or another loved one, Karen would have gone straight for his jugular. But it was her this time, lying on a table, full of cancer, and he was performing a test that would help her. Fear and pain made her vulnerable, and she was angry at both him and herself.

This relentless fear bothered Karen. It wouldn't leave her alone. Every waking moment was dominated by pain and fear. Here was she, Karen Farley, who'd always been so tough, now mindless at times with terror. Where was the brave woman Lynn bragged about? Where was Lorry's "stone" that never cried? Why wasn't that Karen showing her face? The only ones here were scared-to-death Karen, nervous Karen, cowardly Karen. She was waiting for Amazon Karen to stand up and take over, but so far, she was a no-show. The only personalities left seemed to have a streak of pure yellow down their backs.

And the visions, all the time now. She found she could now read people effortlessly. She didn't try; it just kept happening. Feeling as if she had one foot on the physical plane and one foot in the spiritual, Karen was shifting back and forth between the two. Friends came to visit, and she discovered lost articles for them by touching a watch or piece of clothing. Bizarre and scary, but also invigorating. Karen latched onto that feeling. Anything positive was good, and she began enjoying people's shock when she hit on a truth.

Coming to see her after the surgery, Scott De Simone was one of these.

They talked pleasantries and bad news together for a few minutes; then she told him about her strange entity vision.

"I've always been psychic, Scott, but it seems to be escalating now."

"Huh?"

"I'm psychic. I can read people."

"Karen ... "

"I always thought it was just my weird imagination taking control, but there've been way too many coincidences for me to believe that anymore."

Oh, no. She's really lost it. Poor Karen. What else is going to happen to her?

Scott realized, more than most, the trauma this dear girl had gone through. He'd known her for fifteen years. Who could blame Karen if she had a breakdown now, after such a life?

Karen grinned.

"I know, sounds like I'm nuts, but I swear it's true."

"So ... " he was struggling. " ... how are you psychic?"

"Hand me something of yours that's important, something I don't know about, and I'll see if I can get anything from it."

Scott fished in his pocket. Hell, she'd been through enough. He'd humor her. His hand touched his keys, and he pulled them out.

On the key chain was an old dog tag. Smooth and weathered, it didn't look like a dog tag at all, just a simple round metal disc. The engraving had worn off long ago. It'd belonged to the most beloved pet Scott had ever had. A family dog who'd disappeared years ago, long before Scott met Karen. He'd never talked about the animal. Even today, the loss was hard felt.

Karen took the tag and rubbed it between her fingers. Scott wanted to stroke her hair and tell her everything would be all right, but he knew Karen. Very reserved in the face of tragedy. She always had been. Maybe she'd finally snapped. It was perfectly understandable; Scott knew he'd never be able to handle ...

"Kirby."

He jumped like a scalded cat, and his eyes flew wide.

"I don't know if this'll mean anything to you, but I see the letters K-I-R-B-Y. Kirby."

Scott's heart started hammering.

"I see a dog. It's walking ... "

Holding his breath, he waited for her to continue.

"He was lost. Kirby was lost. Running, just having a good time. He was only a few blocks from home, but he panicked. He didn't know where he was."

Scott sat forward, all semblance of disbelief gone. He didn't care about the odds of such a vision, didn't care what happened to bring it about. All he wanted, at that moment, was for Karen to keep talking. He had to know. What happened to his dog?

"He started running in the wrong direction. So scared. Where's home? Where is it? Then, a little boy saw him and gave him some of his sandwich. He was nice, a very nice boy. He brought him home. Kirby followed him home."

Scott's eyes welled with tears.

"He didn't die, Scott. Wasn't hit by a car. He was fine. They adopted him. He lived for a long time, only a mile-and-a-half from your house. I see the number fourteen, which can mean he lived another fourteen years, or he was fourteen when he died. He was happy. Don't worry about it anymore. He was happy. Missed you, though."

Lost for words, Scott stared at this remarkable woman and wondered at depths he hadn't imagined.

Karen grinned.

"How do you do this? Do you see Kirby?"

"Well ... initially, I saw an image of a dog. It's like I'm inside his head, seeing what he sees, feeling what he feels."

"He lived for fourteen more years?"

"Yeah. He was one old dog."

"How do you know his name?" Scott laughed, amazed. "It's the weirdest thing."

"I see a big curved stone, like granite or something, and in big fiery letters it spelled out K-I-R-B-Y. They just sort of etched themselves into the rock face."

"I can't believe it."

"I told you."

"Does Richard know?"

"Yeah. He knows all about it."

"Do you read him?"

"Sometimes. I try not to read people if they don't want me to. With Richard, things just come. At times, it gives me a headache. It's very draining; especially in a room with a lot of people thinking loudly."

"That is amazing."

Word got out about Karen's abilities. Soon the night nurses were lined up for readings. She enjoyed the attention, and it kept her mind occupied. Reactions were never mixed. Every person was stunned at her accuracy.

The chemotherapy began less than two weeks after her surgery. She used the oncologist Doctor Weil suggested.

He also encouraged her to shop around for other opinions. "Get a second, third, and fourth opinion if you want. It's always wise to do your homework. In the interim, you can begin Doctor Webster's treatment."

Webster was a pleasant woman, very friendly. She seemed more than capable as an oncologist, but Karen felt uncertain. The knowing whispered that this was the wrong choice.

Doctor Webster mapped out a horror of a future plan. One year of chemotherapy, then radiation, then a bone marrow transplant. Overwhelmed, Karen thought she'd better start taking matters into her own hands.

Lorry and Richard were both present for her first chemotherapy infusion.

Scared to death, weak in the knees from memories of Rita's violent nausea, Karen began the treatment.

Lorry put on a brave face and amused her sister with jokes, entertaining Karen for the two-and-a-half hours it took for the infusion to flow into her arm. "Try visualization, Karen. Imagine the chemo going everywhere, cleaning out the cancer. Or, if you'd rather be physical, imagine kicking the lymphoma's ass. Surround yourself with white light."

By this time, Lorry had fully embraced the transcendental world. Approaching the founder of the Metaphysical Learning Center in Levittown, she'd informed him that she wanted to take classes but was hampered by circumstance.

"I'm a single mother with two children. I have Systemic Lupus, and I'm helping a sister battle cancer right now. I can't attend any outside classes." Lorry took a deep breath and plunged in. "I'd like to start a group in my own house. How do I do it?"

And as simple as that, Lorry became the Wednesday hostess of a group class on the metaphysical. Every conceivable type of strange human being walked in her door on Wednesday evenings. Lorry began to think, sometimes with delight, sometimes with trepidation, that she was living and breathing a real, live science fiction show.

There were classes on reading auras, reading people, past life regression, time travel, the Philadelphia Project, alien abduction, alien offspring with telekinetic abilities, out-of-body astral projection. Meditations on Atlantis, the healing art of music and tones, mantras and chanting. Aromatherapy, Bach flower remedies, angels and healing rays, the importance and placement of the body's chakras, and the effects of the full moon. There were topless Lo Mei Lo Mei dancers, Hawaiian healing techniques, Native American medicine men and the strangest of all, the man with the gong.

Lorry picked him up from the train station. When she asked him on the phone, "How will I know you?" he answered quite dryly, "Simple. I'm the man with the gong."

When she got to the train station, Lorry spotted him immediately. The gong was three feet wide in diameter. Healing took place, theoretically, with the vibrations of the gong being struck while he blew on a conch shell. Lorry got blown, gonged, and was paid for the strange pleasure of it all.

She was in heaven. Repressed all her life, Lorry suddenly found herself surrounded by the freakiest, weirdest, most hilarious and wonderful bunch of people in the world. She tried it all, and a basket at the front door was filled with donations that reimbursed any expenses she had. Lorry felt as if she'd stumbled onto her destiny, and it was straight out of the Twilight Zone. Laughing at it all, she distilled her learning into sessions of healing with a skeptical Karen. Lorry didn't care about the general reaction of cynicism to what she was doing. This was something she was passionate about, and the passion sustained her. That, and the belief that by doing so, she could help to heal not only Karen, but perhaps herself. So, Lorry endured the sarcastic gibes of family and friends and went on with her classes.

Karen, remembering Bill Kelly and all he'd put them both through, worried endlessly about her two young nieces and the parade of oddballs filtering through Lorry's house. What characters marched through the doors didn't matter, so long as her nieces were safe. She thought, uncomfortably, about Rita and Toni's bedroom, right across the hall from the bathroom, and asked what type of screening Lorry was doing to protect them.

"My friend Janice stays and watches over everything while I'm in class. She's usually in the kitchen making tea or whatever. The kitchen's right by their bedroom."

"Okay. I'm glad you've got a friend watching them. You know me, Lorry. I hear about the gong man, and I worry."

"Yeah. He was hot, though, with that gong."

Karen burst out laughing.

Lorry carried humor like other people carried their wallets. She took her new knowledge with her whenever she was with her sister, using it as a source of both amusement and inspiration to Karen during the chemo sessions.

The first two weeks of infusion were with the MOPP combination drugs. The IV the first day, the pills the remaining six, then the IV again, and pills to the end of the second week. Then a two-week rest period, and the cycle would begin again.

With this first experience of chemo, Karen was in the *Gung Ho* mode of wanting to destroy the cancer. Afraid, but tempered with the determination to get well. She talked to the drugs as they slid into her vein, telling them where to go, how to fight, how to heal her. Since she'd read all she could find on the traumas of chemotherapy, Karen was in the mindset of naiveté. *I can handle it. I'm ready for it.* Only to discover her own innocence.

Nothing can prepare you for it. Unlike normal knowledge, things didn't get better with experience. In chemotherapy, especially the radically high doses Karen was receiving, they get worse. The patient knows what's coming.

She discovered bumps all over her arm the morning after her second infusion, painful nodules that were hard to the touch.

Doctor Webster apologized. "The bumps are caused by chemo infusion which had infiltrated your arm yesterday. Put simply, the needle must have moved, and some of the chemo leaked into the muscle tissue around your vein. I'm sorry, Mrs. Farley, but you'll probably need plastic surgery to remove them."

Lorry recommended visualization again.

"Just imagine the bumps disappearing, Karen. Use your mind to tell your body how to do it. Give it direction, and visualize the nodules dissolving until they're gone."

Thinking about Lorry's suggestion, Karen knew that she could do it. No voices, no carvings in stone, just a certainty. Yogi masters could do amazing things with their minds, slowing their heart rates, raising or lowering their body temperatures. Tibetan monks, sitting on mountaintops in the dead of winter, melting great patches of snow around them, simply by focusing their minds. If they could do it, why not Karen Farley? She had a powerful mind. She just had to focus and believe. The limitations of a lifetime of learning would be set aside. Karen decided to make herself limitless.

Her first target was the nodules. Staring at her arm for a long time, Karen pondered what course of action to take. "Re-absorb," she whispered, and began her visualization. Faith is a state of mind, a matter of choice. *I can do this.* Karen chose to believe it.

Everything was included in the process. She talked to her immune system, to the cells surrounding the bumps, to the nodules themselves. Like a mantra, she repeated key words, concentrating, focusing everything on gaining control of her body's functions. She ordered them to do what her mind wanted, set her will against the scar tissue. After two days, the pain became less. After three weeks, the nodules began to shrink. After six weeks, they would be gone. She never had surgery.

* * *

At Karen's request, Doctor Weil recommended another oncologist, one with a string of credentials. Chairman of the oncology department of a major hospital in Manhattan, his specialty was lymphoma cancers. Karen was in the two-week interval between chemo regimens. During that time, she got three additional opinions.

Richard took her into the city, where they met the doctor in his office.

Having reviewed her case, his words were blunt and pessimistic. He was also very busy. "Your doctor's got you on MOPP therapy," he began. "Now, before I give my opinion on how I'd treat your case, I want to tell you what I think about the therapy you're on now.

Over twenty-five years ago, MOPP was the standard therapy in treating your type of cancer. Today, it's archaic. If that's all you're going to use, your chances of survival are zero. Even if the cancer goes away, there's a high chance of reoccurrence.

What I suggest, and I think it'll give you about a twenty percent chance of survival, is the combination of ABVD. It's a very aggressive chemotherapy, probably the second most aggressive regimen known to man. You'll be very sick, and your hair'll fall out, but I think it's the best choice. You'd have a better chance with this. I would tell you to receive the treatment in the hospital, in case of any complications. You go in a couple days, then you come home."

Karen and Richard just stared.

"Could you back up a minute?" Karen asked. "Did you say that I had a twenty percent chance of survival *if* I do the medication that you're suggesting, but zero percent if I only do MOPP alone? The treatment I'm doing right now?" This was the first time anyone had quoted odds to her.

He nodded.

No words could describe Karen's emotions. She found that there were stages of reality she knew nothing about. The physical pain of the cancer had been one wake up call. This latest one tore off her rose-colored glasses and exposed her completely, raw and open. Reality forced her to see something she'd refused to look at, and now she couldn't turn away. She broke down.

Richard wrapped an arm around her, fighting devastation himself. For long minutes, neither could get past the figure of twenty percent. It ran around the room like a sentient pair of digits, terrifying, laughing, and loud.

After the bout of hysteria was over, Karen switched to survival mode. Her present oncologist was not for her, but neither was this man. She appreciated his honesty. In hindsight, it might help save her life. But she needed to find someone she could have absolute confidence in, and Karen wouldn't stop until she did.

During the interval in her chemotherapy regimen, Karen thought often about Uncle Marco. Bothered by the bad blood, she wanted to heal the breech. He was family, and Karen had precious little of that left. She had cancer, was fighting for her life. Marco needed to be forgiven. This was a golden opportunity for him to be forgiven.

"Call him," the voices whispered, and she looked up. "The things are not important. They're just things. This is for Marco. Do this for him. Give him this chance."

She struggled with the idea. After Mary Lorenzo's death, it was discovered their grandmother, riddled with guilt, had added a codicil to her will, which left Lorry and Karen a small property in Florida and several bits and pieces from her house. It was a codicil Marco chose to ignore. Neither sister wanted to pursue it. Their lives were preoccupied with other things now.

It was very difficult, the thought of forgiving a man who'd betrayed her, her mother, and her sister so utterly. *And for what? For little bits of nothing.* The thought of leaving herself open to rejection was difficult.

Still, life was too short to fill up with anger, and it had just gotten a whole lot shorter. Karen wanted to let go of her rage, give it back to Marco, maybe even give him the chance to dispel it.

She called Lorry about the idea of healing the breach, and Lorry praised her for her spirituality, all for healing of any sort.

Karen dialed the number. Marco answered.

"Hello?"

"Uncle Marco, it's Karen."

Silence.

"You know what I've been going through, Uncle Marco. About the cancer and all. A lot of things have been running through my mind. I want you to know I'm willing to work at a new relationship between us, if you are too. We're family, Uncle Marco. I really want us to be friends."

Karen meant every word. Anything would be better than the soured animosity they now had.

Uncomfortable with such talk, Marco considered her words. If Karen had been well, perhaps he'd have lashed out, but the cancer made him hesitate. He knew his niece was dying.

"Karen ... you know I never wished for anything bad to happen to you or your family."

"I know, Uncle Marco."

"You and I just never saw eye-to-eye about things."

"I know. When I don't agree with something, I have to say it. It's how I am."

"Well ... you're a fighter. I'm sure you'll stay tough and fight the cancer."

"Yeah," Karen laughed weakly. "So, what do you think? Do you want to try again? Have a relationship with me?"

Karen sat and waited on the phone, her heart pounding. Marco was silent for a long time. Then, she heard him sigh.

"I'll have to think about it," he said.

They never spoke again.

The two-week interval was going quickly, and Karen was still looking for a new oncologist.

Lorry's connections and good memory came to the fore. Karen told her about the twenty percent chance man, and the zero percent woman, and Lorry suddenly remembered a friend of the family, Bob Goldstein, who'd survived advanced leukemia for twenty years now. He'd gotten to the stage of one-hundred-and-six-degree temperatures and coma before proper diagnosis and chemotherapy but had still survived. Even beating the diagnosis of sterility, he was the proud father of a little girl.

For the first three months of his illness, he'd been misdiagnosed with mononucleosis. The doctor who helped bring him back from the edge was named Bidnold.

Doctor Joseph Bidnold, in his late sixties, walked with a slow stiffness from his own battle with colon cancer. He'd been in remission for three years.

Bidnold had a no-nonsense manner which grated and reassured at the same time. He reviewed Karen's case, and disagreed with both the other oncologists.

"Well, the way I think you should go is a hybrid of both MOPP and ABVD. An incredibly high dose of chemo, but I think that'd give you the best chance of survival. I also recommend a pneumonia vaccine. They last for ten years."

Something clicked. Karen stared at him, assessing his personality, reading bits and pieces about the man from his body language and self-confidence. With credentials beyond reproach, plus the fact that he'd saved Bob Goldstein from fourth stage leukemia, Karen felt she'd found her oncologist.

"I'd like to suggest another thing," he said. "There's a new drug on the market called Neupogen which stimulates the white blood cells in the bone marrow."

"Why is that important?" Karen asked.

"Sometimes, when you're on such an aggressive regimen of chemotherapy, you may not get treatments on time because your white blood cell count might be too low. Neupogen can possibly help with this by stimulating the growth of white blood cells in your bone marrow. The downside is, it's very expensive. Some insurance companies won't pay for it. Also, you have to give self-injections at home. Your blood cell count has to be monitored once a week, maybe more, to make sure that you stop the Neupogen once your white count gets too high. It can skyrocket very quickly in some people, so the monitoring is essential."

Talk of expense always made Karen nervous. When a doctor says a drug is so expensive that the insurance companies refuse to pay for it, she felt tentative and worried.

Richard brushed aside her concerns. "Don't worry about it, Karen. If you need it, we'll get it. Just leave it to me."

He took her home, went to the office, rolled up his sleeves, and picked up the phone. It took weeks of constant nagging and bureaucratic, evasive nonsense on the end of the insurance company, but Karen got her Neupogen. Richard resorted to half-threats to get it; he wouldn't take no for an answer. It cost the insurance company six thousand dollars a month.

Karen went home and did homework, studying the side effects of every chemo drug in the regimen. The *D* in ABVD had negative side effects on lung tissue. With her history of asthma, Karen decided against *D*, choosing to go with just MOPP and ABV chemotherapy.

Years later, a gastroenterologist told her the decision probably saved her life.

The second regimen began. Karen had been told that the ABV was a stronger set of drugs, and she was very nervous. *I barely handled the MOPP. How am I going to deal with something stronger?*

As luck would have it, her body responded better to the ABV than to the MOPP. The cycle was the same: a week of MOPP, a week of ABV, two weeks rest, then repeat.

Always cool and arrogant, Doctor Bidnold brushed aside questions about mind/body connection and alternative medicine with a disdainful hand. When pressed, he did admit that studies were being done on positive thinking, and he himself had noticed that optimistic patients seemed to do better. "But," he said, "it's the chemicals and doctors who save lives, not happy thoughts."

Despite this close-minded opinion, Karen admired his credentials and his brain. Bidnold was obviously very intelligent, and he truly wanted to cure her, was concerned about her well-being. That, in itself, was well worth a little arrogance.

By this time, Karen could no longer walk unaided. Lorry gave her their mother's cane. She had used it herself during Lupus flares. Karen felt strangely comforted by it; by Rita's and Lorry's acrylic cane.

"I can feel my skeleton, Lorry. It's too heavy. I can't hold it up anymore."

The loss of strength in her limbs depressed her. Karen worried about the atrophy already setting in. Remembering Lynn's advice, she bought a treadmill and used it as often as she could, if only for a few minutes.

Despite the positive words, despite any vision to the contrary, Karen was, of course, sometimes terrified that she was going to die. When she'd told Bidnold about all her health problems, starting with an ovarian cyst at the age of twelve, a peptic ulcer at fifteen, the asthma and panic attacks, he'd nodded.

"Classic history for cancer patients. This isn't uncommon."

His dry solemnity never failed to depress her. Searching for optimism, she had to dig deep inside her heart to find it.

Books about terminal cancer patients, who lived despite the odds, were her favorites. Five volumes, in particular, stood out among the rest.

The first was called *Getting Well Again,* written by Doctors Carl O. and Stephanie Simonton. Lorry had bought that one years ago for Rita, who'd never followed it. *I'm too tired, Lorry. You do it for me.*

Karen embraced the book, impressed by doctors who were open to the idea of visualization, positive thinking, faith, and hard work. The patient was not only encouraged, but expected, to take an active role in their own healing.

The second and third books were about philosophy and diet. *The Zen Macrobiotic Way,* by Michel Abehsera, was about the belief that diseases are caused by an imbalance in the body, which could be realigned with certain foods. *The Macrobiotic Cancer Prevention Cookbook,* by Aveline Kushi and Wendy Esko, told of the power of specific foods for healing. The macrobiotic diet was used all over the world to cure a host of ills, not just cancer. This impressed Karen. Diet was something she could see, something she could change immediately.

The fourth book was by Doctor Bernie Siegel, called *Love, Medicine, and Miracles.* Karen referred to it often. Here was an oncologist surgeon, well known in his field, who had taken the time to instruct his patients to think positively, to see the chemo as a wonderful thing, sent to heal, not poison sent to destroy. He encouraged art therapy so he could understand their feelings better. Using many different unconventional means of self-help, the results were impressive.

The fifth book was Louise Hay's cancer healing audio book. At times, it was easier to listen to a book than to read it. It was difficult to concentrate.

Karen thought about the hybrid of MOPP and ABV as the proper chemotherapy cocktail for her particular case. Not MOPP alone, and not ABV alone, but a combination of the two. The Simontons wrote of patients healing themselves with visualization alone; Abehsera, Oshawa and Kushi wrote of cures through macrobiotic diet alone. She'd become interested in juicing after reading about its benefits. After buying expensive juices at health food stores, she was so impressed with the results, Karen bought her own juicer and added it to her daily regimen. Alternative medicine or conventional medicine. People tended to be loyal to one or the other. Why not a hybrid of both? If positive thinking were united with healing foods, wouldn't that be stronger than just one or the other? If conventional medicine were combined with these alternative philosophies, wouldn't that be more powerful than any one thing?

Karen decided to do it all. Every single thing that went into her body, or was visualized with her mind, would be there as backup for everything else, reinforcing each separate endeavor to heal. She'd knit herself an interlocking net of mind, body, and spirit, working together, to heal everything as a whole. Nothing separate, nothing taking precedence. All would be of equal importance, and all would support each other. Karen would become a student, and the subject would be herself.

Where to begin was one fear to overcome, all by itself. Every so often, Karen was suffused with thoughtless well-wishers, coming up and telling her horrific cancer stories that deflated her fragile optimism like a wet taco. Bad enough to pick up a newspaper and read about some new celebrity diagnosed or deceased with cancer. But individuals with this or that dead friend or relative, who felt they had to share their story with her, were too much. Karen had had no idea of the sheer magnitude of terminal cancer stories that were out there, and some people felt it was their duty to share them all.

Licking her wounds after a barrage of these horror stories, Karen realized that it was her own responsibility to stop them. In mid-sentence, if need be. Bent, almost crippled, and losing her hair, she had neither the strength nor the inclination to hear such lost causes. She had to find the courage to interrupt clueless anecdotes.

Loved ones were important. Each had their own strength to give, bracing Karen up with gifts as individual as fingerprints. Richard was there with his unshakable belief and dogged resolve. Lorry was there to encourage with both words and her own rapidly improving health. Initially as a support, Lorry shared everything Karen did. The diet, the alternative mindset, the juicing; she wanted to help her sister and ended up benefiting herself. "I always knew you'd find the answers, Karen," she said. "Not only are you saving your own life, but you're saving mine, too."

And Lynn Wuest. Lynn knew, almost before Karen did, exactly when she was needed. Karen drew endless strength from her steady encouragement.

Doctor Weil gave her the name of a psychologist named Andrea Gould, whom he thought could help Karen in coping with her predicament. Lorry went with her to the appointment.

Andrea was like no psychologist either sister had ever seen. She ushered them into her office on a curling wave of incense. Adorned with plants and little waterfalls, Chimes hanging from the ceiling, her office was illuminated with candles. A sofa stood in the corner, or if you preferred, several comfortable chairs. All very spiritual, very non-threatening and inviting.

Doctor Weil was an old friend of Andrea's, and she was somewhat acquainted with the case when Karen first called. She knew of the family's terrible losses to illness, and was intrigued by Weil's description of Karen Farley's determination to survive.

Walking with a cane, Karen hobbled over to the sofa, assisted by Lorry, and laid down. Her sister never left her side.

Hair falling out, color pasty, the illness was glaringly obvious. Andrea watched Karen's blank expression. She was in an almost trance-like state, a common occurrence in a person facing a life or death situation. It was not, however, the trance of a woman giving up. More akin to a woman giving birth. Focused. Karen was determined to live. Nothing else mattered. She was there in Andrea's office to help herself live.

Details regarding her past and present were discussed. Straightforward about her uncertainties, Karen was equally direct about her confidences. She believed that other people had healed themselves, but distrusted her own ability to do so. She wanted to cope with the anxiety attacks, which hovered just below the surface; she wanted, somehow, to just slow down and rest. All was noise and chaos and tragedy, eating away at her emotions.

Andrea listened as Karen poured her heart out in a manner one would discuss the weather. She was defensive, wounded and on her knees, but she wasn't down. Andrea saw a glimpse of incredible strength hidden in all that fear and anger. *Now I realize what Doctor Weil was talking about.*

Andrea began speaking. "Karen, it seems to me that you're at a crossroads right now, feeling like you have to choose between two worlds. There's the world of traditional medicine, which your family followed, but that wasn't enough. Then, there's the world of the spiritual, where everything is done with the mind and soul. Why would you limit yourself to one or the other? You need to find a path that you can trust, a path that is yours alone. I feel in my body that you need to walk with a foot in both worlds."

Karen was surprised. This was no phony psychologist mumbo jumbo, or the hazed reasoning of an extremist or hippie. Where was the cold calculation Karen had been taught existed in all therapists and quack shrinks? She studied Andrea's face. Truth, caring, and intelligent consideration. Karen liked what she saw.

The pain hit, and Andrea saw the blow scream across a face frozen in denial. Anger clenched Karen's jaw, and Lorry was there instantly to help. Andrea observed their interaction. *That's going to have to be temporary. Courage can be borrowed for only so long. Then you have to find your own.* For now, Lorry was necessary.

"I started getting interested in meditation because of the Beatles," Andrea said.

The distraction worked. Karen looked up.

Andrea continued. "I studied under the Maharishi Mahesh Yogi. He was a master of transcendental meditation, which is what I was interested in. I wanted scientific proof of its merits. Studies had already proven that the body produces less lactic acid due to stress. Appetite can be suppressed, hypertension relieved, sleeping habits improved. All by slowing down and just breathing."

"How can that cure a person?" Karen asked.

"Meditation is the first step to silencing all the traffic in your head. How can you concentrate and imagine if you're always in a state of chaos? You have to slow the brain down, silence your thoughts. Then you can drop whatever you want into the stillness."

"I don't know how."

"We can learn right now, if you want."

Karen nodded.

"The first thing is to learn how to breathe. Deep breathing is essential to cleanse the system and oxygenate the body in preparation for meditation."

Her patient had a hard time concentrating. Andrea walked her through the breathing exercises, but Karen was very agitated. Squirming, scratching her head, complaining about pain or light from the window. She apologized for forgetting to take off her shoes on the sofa, asked what time it was, thrummed her fingers impatiently. It wasn't working.

"I can't do it!" Karen cried. "How can anybody concentrate when they hurt like this?"

"Let me put some music on. That might help."

Andrea put a tape in the cassette player, then came back to where Karen lay stretched out on the couch. Arranging the three of them, Lorry at Karen's feet, Andrea at her head, the psychologist tried something else. Speaking in a gentle singsong voice, she started again, giving instructions to Lorry as much as Karen. "Relax your forehead ... breathe ... Lorry, massage her feet ... let your mind go empty, Karen, you don't have to think ... "

Obediently, Lorry began stroking Karen's feet and ankles, while Andrea smoothed her forehead with gentle fingers. Karen's face began to relax. Andrea smiled. *Good. She's a tactile person.*

They worked on Karen together. Calming her panic, silencing doubt, creating a circle of quiet for her to be safe in, a silent refuge from her own thoughts.

The music in the background was hauntingly beautiful and very lonely. Like Karen's soul. Suddenly, she was crying.

Catching the psychologist's eye, Lorry smiled. Her sister, *the Stone*, was opening up.

"Why are you crying, Karen?" Andrea asked.

"Because I feel like ... I feel like I'm coming home."

Why did she say that? A spur of the moment statement, but on reflection, it was correct. She did feel as if she were coming home.

Afterward, Karen was glowing. Her skin, abdomen, joints, even the nausea felt improved. *If this is what it's like after just one session, what'll I feel like if I do it every day?* She wanted to know if Andrea sold those tapes. A copy of the music would be fantastic to meditate with.

"I can tell you where I bought this one," Andrea said. "There's a store in Huntington called *Enlightenment*. They've got it there."

"What's the music called?"

"The Journey of Lazarus."

Karen liked that. "Lazarus, raised from the dead. Thank you, Andrea. See you next week."

In the parking lot, Karen couldn't stop talking. "I want to go get that music right away, Lorry," she said as she fastened her seatbelt. "There's something about it. I just have to get it today."

"I know that place. Let's go."

The shop was upstairs. Karen cursed as she pulled herself up the steps, reminding Lorry of her own long climb to Norma's rebirth class.

Passing through a shimmering bead curtain in the doorway, they hobbled into the store. Sandalwood incense and piped seagull music greeted them, and Karen was irritated enough by the climb to cast a jaded eye.

A woman stood behind the counter. Glancing up between gasps for breath, Karen found herself staring into a pair of riveting blue-green eyes. The woman didn't look away. Her expression was frozen, as if she were startled by something.

Karen sighed. Wherever she went, people gawked at her, open-mouthed. *Look at her. What's wrong with her? She's so young. Must be cancer.* Always cold now, she wore a heavy coat, despite the warm weather. Devoid of makeup, her face was the color of oatmeal, and her hair was patchy.

The woman was still staring.

Never comfortable with the inevitable stares that accompanied a grave illness, Karen moved toward a display table. Lorry was over by scented oils.

The Journey of Lazarus. She found the tape, chose half a dozen crystals because they were pretty and felt good, and was standing in front of the herbal tea rack when the owner approached her.

"Hi. My name is Elizabeth. My guide Jesus Christ sent me over here. He told me you had to be healed."

Karen took a nose dive back into the Twilight Zone.

"What?"

"You. I'm supposed to help you. You must be healed. This is very exciting. It's never happened before. Hundreds of people come into the shop, and nothing. For some unknown reason, my guide told me you have to be healed. He told me to come over and tell you about Michael. He said, *Send her to Michael. Michael needs to help her.*"

"Who's Michael?"

"He's our healer in the store."

"Healer?"

"He's a hands-on psychic healer. He works through our store."

"Okay," Karen said, cynical. "How much does he charge?"

Elizabeth looked affronted. "Nothing. Jesus told me you must be healed. We won't charge you anything."

That threw her. "I don't understand. Why would you do that? You don't even know me."

"I have to. They told me you have to be healed, and I have to help you."

Lorry, who was listening, joined them. Karen looked at her.

"Should I should try it?"

"Are you kidding? Of course. Don't go alone, though. You don't know this guy."

"I promise you, Michael is completely legitimate. He's an amazing healer."

Lorry nudged her. "Go on, Karen. Do it."

"Well, why not?"

Pleased, Elizabeth turned. "I'll see if he's free. Browse, enjoy yourselves." She went down a hallway into the back room to confer with the mysterious Michael. Karen turned to her sister.

"Is this a little weird, or is it me?"

Lorry laughed. "It's you, and that *is* a little weird. I think this is cool."

Elizabeth came back. "He can see you right now, if you want. He's between clients."

Between clients, huh? I'll bet.

As she followed the shopkeeper down the hall, Karen remembered the entity's words. *Stay on the path, and what you need will be provided.*

Subdued and soft-spoken, Michael was a shy man with watery blue eyes. He spoke very little, letting the client do the talking. When Karen admitted she was doing very poorly, he nodded, led her to a table, and helped her lie down.

Allowed in the room so long as she didn't stand too close, Lorry sat on the

floor against the wall. Michael sat down next to the table and explained channeling energy.

"Don't be frightened if you feel my hands getting hot, or a burning sensation. It's a normal part of the healing process."

Michael put some music on. When Karen heard what was playing, she tensed.
The Journey of Lazarus, the same music they'd come here to find.

Michael rubbed his palms together, blew into his hands, and laid them on
Karen's abdomen. She grimaced at the thought of this strange man touching her,
but tried to relax into it, counting the seconds until it was over.

A warmth began pooling around her ribs, like the welcome heat of a hot water
bottle. The sensation was concentrated around the spots Michael touched. His
eyes were closed, his head bent low into his chest.

The heat increased, and Karen closed her eyes from the sheer pleasure of it.
The pain was better, and she didn't care if it was only temporary or not. Now
was enough. The healing brought back thoughts of the entity, and she felt as if
the warmth were coming from somewhere else and not Michael, as if he were
merely a conduit. *This is God's warmth,* Karen thought, and visualized it melting the cancer like hot tallow.

They set up another appointment in two days. At first Michael didn't want
Lorry in the room again, but she was anxious to watch and learn, and Karen was
anxious for a chaperone.

The healing room was simple and sparse, with only a lit candle, a cassette
player, and a chair beside the table. Michael wore regular clothing, nothing dramatic or flashy, just understated comfort. He didn't ask how Karen felt, he simply brushed his hands over her aura and began to work.

Karen was tense for the first few sessions, ready for him to reveal himself as
a pervert or deviant, but Michael's touch was sexless.

It was also very powerful. Karen knew something was happening. She
could feel it. Similar to the way she felt when Lorry tried to heal her, but on
a larger scale.

Thrilled with everything she was learning and happy with the obvious
progress, Lorry accepted his gift without question. It didn't matter how it
worked, just that it did.

Karen viewed the healing sessions in a different way. She didn't want to
cloud her intellect or logical side by embracing Michael's powers without
proof. To her, the sessions were to be enjoyed for the moment. They didn't
take much time, and they gave temporary relief. Were they really healing her?
Karen didn't believe one way or the other, at first. She only knew that they felt
good, that she was somehow growing spiritually inside with each session. For

now, that was enough.

Puffy from the cortisone, crippled from the pain, and sick from the chemo, she went to see Michael as often as possible.

He never took money or turned her away, despite a continuously full schedule. His guide, he told her, had instructed him to heal her, too.

A born skeptic, Karen wanted to believe that some unseen being had whispered words of good deeds to these kind souls. But life had always thrown reticence into her demeanor, and she struggled to accept Michael's story without question. Instead of concentrating on his history, she decided to live in the now. The sessions with Michael were making a difference. Karen could feel it. It didn't matter that the healing defied conventional wisdom or that family and friends turned a patronizing ear to her descriptions about Michael. It was helping. The pain was better. Karen contented herself with that.

The rest of her hair fell out in one huge drop the day after Dana's baptism. Karen had fixated on the need to have hair on her head for her baby's baptism.

"It can all fall out afterwards, but I have to have my hair for Dana's baptism." This is what she told herself. A strange wish to hold onto.

The baldness seemed to hit Lorry harder than Karen.

"I feel so bad for you, Karen. If it happened to me, I don't think I could handle it. I'd just look like an Italian Yul Brynner. But look at you. You're gorgeous."

Karen saw the hair loss as part of the healing process. It'd grow back.

Deep into her second month of treatment, Karen's every waking moment, and many of her sleeping ones, were dedicated to healing and study. Thoughts were never bent toward the so-called inevitable, only the seemingly impossible.

When first diagnosed, tumors were found on every organ in her chest, abdomen, and pelvis. Cancer was in both sides of the bone marrow. If she listened to sensible advice, Karen should lie down and die. Nobody recovered from fourth stage cancer.

The disease didn't allow time to think about all those negatives, so she chose to disregard them. The impossible was her goal now. Life. She fought to live. Her armor consisted of friends, family, food, Andrea Gould, chemotherapy, and faith. Karen read books about cancer survivors, asked for any ideas or remedies, no matter how absurd, then shuffled them all into her own unique deck of cards. She was studying how to get well, and people were amazed by her stamina and strength.

Then, there was the P.O.W. food.

Richard dubbed it thus. The macrobiotic diet. No sugar, caffeine, bread, or pasta. Karen ate brown rice, beans, seaweeds, vegetables, fish, and poultry.

Everything was organic. Combined with juicing, it gave her the stamina needed to survive.

Digestion requires enormous energy. Everything that went into her mouth had to count. She couldn't afford to waste energy by putting non-healing foods into her body.   Lorry followed the same healthy diet. Whereas normal people swing by a drive-through for a burger and fries, the sisters stopped for a nori roll with brown rice and kale juice. Lorry commented that the macrobiotic menu tasted like dirt.

"How can we eat this?" she teased. "I'd rather swallow dog food. Now, there's an idea, Karen. Isn't there a drive-through for canines? I've got a craving for some Mighty Dog."

"No, but there's a rawhide bone in the glove compartment. Knock yourself out."

"Oh, ha, ha, ha." Lorry took a bite of her roll, and a blob of brown rice glopped in her lap.

"Think of it as medicine, Lorry. We're taking our medicine. This food will heal us. Doesn't matter what it tastes like. Medicine never tastes good."

"Yeah, but I don't even get my spoonful of sugar."

Karen took a bite. "Mm. Delicious. Let the healing begin!"

"I'm ready."

Miso soup, seaweed, kale, adzuki beans, short grain brown rice, and juicing. Parsley juice, kale, spinach, celery, cucumber, wheat grass, ginger, and garlic juice, periodically. Green cabbage juice for stomach pain from the vomiting and the chemo.

Karen also utilized a variety of teas. Organic Kukicha, Bancha, Pau D Arco, Red Clover, and most importantly, blended green tea. These were all known as anti-tumor teas that boosted the immune system. In theory, they prevented cancer cells from bunching together and forming tumors. She ate thirty almonds a day for their natural laetrile. Karen tried everything.

Within reason. Many of the more outlandish healing techniques were avoided. She didn't wear pyramids on her head, as someone suggested. She didn't work incantations, or pin money to her shirt and go into New York City at midnight, as one psychic demanded. "Gong Therapy" just wasn't for her. She tried anything that seemed to make sense in a logical manner, with some kind of scientific foundation. Karen simply mixed and matched what she thought would work for her, and *followed through with it*. She never gave up.

Positive thinking. That was sometimes the hardest. A lifetime of insecurity reared its ugly head, whispering failure and inability like tepid raindrops, drenching her late at night when everybody else was asleep. There were chinks in the armor, but Karen was determined to have faith in herself. All day, every day, even through the vomiting and the pain, the medical scares and emergency rooms, Karen was chanting a mantra of self-healing to herself.

"I'm getting well," she said. "Everything I eat, drink, smell, breathe, think, feel, is helping me get well."

All bodily functions had a healing purpose. Sweat was her body detoxifying. Bathroom visits rid her of deadly cancer cells and chemotherapy drugs. Vomiting cleansed poisons from her system. Each bite of food was healing energy directly targeting the cancer. Every sip of water or juice washed the malignancies away.

Cleansing the body was an unequivocal undertaking. Cleansing the spirit was trickier. Karen continued with Andrea Gould, detoxifying emotions from her riddled past as well as her present.

Lorry, through her psychic training, carefully monitored Karen's progress. The gold nodules were fading.

This was frowned upon at the Metaphysical Learning Center. They warned Lorry about *transference*. She'd been trying to heal Karen by willing the sickness out of her. A friend at the center said she was going to kill her sister, and probably herself, by transference.

"Hands on healing exchanges energies between you and your subject. You're going to give Karen Lupus, and she's going to give you cancer. Learn to do Reiki. No transference between healer and subject."

Reiki is a form of healing where energy passes through a person into the subject. Both channeler and patient benefit. There's no exchange of illness or negativity. Understood as a type of green-light healing, it's considered completely benign."

Lorry's goal was to achieve Reiki master status. Starting slow, she signed up for the beginner's course of Reiki I.

* * *

"There's a figure behind you, Karen," Lorry said. "I can see it."

They were in the healing room with Michael, halfway through the session.

Karen, the chronic doubter, had to admit she often felt a presence in the room, assisting in the healing. Strangely familiar, it felt like something that had always been with her.

In the three weeks since they'd been coming to Michael, she'd yet to have a name for this presence.

Lorry talked a lot about her own guide, and what a comfort he was during meditation. Michael said his guide healed through him.

Thinking about the entity in the hospital and the voices she called her *friends*, not to mention all the stones and their prophetic carvings, Karen wondered about her own guide. Before the session began, she'd asked Michael to help.

"Michael, could you find out the name of the entities that talk to me?"

"You don't need me to do that. While you're meditating, when you feel them, just ask."

"I've tried that, but I only hear, 'My name is unimportant'"

"Sometimes they don't answer right away. They will, eventually. Just keep asking."

Now, Lorry was seeing a presence behind her.

Deep in meditation, Karen asked the entity its name.

"Who are you? Please tell me who you are."

The stone appeared in her mind's eye. Fiery letters began carving themselves into its rough surface. O-B-E-D-I-A. The voices whispered the pronunciation into her memory. "OBEDIA. We are healing you."

After the session was over, Karen described the stone and the letters scratched out. Michael's face grew blank with wonder.

"How do you know that name? That's my guide."

"Only it was spelled strange. There was a loopy symbol in the beginning and again at the end. The *E* looked like a backwards *C* almost, with a slash through it. That's how I know it was an *E*. What does that mean?"

"I don't know, Karen." he said.

She looked at Lorry, who shook her head.

Happy to have a name for her entity at last, Karen tried to imagine a history behind it. Maybe Obedia was some Buddhist holy man from the past. *That'd be wonderfully weird. Lorry'd get a kick out of that.*

Karen was gradually losing her fear about her strange abilities. She was beginning to open up.

"Karen." Michael's voice interrupted her musings. "Can I talk to you?"

"Of course."

He looked at Lorry. "Could you step out for a minute?"

Lorry blinked, startled at the request. "All right," she said reluctantly, "I'll be out in the shop."

As soon as the door closed behind her, Michael winced as if in pain. His face was red, making the pale eyes stand out in vivid contrast.

"I have some bad news. I hope I'll be able to continue with my work. It's so important."

"What? What's wrong, Michael?"

"I've just been diagnosed with leukemia."

"No. It can't be."

"The test results came back today. I don't have health insurance. I can't afford the medicine.

The pain is so terrible, Karen. I'm telling you this because you know. You're going through it yourself. My concentration is way off. It took everything I've got just to get through your session today. Please don't tell Elizabeth. She's like a mother to me. This would break her."

"Of course."

"She can't know. The poor woman would just try to pay for my pills herself, and she can't afford it."

"Isn't there some other way for you to get treatment? Maybe an agency you can go to?"

"I can heal myself of the leukemia. It'll take a long time, but that's not the problem. The problem is, I have so much pain. I just can't control it anymore."

Karen watched as a bead of sweat ran down his face. Her heart went out to him.

"If I can't control this pain, I may have to stop working for awhile. That can't happen. So many people depend on me. You wouldn't believe how much suffering comes into this room, and I'm the only one who can help them. I can't stop doing that, Karen. My work is too important. God gave me this gift for a reason. I've got to help people."

"You do help people, Michael. Look what you've done for me. I'm so sorry this has happened. If I can do anything ... "

The threads shifted so slowly, so softly around her. Michael wove words of sorrow like a spider weaves a web, trapping Karen with her own sympathy.

Wracking her brain for a solution, an idea dawned, clear and bright. He saw it in her face.

The trap was sprung.

"What can I do?" Karen's eyes were earnest.

"If you can help with the pain, that's all I need. Would you have any extra pain killers? Just a few to get me through the week."

She nodded. "I've got bottles of them at home, just sitting in the cabinet."

"Do you have any with you? In your purse?"

"I really don't take them."

"Can you bring me some?"

"Of course."

"Oh, God, Karen. Thank you. Are you sure it's not too much trouble?"

"Don't worry, Michael. We'll get through this. You've helped me so much. Please, let me do this for you."

From then on, Karen brought him a little comfort with every session. Starting with just one or two pills, it quickly escalated. The more she gave him, the more he seemed to need.

Lorry was ignorant as to the amount, but she knew of the furtive transactions. She didn't question them too deeply. This man, for all his faults, had a genuine gift. He was helping Karen. Lorry knew that. If he needed pain killers, so be it.

* * *

Karen found a book on Edgar Cayce, the so-called Sleeping Prophet, and the remedies he'd passed on during his lifetime. Unorthodox but effective, she added them to her healing supports.

Saturating a white linen cloth with castor oil, Karen placed it on her body, over spots where tumors had been noted. The cloth was then covered with a hot water bottle. Meditation was to accompany this Cayce remedy. Karen visualized the castor oil seeping through her skin, pouring over the tumor, and breaking it up.

Bathing became a healing ritual. In macrobiotic philosophy, the skin is of the utmost importance. Being the largest organ in the body, skin is responsible for a vast amount of waste removal through the pores.

Karen scrubbed herself daily with baking soda water and a dye-free white cloth. This helped to remove the dead layers of skin, allowing the toxins to pass through more easily.

Seaweed baths. Seaweed wraps were a common luxury in spas, but with the chemotherapy, Karen's immune system was compromised. It wasn't safe to expose herself in public. Too many people with potential diseases. Even a simple cold was dangerous to a weak immune system, so public spas were out of the question. That, and the expense. Seaweed wraps were outrageously expensive, often hundreds of dollars each. Karen refused to limit herself.

A local health food store carried dried Kombu and Wakame seaweeds. These were essential in macrobiotic cooking. If drinking the seaweed helped heal her from the inside, Karen figured her skin would benefit from their nutrients as well.

She ran a scalding hot bath, threw in six cups of baking soda, two cups of sea salt, and half a package each of Wakame and Kombu.

As the mixture cooled, the seaweed expanded, turning the water green. As soon as the temperature was bearable, she'd climb in and soak for thirty minutes. Picking up handfuls of the seaweed, Karen rubbed it over her skin. A dye-free cloth covered with baking soda helped exfoliate more dead skin cells, and she'd step from the bath feeling at least somewhat rejuvenated. The mixture was a concoction of her own. Karen did this religiously, especially when she was weak from the chemotherapy.

Time was not on her side. Cancer doesn't wait. Everything took second place to the concept of healing. That was now her job. No self-deluding guilt of work, or children, or home, or housework, no friend's emotional troubles or loved one's tragic history could interfere with her job. Karen knew there was no second chance, no lukewarm philosophy or past self-destructive patterns that could come between her and her body. Everything was second to the overwhelming priority of battling cancer. Here. Now.

Richard hired a woman to come in and help around the house, leaving his wife free to concentrate on getting well. With strict instructions not to bother Karen during her meditations, which she did three times a day, he left her alone to heal herself.

The power of human touch was proven to Karen when her loved ones put their hands on her. Richard stroking her arm could calm her faster than any drug, and his warmth at night was a blessing.

But the children. They were something more. Whether it was maternal instinct or simple adoration, the mere presence of her babies worked wonders. In some of her darkest hours, when the pain was almost unbearable, her children could simply touch her, and it would drift away.

Things weren't always positive. Depression hit so hard and fast sometimes, Karen was blindsided by it. *God, I'm so sick. I can't do this. I can't fight anymore.*

Lorry knew her own job. When Karen's confidence floundered, she was there. "Remember the entity, Karen. Stay on the path. You saved my life. Matt's life, too. You'll save your own. Don't forget the visions, and have faith. You're the most powerful person I know, your mind can do anything. Believe it, Karen. You said I was going to be okay when I was dying. I know you don't lie. You gave me hope. Now I'm telling you, you're going to beat this. Remember Norma's seance? Daddy said you'll beat it in three months."

Karen held onto those words, especially late at night, when the whole world was asleep and the minutes felt like hours. Sleep eluded her. Late night television consisted of infomercials, soap opera reruns, bad B-movies, and talk show repeats. Karen needed something else to get her through the nights.

Doctor Bernie Siegel and Louise Hay came to the rescue. Comforted by their philosophies, Karen found the night lost much of its frightening aspect with the simple addition of a tape recorder and set of headphones.

Meditation was easy now. Once learned, it was like riding a bike. Karen meditated at least three times a day. Before beginning, she wrapped all her senses in soft pleasure, distracting them into relaxation. Music for her ears, aromatherapy for her nose, comfortable pillows for her body. A cup of green tea and a light meal beforehand, so the stomach was distracted neither by hunger, or over stimulated by heavy digestion. The telephone was switched off, the lights dimmed, and Karen had a little sign that she hung on her door. It read simply, *In Meditation.* Everyone knew not to disturb her when the sign was up, under any circumstances.

She always began a meditation with a set of prayers. The "Lord's Prayer" and "Hail Mary" were her favorites. Then Karen would ask for help from the other side, to be with her, protect her, and guide her. Her parents, Patty, Jesus, the Virgin Mary, Padre Pio, Obedia, and Saint John Neumann, a patron saint of illness, anyone who might help or comfort her from the spirit world. She protected herself and her loved ones with a mental circle of mirrors that faced outward. This would reflect back anything negative or bad. Only good could pass through.

Humor, also, proved to be a powerful ally. Lorry, setting out to amuse her, watched as Karen's face flushed with healthy color when she laughed.

They rented funny movies and laid down the law with everybody about acceptable subject matter. No one was to unburden their problems on Karen. They both remembered Rita and Angelina. Rita had always said "Angelina's killing me. Her sadness is killing me."

Karen wasn't going to shoulder that type of burden. Everybody has problems, but she was fighting for her life, and hers was not the ear that could listen now. People's sorrow was an obstacle she would shoulder later.

Obstacles. Karen simply refused to believe they existed. When her veins started to collapse, she had a port inserted in her chest. The chemotherapy could then be injected straight into the major vein of her heart.

She chose to see the port as a positive thing. Choice became everything. Karen sifted through the bad and pulled out a positive. When the port in her chest reminded her too much of her mother, Karen gave it a spin. "This is the doorway through which my healing potion can come in," she told herself, "Now, instead of a two-and-a-half-hour IV drip, I can get all of my chemo in twenty minutes, and get the hell out of here. I've saved over two hours."

When her body became so poisoned from the chemotherapy, she chose to laugh about it, relating her favorite tale of revenge.

One morning she woke up to find a dead mosquito sitting on her chest, its proboscis still imbedded in her skin. The level of toxicity in her blood had killed it.

"Richard, look at this," she laughed, shaking him awake. "After years of these damn things biting me, revenge!"

When people were bothered by the sight of the port in her chest, Karen donned a bathing suit, a glamorous straw hat and had her photo taken on the beach. She was re-inventing herself after the years of negative thinking and tragedy that had been her past.

Impressed by Karen's optimism, a friend gave her phone number to a woman named Helen. She'd been diagnosed with second stage breast cancer. Hoping to be inspired, she called Karen.

Their backgrounds were similar; the woman had two small children, and she wanted to live to see them grow up. When she first called, Helen was very depressed.

"How can you be so positive, Karen? You just told me you were given a twenty percent chance of survival. Your cancer's a lot worse than mine. I have an ninety percent chance, and I feel so hopeless. I just don't understand."

"Well, number one, I'm not just another statistic," Karen said. "When my doctor dropped the bomb about the twenty percent, I was devastated. After the initial panic wore off, I decided to devise my own set of statistics. I'm taking vitamins and supplements. That's got to be worth another five percent. Macrobiotic foods; another five. Fresh vegetable and fruit juices; that's five. Organic foods are another five. I drink filtered water. Five more. See, the doctors put me in a general statistic which included all ages and habits. Some individuals smoke, drink, or have some other unmonitored bad habit. Others don't even finish their chemotherapy regimen. I haven't smoked or had a drink in years, and I'm young. That's got to be at least five. A positive spiritual and mental outlook; a good ten percent for that. My children need their mother. That's another ten percent. Belief in myself and all my choices. That's ten at least. And, maybe most importantly, I use guided imagery and meditation. That's about fifteen percent. The way I look at it, I now have a ninety-five percent chance of surviving."

Helen wasn't convinced. "How did you get such a positive outlook? Were you born with it?"

"I was given a gift of knowledge through some, shall we say, extraordinary circumstances. I needed to find something other than conventional medicine to inspire me."

Karen outlined everything she herself was doing to fight cancer. It was a long and informative phone conversation, but Helen was still negative when she hung up. Karen feared for her.

Within a week, she called back. She couldn't do the diet, the seaweed tasted disgusting and made her sick. She couldn't drink the juice, it tasted awful. The books were no help, reading hurt her eyes. The audio tapes made her dizzy. She couldn't meditate, she was in too much pain.

Helen was giving up. Karen could hear it in her voice. She tried to convince her to keep trying, don't quit, but it was futile. No pep talk or logical reasoning had any effect on Helen's supreme pessimism. Even the suggestion of trying it for just one more week was met with a wall of resistance.

Within months, Helen was dead.

Sobered by the news, Karen struggled to keep it from overwhelming her. *If only* was a phrase she couldn't afford to indulge in right now. Her own battle wasn't over. She'd done all she could for Helen, but it hadn't been enough. Even Karen's own enthusiasm couldn't force a person to do anything.

Worried about the future, Karen was torn. Should she make plans? If the worst happened, and she did die, her children must know how much she loved them.

She made a secret video will the next day, touching on subjects that her children might need help with, in a possible future without their mother. To Matt, she said, "Always be kind. I know you're sensitive. Don't hurt anyone, and take care of your sister." To Dana, she said, "I love you very much, my little girl. Don't let anyone hurt you, or make you feel bad about yourself. You're beautiful, and Mommy loves you very, very much." She wore a wig during the filming, then meditated for a long time afterward.

* * *

Karen was getting heartily sick of well-meant advice.

Andrea found herself constantly repairing the damage of a few poorly chosen statements such as "I just don't want you to get your hopes up" or "I wish you wouldn't spread yourself so thin. Just focus on the chemo, and not all this other stuff. Who knows if it'll help? Maybe it's even hurting you."

And there were many others. Karen kept a list of the most common.

"You know, maybe this is God's way of bringing you back to the church."

"Did you tell your doctor about these weird things you're doing? Maybe he doesn't want you taking all those vitamins. Does he want you juicing or changing your diet?"

"Leave your health in the hands of professionals, not some metafuzzy in a health food store."

"If I had the cancer you had, I could never do what you're doing. I'd be paralyzed with fear. You must be so afraid for your children."

"I'd hate having to take chemotherapy. I know someone who took it, and it did terrible things to them. It just destroys your entire body."

And Karen's all-time favorite:

"Aren't you afraid it'll come back?"

Karen called a Reiki massage therapist whom someone had recommended, but the woman refused to work on her when she found out Karen had cancer. "I don't want to touch you and pick up any of your bad energy. Your aura is dark and murky. That's what it looks like right before a person dies."

That one infuriated Lorry.

Even the gentle teasing about her macrobiotic diet could exhaust Karen when she was having a bad day.

Andrea helped put things into perspective, giving her a fresh dose of optimism by showing her a different outlook.

"Andrea, I told my oncologist some of the things I'm doing, and he pretty much negated everything. All these doctors, they're always negating anything I do that they didn't tell me to do themselves. Doctor Weil's the only one who encourages me. Nobody else does. They don't realize how hard it is to just get through the day sometimes. I guess it would be nice if Doctor Bidnold acknowledged, even a little bit, some of the things I'm doing."

"Well, Karen, why did you hire this doctor?"

"He was referred by a friend of the family."

"Okay. So you hired him for his medical expertise. Why don't you just leave it at that? His job is to help design the medical treatment for you. You feel confident in his ability to do that. That's what his purpose is in your healing. He's there to design the best course of medical treatment, and that's what his job in your life is."

"So I shouldn't have any expectations other than him helping me make medical decisions, or I'll be disappointed?"

"Exactly. You see, Karen, you're developing several support systems for yourself. That's your first support system. Put it into perspective. Draw a circle with the words "Karen's Healing" in it. Then draw lines radiating out all around it. At the end of each line is one support system. Chemotherapy, juicing, guided imagery. Here's meditation. Macrobiotics, organic foods, hands on healing, positive thinking; the list is endless. If a support fails, you have all these others to back you up. Your doctor is only one." Andrea held up a finger.

After that, Karen was able to see her oncologist in a new light. She no longer set herself up by caring about his opinion anywhere but in his own specialized field. He'd been in this profession for over fifty years, and was set in his ways. Karen knew Bidnold cared for her in the best way he knew how, and that was enough for her.

* * *

After her fourth cycle of chemotherapy, Karen's red blood cell count fell dangerously low.

"You have to go into emergency today, Karen, and get a transfusion," Bidnold told her.

Karen shook her head. Blood screening at that time wasn't good enough for her. She didn't want to beat cancer, only to succumb to AIDs or hepatitis because of an infected blood supply.

"I'm telling you, you don't have any choice. You've got to get that transfusion right now."

"I don't want strangers' blood." Karen shook her head. "Can't I have my husband or sister donate?"

"Spouses can't donate. Besides, there's no time. It takes four days to screen the blood. You can't wait that long."

"Then give me twenty-four hours. I'll work on it myself."

"Karen," the oncologist was getting agitated. "I'm telling you, you don't have time to play around like this. This is very serious."

Karen just looked at him and said nothing.

He sighed, exasperated. Bidnold knew that look. "All right. But if you feel yourself losing consciousness, have someone bring you to the emergency room immediately. Do you understand? Immediately."

She nodded.

"I want to see you in my office tomorrow afternoon."

Lorry drove her home. Karen looked up blood builders in her juicing book. Kale juice and blue green algae.

The next twenty-four hours were red. That's all she meditated on, all day, breaking the meditations up into six separate, one-hour sessions, juicing in between each one. She had a sitter watch the children. The house was taken care of. Nothing was going to distract her from this all-important goal.

Karen meditated on red. The color red. Crimson floods and thick apple red, ruby lakes of healthy claret; bright sunsets of deepest rose. Red, red, red. It swam before her eyes, poured into her senses, filled her veins with color. She slipped into guided imagery without a second thought, murmuring descriptions to herself of fat red tomatoes, growing plumper and plumper, until they burst their skin with riotous red. Red blood cells reproducing like rabbits, flooding her body with legions that grew larger and larger, until her skin felt stretched with it. Everything was a world of aggressive crimson, and Karen saturated her mind, body, and spirit with it. Hot spots were all over her. Feeling them, she knew healing was taking place.

The next day, Lorry drove her into the doctor's office, where they drew blood again. The test came back quickly.

"I'm glad to see you took my advice, Karen," Bidnold said, looking at the results.

"What do you mean?"

"You had the transfusion. Your red blood cell count is back to normal."

Lorry looked at Karen and grinned.

"I didn't have a transfusion," she told him. "I went home and drank kale juice and blue green algae, then meditated."

Bidnold was clearly skeptical. "What are you talking about? Your count is normal." He turned to Lorry. "Didn't you take her for a blood transfusion?"

"No."

He couldn't understand, but decided not to pursue it any further.

"Hm. Well ... maybe the first test was wrong."

His disbelief slid off Karen like water from a duck's back. Andrea was right. Karen was there for conventional medical support, not a pat on the head. She was learning. She was also very happy. This was a reinforcement of everything, a proof of how powerful the mind can be.

The visits with Michael ground to a halt. After exhausting all the painkillers Karen had, he'd only grown more demanding, telling her to refill the prescriptions so she could give him more.

With her health improving, Karen saw past manufactured illness. Michael was lying. He was just a drug addict. Had he been lying about his gift as well?

She felt dirty. Michael had used her, milking her sympathy and fear for his own purpose. Karen felt almost as violated as if Bill Kelly had put his hands on her.

For one awful moment, she feared the healing itself, having come from such a flawed source. Guilt lent a twist to the mix as well. Karen blamed herself for not seeing it earlier.

Then she remembered the entity. The energy, the warmth, was not from Michael. He was only a vessel through which it traveled. Flawed he may be, but he was graced with a gift, and he'd had an important purpose for her. Maybe she was supposed to learn a harsh lesson from all this sordid business. Maybe, like the voices had told her with her Uncle Marco, maybe she should let the feelings of violation go. *"It's just things. They're not important. Stay on the path."*

Word had gotten out. Karen found herself inundated with phone calls from other cancer patients, asking for advice and inspiration. An optimistic person with fourth stage cancer was a rarity indeed and a pearl beyond price.

Karen doled out remedies for throat lesions, walked people through the philosophies of guided imagery, and handed out macrobiotic recipes almost daily.

The ability to help people, and the surprising need of so many, touched something inside Karen. She thought of the entity in the hospital, and all it had foretold. Maybe she could do something for cancer patients, after all.

Three months after she was diagnosed, Karen felt … clean. It was a strange sensation, as if the cancer were a dirty stain she'd tried to scrub out, and now it was gone. Lorry, too, said she felt no illness in her sister when she laid her hands on her.

Bidnold was reticent to order a new CAT scan.

"It's too early to see any difference yet, Karen. Give it time. You're doing fine."

She was adamant.

"Doctor Bidnold, I need to have a CAT scan done. I want to know if the chemo is working. Are the tumors shrinking?"

"Karen, it's too early. We don't even know if the tumors have reacted to the chemo yet, it needs more time. Let's wait until after the sixth cycle of treatments. By then, we should see improvement. I don't want you to be disappointed."

"I feel that the cancer is being destroyed, and I need to know that the chemo is working. I also want to take as little chemo as possible. If the cancer is gone now, then I'll only need five treatments instead of eight, and that'll be less damage to my body."

"Well, I think you're jumping the gun here. You should wait the full six months before having the scan."

Karen shook her head. The months of meditation and self-reflection had given her a new understanding of her body and its workings, and she needed to have that knowledge confirmed. It was now three months since her diagnosis. She felt clean. She wanted the test.

Grudgingly, Bidnold agreed, but only halfway. Karen agreed to one more cycle of chemotherapy. The CAT scan would be done after the fourth cycle. Doctor Bidnold warned her again.

"In my opinion, you may not even see a change yet. You're going to be disappointed."

"I understand. I still want to do it."

Karen went into her fourth cycle of chemotherapy with mixed feelings. On the one hand, she was excited to be near an answer, proof about all she had worked so hard at; on the other, it was two more weeks of dry vomiting and throat lesions, and the fear of damage from another infusion of MOPP/ABV. Knowledge, she discovered, could be a double-edged sword. She knew the possible side effects of every drug entering her body. And after a two-week cycle, the two-week rest period.

It was the longest month of Karen's life. All her old doubts and fears came roaring back. Friends and family rallied to her side.

Richard was optimistic. Lynn was a constant source of reassurance. Andrea was also very supportive.

Lorry was there, repeating the mantra, "You're getting better. You're getting better, Karen."

They decided to make a trip to Enlightenment. Despite how he'd used her, Karen wanted Michael to know that she was doing so well. Fate had put him in her path, and she wanted him to share the moment. Even Lorry, who was fiercely protective, agreed that it would be good to see him.

Elizabeth greeted them with a face ashen and grave.

"Michael passed away," she said without preamble.

"What?"

"He committed suicide. Karen," Elizabeth looked sick. "I need to ask you something. Did Michael ever ask you for your prescription drugs?"

Karen's guarded expression was all the answer she needed.

"Oh, my God. You're not the only one. Another customer said Michael told her that he had cancer. She gave him some of her painkillers. I dismissed him a while back. It's only recently he committed suicide. I'm so sorry."

Karen and Lorry took the news hard. Despite his callous manipulations, Michael had once meant a great deal to them. To Lorry, he'd been the man who kept encouraging her pursuit of healing. She'd looked up to him. To Karen, he'd been a conduit for her own healing. That he could throw it all away to his addiction was a tragedy that touched them both.

The night before the CAT scan, Karen couldn't sleep. Nausea and excitement had a civil war in her belly, and she literally vibrated with the strain.

Lorry drove her to the radiologist's office Monday morning. They both wiggled and twitched, like two children on a long car ride. Richard met them there.

Karen drank the Barium, and the dye slid into her veins through the IV. She visualized it as an illuminating map, pointing out all the clear and cancer-free areas in her body. The technician administered the CAT scan.

When he was finished, Karen was far too keyed up to wait for the radiologist's report.

"Okay, Mrs. Farley, you're finished," the technician said. "We'll let you know the results when they come in."

"Please, I can't wait. Can't you tell me now?"

"We're not allowed. Your oncologist will let you know. He'll have the results sometime this afternoon."

"I can't wait until then. Please. Tell me something!"

The technician looked undecided, then said, "Wait here. I'll see what I can do."

He was gone for a few minutes. As she waited, every murmur in the hallway, every rustle of her clothing when she moved, seemed exaggerated and over-loud.

The door opened, and the technician came back in.

"What? What did he see?"

"I'm not supposed to tell you this ... "

"Please! Please, tell me."

A slow smile spread across his face, and the eyebrows went north as he told his happy secret.

"It looks good. It looks real good."

"What does that mean? The tumors are smaller?"

"They don't see any tumors at all. Nothing abnormal." He grinned. "Congratulations."

If Karen had been standing, she'd have fallen down. "Is this true? How can it be so fast?"

"You're a very lucky young woman, Mrs. Farley. The scan was clear."

Karen started to cry. "Oh, thank you! Thank you so much."

She ran out and gave Richard and Lorry the news.

"We've got to celebrate," Richard said, beaming. "What do you want to do, Karen? We've got to celebrate!"

The next day, she began the four-day Gallium scan. The first day was comprised of an injection of radium. The remaining three days looked for individual cancer cells by a long series of one-hour X-ray sessions.

Once again, Karen asked, each day, what was found. Once again, the slow smile and a look quite rare on the faces of the medical profession. Pure wonder.

On the fourth day, all the test results were in. Karen sat in her oncologist's office, watching as he silently poured over the X-rays. Doctor Bidnold studied them and shook his head.

The results were no less than astonishing. No trace of cancer could be found anywhere in Karen Farley's body. No tumors, no individual malignant cells swimming around, no cancer hiding in the bone marrow.

They did a barrage of tests, almost stubbornly searching for what they knew to be there. The lymphoma had been far too extensive for these to be correct. But test after test showed no malignancy anywhere.

Karen Farley was cancer-free.

She felt a great surge of exhilaration and a limp sag of relief at the same time. It was a euphoria Karen had experienced only once before, when Matty's surgery proved successful and she knew he'd live. After all the fighting, all the effort, all the endless battles with doubt and worry, pain and sickness, it was over. Despite its being foretold, Karen was still a skeptical creature, deep inside. She hadn't been completely willing to place her faith in a gleaming butterfly entity floating above a hospital bed, any more than she could lay her trust in the hands of one doctor and one doctor alone.

When the last test was done, Lorry cried with relief. Karen was healed. She wasn't going to die.

Riding on the heels of that revelation was the thought that *she had time now*. Her sister was safe. Karen would live. Lorry had time now to concentrate on her own healing. She'd done the diet, the meditation and juicing for her body. Now it was time for the spirit.

It would be a hard road, the path to self worth, but worth it. Bolstered by the knowledge that she'd stumbled onto her own strange and wondrous destiny, and knowing that Karen would now be all right, Lorry plunged headlong into self-healing.

When she'd first begun meditating and using guided imagery, Doctor Alguta had noticed a marked difference in her health almost immediately. She told him about her daily meditation, and he encouraged it, soon lowering her dosage of Prednisone. When she'd begun the macrobiotic diet, with Karen cooking food for them both, Lorry's symptoms once again improved, and she was taken completely off the Prednisone.

Now that Karen was healthy again, Lorry could concentrate more on herself; perhaps escalate the healing. In helping Karen, she had also helped herself. Karen had shown her selflessness; sharing everything in her desire to heal not only the cancer, but Lorry's Lupus as well.

I don't have to worry about you any more, Karen. You're going to be fine.

When first diagnosed, Lorry had started out with three potentially danger-ous prescription drugs. She was now down to two. That was the number one priority. If at all possible, get off those medications.

The first thing to do was to advertise for group meditations. Lorry found those the most beneficial to her. She loved being in a group, with everyone focused on healing. The Wednesday night classes were marvelous, but they were always changing. She wanted a healing meditation group. The room always felt charged with positive energy during a session, even long after it was over.

She put flyers up in all the local health food stores. They advertised a group meditation, which would be held on Monday nights at her home.

People flocked to her door, looking for advice and guidance as well as a ses-sion of meditation. Finding herself a teacher almost before she knew it, Lorry strove to pass on the knowledge she'd gained from all those Wednesday nights, all those books and tapes and guided imageries she'd practiced. Everything she and Karen had done together.

Leading the Monday night classes through her own unique versions of meditation, Lorry had a soothing voice and a flair for the imaginative. No two meditations were the same, and she rarely bothered with a prepared script. No set ritual, no rigid standard of conduct. Lorry was funny, mouthy and open. She learned to read people empathically, knowing intuitively how to put them at ease.

Word spread. More and more people were drawn to her Monday night ses-sions. Whispered comments of channeling and impressive healing abilities began coming back at her, and Lorry felt topsy-turvy with the old conservative voice inside her growing quieter, giving way to a new one. Her spirit was being freed from the blocks placed there by the traumas of her childhood, and Lorry's true self was slowly unfurling.

By this time, she'd been initiated in Reiki II, which she demonstrated to her Monday classes, with encouraging results.

She tried not to get carried away. One night she was practicing Reiki on an extremely enthusiastic client who said, "I can feel it. I can really feel the heat;"

Lorry tapped her shoulder, pointing over her head. An electric heater stood next to them, radiating warmth.

Ten members of the group pooled their money and sponsored her final training. They wanted her to become a Reiki master so she could initiate them. It was a fast-growing field.

Lorry's energy was returning, and she was able to go shopping for longer periods of time. Lifting her daughters, once impossible, became a common-place joy.

She was initiated as a Reiki master and held her first class in Reiki I, where she initiated all her sponsors.

A short time later, she gave her first master training class. One student. Evelyn Waters was in her seventies, and very demanding. Nervous, Lorry dug in her heels and answered every question.

Evelyn came away impressed, initiated, and grateful. She wanted to give Lorry a gift.

Still unable to afford a massage table, Lorry worked on people on the floor of her home, stretched out on an old patio mattress covered with a sheet.

Evelyn called her and asked Lorry to help her pick up a massage table she'd just bought. They were too heavy for the older woman to lift alone. Now that Evelyn was a Reiki master, she needed a massage table for herself, to work on clients. Swallowing her envy. Lorry agreed to help.

The table was at a store only minutes away. Evelyn paid for it, and they carried it out to the car. Lorry could lift it with relative ease. Just five months before, she had trouble getting out of a car.

As they were sliding the table into the back of Lorry's van, Evelyn said, "This table's not for me. It's a gift for you, Lorry. I want you to accept it without a lot of talk. Don't even say thank you, and don't try to refuse it. You need a table."

Then she settled back to watched the emotional show.

Lorry didn't disappoint her. She burst into tears, sucked her lips together to hold in the *thank you's* that were trying to escape, and floundered about awkwardly, trying to deal with this unexpected kindness. She had gotten gifts before, but always for a reason outside of herself: getting pregnant, being beautiful, owning a restaurant. This was the first present she'd ever received for being talented, for having a gift of her own, one that was intrinsically hers, and no one else's.

She drove home in a haze of watery vision.

Her following grew quickly, and Lorry's health improved with it. The happier she got, the better she felt. Doctor Alguta took her off the Procardia, and the only medication she was on now was the Plaquenil.

"You'll have to take the Plaquenil for the rest of your life," Alguta warned, "But don't worry about it."

Lorry was fine with the idea of taking just one pill. It was like taking a vitamin. She felt that, like Karen, she had healed herself. For the first time, Lorry had positive thinking, and she wanted to share it.

She became a regular lecturer at a bookstore in Levittown, leading group meditations on stress management. People who could never meditate before, found themselves sliding into it inside a crowded bookstore, with Lorry leading the way. She became the store's exclusive Reiki master. Lorry learned the art of public speaking the hard way. The experience bolstered her slowly growing confidence.

The Lupus symptoms had virtually disappeared. She looked forward to each new day as a positive challenge and not a fearsome obstacle to overcome anymore. Instead of viewing the countless faults she had seen all her life, Lorry was grateful for the unexpected gift of happiness which she, herself, was now bestowing. Inspiration had been in the form of a beloved sister, and Lorry could now inspire both herself and others.

She was happy. Karen was healthy, her children were healthy, her niece and nephew were well. No one was dying. No one was even sick. *Including me.* Lorry laughed out loud at the thought.

She'd finally discovered her place in the world. No longer simply existing, waiting for life to end. She had found her purpose. This is what they were talking about, all those years ago in the tunnel, when she'd reluctantly returned to life after swallowing a bottle of aspirin. This was what she was here for. Destiny. Call it strange, weird, and wonderful, she was happy. Lorry was a healer, and she would make it her calling for the rest of her life.

A routine check-up with Doctor Alguta was the final icing on the cake.

"Well, Lorry, I don't see any reason for you to take the Plaquenil anymore. I'm going to take you off of it."

"What?"

"There's no reason for you to be on it."

Lorry looked up at him, and felt ... free. She grinned the grin of a free woman. An unexpected and beloved gift, those simple words. She was in remission from Lupus, a state virtually unheard of in the history of the chronic illness, and she was going to remain in remission. Lorry knew it in her heart. *There's no reason for you to be on it anymore.* She had told Doctor Alguta, years ago, that his words would create for her. "Use that ability wisely," she had said. "Use it to heal me. Whatever you say to me, I'll believe, and create within myself." Lorry always told her doctors this. "Be careful what you say. I will believe you."

Doctor Alguta had been more than careful. He'd been an artist with his words, and Lorry had bloomed under them.

She drove for hours afterward, face shining, full of the wonder of a child. The sunset was the most beautiful she could ever remember, and Lorry found herself taking the exit to Jones Beach, Field Five, where she, and her mother, and her sisters had all gone so often, all those years before, when they were naive and thought they knew tragedy, when real tragedy had not even sipped at them yet.

Lorry got out of the car and leaned against the hood, watching the moon rise over the water, feeling her mother's presence so strongly, she thought she caught the tail end of Rita's perfume.

"I love you, Ma," she whispered. "I don't hate you or Dad, or anybody anymore. You never got the chance to see life, but somehow, you gave it to Karen and me. I stuck by her, Ma. I stuck by Karen, like you asked me to, and she saved me as much as I saved her. We're alive, Ma. We're finally alive."

A gull screeched somewhere over the water. Lorry let the breeze lift her hair and wash her clean of all the years of misery and suffering. Life had lit a path before her, and she could see it clearly. "Stay on the path," Lorry grinned, the words a slow delight on the tongue as she finally understood what Karen's voices had meant.

Stay on the path.

She drove to Karen and Richard's to pick up her kids. They were all sleeping together in the back bedroom. Karen answered the door, glowing and vibrant with health, her hair a shoulder length bob of gold. Lorry told her about the visit to Alguta.

It was news that didn't surprise Karen. She'd seen the change in her sister, as she'd seen the change in herself, and Karen was no longer surprised by anything that happened. They had done it. They'd both faced their demons, and with hard work and faith, conquered them. Now they could face life and all its miracles. Two sisters, two diseases, two remissions. After all their years of shared tragedy and incredible misfortune, a terrible death seemed to be the only logical ending for both of them. It would have fit.

But somewhere along the line, they must have picked up a love for life, to have struggled so hard and fought for so long. Maybe that's why they were both graced with their beautiful children; to give them something to live for. It was Rita and Toni, Matt and Dana, and even Kyle, who were perhaps responsible for saving Lorry and Karen. Without the children, they might have slipped this mortal coil with a grateful sigh of relief.

But children made all the difference. It was their children that Karen and Lorry clung to as a reason to live in those dark first days. Everyone has to have something to live for, but the best reason of all, if a human being can only find it, is to live for yourself. At the time of their diagnosis, neither sister had much self-love, so their children were a gift in far more ways than one. It was love, in the end, that drew them back from the brink, that had created a circle of quiet for them to heal in. Love, not for themselves, which they'd have to learn, but love for their children. By facing death, by finding something worth living for, the two sisters discovered a truth they hadn't even imagined. It wasn't an absolute that one's luck always remained the same. A person could make a difference in both life and death, if they only believed. Experience was a true gift. Be it good or bad, something positive could always be gleaned from it.

They went into the back bedroom and saw their children, all sprawled together in a tangle of flannel and soft baby skin.

Rita.

Toni.

Matthew.

Dana.

Kyle.

There was a kiss for each one of them.

Karen thought of the video will she had made. It was a comfort to think they would never see it. When she'd made it, her spirit was at its lowest point. She thought of Lorry, with her crippled body and spirit when she'd first been diagnosed with the Lupus and not expected to survive the night. Karen had seen both panic and relief in Lorry's eyes, that the whole, ghastly experience of living was soon to be over. She remembered her own fear of losing her sister. Of the cancer. Looking back, in this euphoric moment, she felt compassion for herself, and everything those two sisters of the past still had to face.

"But it was worth it," she whispered, smiling at Lorry. "It was all worth it."

Lorry wrapped her arms around her sister Karen, and laughed.

Bibliography

Abehsera, Michel. *Zen Macrobiotic Cooking.* Avon Books, 1976

Balch, M.D.,James F./Balch, C.N.C., Phyllis A. *Prescription for Nutritional Healing.* Garden City Park, New York: Avery Publishing Group Inc., 1990

Burka, Christa Faye. *Clearing Crystal Consciousness.* Albuquerque, New Mexico: Brotherhood of Life, 1985

Colbin, Annemarie. *The Book of Whole Meals.* New York: Ballantine Books, 1983

Cousins, Norman. *Anatomy of an Illness.* New York, London: W.W. Norton & Company, 1979

Davis, Adelle. *Let's Cook It Right.* New York: Signet Books, 1970

Elias, Thomas. *The Burzynski Breakthrough.*

Epstein, M.D., Gerald. *Healing Visualizations: Creating Health Through Imagery.* New York, Toronto, London, Sydney, Auckland: Bantam Books, 1989

Hay, Louise L. *You Can Heal Your Life.* Santa Monica, California: Hay House, 1984

Howell, Dr. Edward. *Enzyme Nutrition: The Food Enzyme Concept.* Wayne, New Jersey: Avery Publishing Group, Inc., 1985

Karp, Reba Ann. *Edgar Cayce Encyclopedia of Healing.* New York: Warner Books, 1986

Kushi, Aveline, Esko, Wendy. *The Macrobiotic Cancer Prevention Cookbook.*

Martin, Joel, Romanowski, Patricia. *We Are Not Forgotten.* New York: Berkley Books, 1992

Pauling, Linus. *How to Live Longer and Feel Better.* New York: W.H. Freeman & Company, 1986

Pert, PhD., Candace B. *Molecules of Emotion.* New York: Simon & Schuster Audio, 1997

Ray, Barbara Ph.D. *The 'Reiki' Factor.* St. Petersburg, Florida: Radiance Associates, 1988

Read, Anne, Ilstrup, Carol, Gammon, Margaret. *Edgar Cayce on Diet and Health.* New York: Paperback Library, 1969

Reilly, Harold J./Brod, Ruth Hagy. *The Edgar Cayce Handbook for Health Through Drugless Therapy.* Virginia Beach, Virginia: A.R.E. Press, 1975

Roman, Sanaya. *Spiritual Growth.* Tiburon, California: H J Kramer Inc, 1987

Santillo, Humbart. *Food Enzymes: The Missing Link to Radiant Health.* Prescott Valley, Arizona: Hohm Press, 1987

Siegel, Bernie S. M.D. *Love, Medicine & Miracles.* New York: Harper & Row, 1986

Simonton, Carl O. M.D., Matthews-Simonton, Stephanie, Creighton, James L. *Getting Well Again.* Bantam, 1992

Sui, Choa Kok. *Pranic Healing.* York Beach, Maine: Samuel Weiser, Inc. 1990

Walker D. Sc., N.W. *Fresh Vegetable and Fruit Juices.* Prescott, Arizona: Norwalk Press, 1978